24 october 1992

# Tinsel Show

For Joan

# Tinsel Show

## Pop, Politics, Scotland

## Patrick Kane

**Polygon**
EDINBURGH

© Introduction and
Editorial selection Patrick Kane 1992

Published by Polygon,
22 George Square,
Edinburgh.

Typeset in Linotron Sabon
by Koinonia Limited, Bury
Printed and bound by
Redwood Press Ltd,
Melksham, Wiltshire

British Library Cataloguing
   in Publication Data
Kane, Patrick
   Tinsel Show: Pop, Politics, Scotland
   I. Title
   306.09411

ISBN 0 7486 6145 X

# ☆ Contents

Series Preface    viii
Introduction    1

*Pop*

The Beggar my neighbour    3
Bloc'n'roll    10
Songs for Europe    13
Nae luck with the Legion    16
Troubles in mind    19
I had a dream    23
Where the music doesn't take me    26
When protest was a four-letter word    30
Rythym and bliss    33
In a bell jar with Madonna    37
Remote from you, now    40

Essay: Pop Life    44

*Politics*

All's fair in love and the class war    67
Obscuring the show of evil    71
Disquiet on the comics front    75
Into the psychiatrists' lair    79
Heroes of the TV revolution    82
Notes from America's underground    85
Marxism today, gone tomorrow    88
Flights of fancy on the business class    92
Revenge of the cyborg trolls    95
Reasons to be fearful    99
Authors who come up with the goods    103
Hitching up to the hype bandwagon    107
Too clever by three-quarters    110
Onward, Christian Socialists?    114

Essay: Banality, Solidarity, Spectacle    117

*Scotland*

Unashamed of kitsch and kin   135
A hitch on the bandwagon   139
Down but not out in London   143
Something to write home about   147
That's why we'll take Manhattan   150
Planning without a concept   153
Why must Bhoys always be Bhoys?   156
A Day For Scotland   160
Balkans raise the Scottish question   163
Soul brothers under the skin   166
Exorcising the royal prerogative   169
Surreal life crisis   172
Nationalism and modernity   176

Essay: Scotland By Starlight   181

Acknowledgements   208

Bibliography   209

Index   212

# ☆ Series Preface

Scotland's history is often presented as punctuated by disasters which overwhelm the nation, break its continuity and produce a fragmented culture. Many felt that 1979, and the failure of the Devolution Referendum, represented such a disaster: that the energetic culture of the 1960s and 1970s would wither into the silence of a political wasteland in which Scotland would be no more than a barely distinguishable province of the United Kingdom.

Instead, the 1980s proved to be one of the most productive and creative decades in Scotland this century – as though the energy that had failed to be harnessed by the politicians flowed into other channels. In literature, in thought, in history, creative and scholarly work went hand in hand to redraw the map of Scotland's past and realign the perspectives of its future.

In place of the few standard conceptions of Scotland's identity that had often been in the past the tokens of thought about the country's culture, a new and vigorous debate was opened up about the nature of Scottish experience, about the real social and economic structures of the nation, and about the ways in which the Scottish situation related to that of other similar cultures throughout the world.

It is from our determination to maintain a continuous forum for such debate that *Determinations* takes its title. The series will provide a context for sustained dialogue about culture and politics in Scotland, and about those international issues which directly affect Scottish experience.

Too often, in Scotland, a particular way of seeing our culture, of representing ourselves, has come to dominate our perceptions because it has gone unchallenged – worse, unexamined. The vitality of the culture should be measured by the intensity of debate which it generates rather than the security of ideas on which it rests. And should be measured by the extent to which creative, philosophical, theological, critical and political ideas confront each other.

If the determinations which shape our experience are to come from within rather than from without, they have to be explored and evaluated and acted upon. Each volume in this series will seek to be a contribution to that self-determination and each volume, we trust, will require a response, contributing in turn to the ongoing dynamic that is Scotland's culture.

General Editor: Cairns Craig

What though on hamely fare we dine,
    Wear hodden grey, and a' that,
Gie fools their silks, and knaves their wine,
    A Man's a Man for a' that,
For a' that, and a' that,
Their tinsel show, and a' that;
The honest man, though e'er sae poor,
Is king o' men for a' that.

                              Robert Burns


If you have understanding and a heart, show only
                              one.
Both they will damn, if both you show together.

                              Friedrich Hölderlin


Diving for dear life
When we could be diving for pearls.

                              Elvis Costello

# ☆ Introduction

This book was originally conceived as part-autobiography, part-analysis of my last six or seven years in music, media and politics. Leafing through my journalistic cuttings over that period, in the last few months of 1991, I realised with a slight shock that I'd effectively written three-quarters of the book already. Memories of particular places where columns and pieces had been hammered out – just before going on stage at Wembley Stadium; just after the most crushing by-election defeat; and just about everywhere else – came hurtling back. Holding the folders in my hands, it seemed as if I had been gripped by some kind of discursive virus. How did I find the energy, the material, the commitment to keep all these columns and one-offs going? Was every spare moment in the tour bus or the shuttle or the jumbo or the hotel room spent scribbling, reading, inputting? I've asked my fellow troubadours, and their response is usually wordless, evoked by hands encircling heads and moving outwards theatrically, the implication brutally clear: You were completely bloody obsessive about it. Nutter!

*Tinsel Show* is the product of a music career propelled by crises and contradictions, a satchel bag full of the latest theoretical tomes, and a country bringing itself (and myself) to an ever-greater sense of identity: that is, of pop, politics and Scotland. I intend the journalism – a selection of the best – to function like on-the-run reports from each of these areas. They should give some sense of the terror and excitement of finding that everything solid melts into air in this mad, media-drenched world; and that to make an instant account of these thrills and spills, disciplined by theory, is one of the only ways to retain sanity, or at least coherence, within one's personal space and time.

I've made attempts at broader sweeps in the three new extended essays on each subject. Their authoritativeness can only ever be temporary; written largely in the aftermath of the General Election of April 1992, in those crashing, crushing months, they are bound to be outstripped by events as they unfold – and to a certain extent, as I and others like me unfold those events ourselves. My music career, with the launch of our new label, Fidelity Records, and my intellectual concerns, with the serious and continuing challenges to Western modernity from both inside and out, are in no lesser turmoil. My hope is that the rendering of this somewhat chaotic life and times is reasonably pleasing in form, and reasonably substantive in content.

I will retrieve a quote from the Welsh socialist Raymond Williams for this introduction; for several years now these words have been inscribed in the Projects divider of my first purchased Filofax – where else? – and they've never seemed more relevant. Williams is aiming at Sartre specifically but the gun fires scattershot:

> The intellectual 'celebrity' or 'character' – moving through many fields, exhibiting his virtuosity – is guilty of a kind of *exposed biographical living*. (*Listener* , 4 February 1988)

I don't *feel* guilty for trying to sing, to think and to agitate all at the same time; I just feel that I'm trying to banish every future regret for the unacted act, the unspoken communication, the struggle unengaged. But I'm in *your* court now, gentle and general reader. May you never reach a verdict.

Some thanks are due. The editors of *CUT*, the *Herald* and particularly Magnus Linklater of the *Scotsman* have given me space and license in my columns with them over the years: for that I am grateful. The receptivity of the London media – specifically the *Guardian*, the *Independent on Sunday* and *Marxism Today* – has been occasional, but worthwhile.

Gregory Kane and Allan McNeill, the 'Hue' and 'and' in Hue and Cry, have been almost completely understanding about every non-rock'n'roll activity I've embarked on. Thanks also to all our music fans; if you've bought this, remember ... I don't theorise on the CDs (or when I do, at least it rhymes and has a hummable melody). I'd like to thank Marion Sinclair at Polygon, Cairns Craig and John Cairney for accepting the idea of the book. As I believe self-determination at the level of the nation should also mean a greater self-determination at the level of the individual, I'm proud that *Tinsel Show* will appear in Polygon's 'Determinations' series.

My daughter Grace is joy and love epitomised and my wife Joan is behind every word of this book, urging clarity, banishing doubt, sharing her wisdom. When the tinsel show finally closes, we three leave together.

Glasgow, July 1992.

# ☆ Pop

And the moment I feel that
You feel that way too
Is when I fall in love with you

Cole Porter

# ☆ The Beggar My neighbour

(CUT, November 1988)

Apart from music, what most occupies my mind in New York is beggary. The initial shock of half-starved humans underneath gleaming corporate towers soon becomes banal. What really keeps the conscience well-wrung is the fact that it's not enough for the poor to be deserving; they are also required to be *convincing*. The begging market is a tough and competitive one, and in this most capitalist of cities, everyone has to have a good pitch.

One-line humour is effective: 'Hey buddy, help me out, I'm saving to buy a condo.' Or a crazed eye and a war-record: 'I'm a Vietnam vet, I have shrapnel in my leg, I'm also an epileptic...' Obvious proof of authentic need is helpful. A tiny, very legless man bluntly informs his Wall Street benefactors 'NO SPARE CHANGE PLEASE' on his cardboard sign. A subway vagrant once passed out a photocopied CV in my carriage, showing his medical record, personal history and a facsimile of his welfare card.

Sometimes you get poetry for your dollar. During the first album, me and Gregory and Jimmy our producer elicited this gem from a sack-trousered black man in the Bowery: 'I ain't got no money, I ain't got no honey, spare a dime, mister?' I wrote that into a song called *Goodbye to Me*, which continues the phrase: 'The beggar is no bad man, The beggar is not me.' Saying goodbye to yourself is sometimes a psychological necessity in New York – otherwise the morality of stealing the desperate art of paupers for your own career project might profoundly trouble you. The nagging doubt of the socially concerned popster: his parasitism on the world's problems, his aesthetic pleasure in the pain of others.

New York makes me torture myself like this all the time. At the exact point when you're feeling most useful and relevant to your environment, something always happens to turn you into a presumptuous fool. Sitting around in the outside queue for the Deconstructivist Architecture show at the Museum of Modern Art, one has to be careful not to disturb the sleeping homeless behind the flowerbeds. A perfectly fascinating discussion on public television about the essential worth of the American Constitution is

precisely nixed by the gunshot crack coming through the window
from Central Park below. To blank out this stuff is to eventually be
crushed by one's own heartlessness; to worry about it risks a
scrambled brain. So the best way to enjoy your killer second album
in New York is learning the art of character surgery: this part is my
leftist guilt, that part is my artistic ambition; this morning I
witnessed the emptiness of Manhattan myth, this afternoon I have
to get a vocal down or the recording schedule's shot to pieces. To
rule yourself, divide yourself. The only appropriate album title
seemed to be *Remote*.

## Laundered Denim

It is some times embarrassing how easily life resolves itself into
opposites and polarities. Take our two New York producers.

Jimmy Biondolillo is as round and satisfying as his name. When
he tells me his brothers are 'big tough guys' working for the
Biondolillo Construction Company, I can believe him; Jimmy is
built like a dumper truck, widewheeled and capacious. He's the
only guy in his family who didn't automatically go into the con-
crete-and-pilings trade: and where I imagine his brothers have
shoulders you could land helicopters on, Jimmy is softer, rounded,
much more sanded off and corniced. A suitable shape for his
mother's musical son in New York: the golden boy who's waved a
baton at Sinatra instead of wielding spirit levels on building sites.
When I grasp Jimmy's hand, I can feel every moment of Mrs
Biondolillo's TLC.

Harvey Goldberg is a thin stretch at 6-foot-slightly-frightening,
generally has a few more angles and edges than Jimmy. I've learned
a lot about the sartorial power of a laundered denim shirt from
Harvey (Jimmy prefers crimson T-shirts with pink dancing bears),
and he uses that very direct but inviting New York stare when he's
talking to you: I like to listen to Harvey's Manhattan-speak, and
Harvey sure likes being listened to. But he has a large whale of a
laugh that would blow Tom Wolfe's cufflinks off for warmth and
infectiousness. And I can immediately sympathise with a man who
has weight problems because of a terminally blissful marriage.

Everybody I've met in this New York music-making social circle
is a confirmed cultural pundit; delivery boys with fast-food film
criticisms, maintenance engineers with their nose in the latest
literary hot tip. Jimmy and Harvey are no different, and no less
characteristically opposed.

Jimmy is involved in a large-scale reconstruction of the year of
his 11th birthday – the year when 'it all started to come together,

when you began to know who you were and what was going on'. This involves long weekends immersed in fleamarkets and curio shops, retrieving *Life* magazines and *Man From U.N.C.L.E* comic books (with the crucial photo cover), baseball cards and old newspapers; snatching these memories out of the jaws of the recycler and into his Cleveland basement. Jimmy has also pointed me in the direction of Raymond Carver and Langston Hughes; and I hope he'll eventually let me look at his 12-or-so short stories, or his screenplay, or his paste-book encyclopedia of commonplace wisdom.

Harvey has introduced me to a world where a baseball card, stuck in the right piece on the canvas, will get you an extra 2K on the asking price: the New York art market. His dear wife Michelle has bought them a canvas-and-paint-splodged cube, by someone who is either an Earth artist or a Neo-Geoist (I think). Perfectly and simply pleasant as it hangs on their whitened wall, the accompanying users' guide (or 'gallery prospectus') reads like an art-theory computer program with a flailing cockroach in its works.

The dinner date with their aesthete acquaintances was one to treasure. Leon worked beside Michelle in the textiles business, but also sidelined as a collector. His attitude to art was so rampantly capitalistic he made a Wall Street raider seem like Mother Teresa in a generous mood. Me and Joan (over for a holiday) let our liberal jaws flap weakly in the wind of Leon's rapacity.

'If I buy a painting, I can do whatever I want with it, it's my property. I could break it over my knee, or sell it at an inflated price ... Nazi art is *very* hot these days, it's so timeless ... Who is supposed to appreciate art – the man in the street? Art has always been the province of the middle classes – they have the education, the money ...'

Later on, over coffee, Harvey and Michelle and Joan and me decided: at least in the music business, for a reasonably cheap price, everybody can get a piece of your art. And that was the best reason for doing it.

## A Meant-To-Be Scenario

To keep the product plugs down to a minimum: the music went well. At the beginning of the year we untangled the tortured knot that Hue And Cry had internally become. No more Pat trying to be a record producer and total media strategist; no more Gregory as the mute muso and all round loverboy. I articulate myself through my words and voice, Gregory through his music and arrangements, and we decided to respect and support each other's talents to the full, rather than resenting or misunderstanding them.

So we sat down to write some songs, in an asylum-like back room in Cava Studios, Glasgow. It was so damn easy. The pressures and disorientations of last year – from major hits to shuffling misses, supporting Madonna to being cable fodder for Murdoch – all this fell away like hard, bad skin. We took 12 of our purest efforts over to Sigma Sound Studios on Broadway, and nestled in with Harvey and Jimmy again, checked out the new James Brown and Full Force photo in the clients' gallery, chummed up with engineers and staff who warmly justified names like Tony Maserati and Fernando Krel and Randy and Hank; and generally felt that this was, as Mr. Biondolillo was wont to say, a 'meant-to-be' scenario.

After a week, I had to get out of there. Wednesday was the worst day; four pairs of hands struggling to stir the musical pot one way or the other, while our bemused drummer peered through the glass like an aquarium owner at squabbling goldfish. When the psycho-history of brothers repeats itself, it's best to take it as farce, not tragedy: the last thing the songs needed were Biblical struggles over hi-hat patterns.

Gregory has a part production credit on the album, and completely deserves it. Each time I flew back to New York to do my vocals and lend my 'fresh ear', I was presented with four beautifully ornamented musical pedestals; all I had to do was sit on them, shuffle the cushions a little to get comfortable, and then let fly. This is how we made our best music yet.

## The Sci-fi Wet Dream

Returning to our I-was-a-New-York-schizo theme, it's a reasonable guess that there are as many bookshops as Uzi guns on Manhattan Island. Five minutes along from the New David 'hot shot gay porn' cinema the brilliant Museum of Broadcasting can find you Martin Luther King or Mary Tyler Moore in its video archives. I now know why so many writers and artists say they have no desire to leave New York; if anything uniquely funky or hyper-urban hits them in the streets, they're only a cab ride away from that East Village minor poet's work who'll put the whole thing *exactly* in context.

For the unofficial capital of a country which worried wee Euro-intellectuals are always calling a 3-D soap opera, this town is incredibly committed to the written word. As a *Saturday Night Live* wag has quipped, there is probably no substance known to man heavier than the Sunday edition of *The New York Times*. And for all the brow-furrowing that goes on about the politics of information in the capitalist mass media, I found two best-selling books which, taken to heart and acted out, would shake the corporate exploiters to their foundations: Studs Terkel's *The Great Divide*, and Barbara Garson's *The Electric Sweatshop*. The socialists must still be out there, if only even to sell books to.

Otherwise, New York mass media is as totally overloaded as you've heard about. Channel-flick spasmodically enough, and a news close up on the bloody remains of a Queens shootout will mentally blend into the haemorrhoids ad and the tele-psychic chat show: nothing surprising really, just your average American info-inferno of dissolving values and unreliable reality. I found the three most warming and reliable shows, and clung to them like pet dogs in a rabies epidemic. *Star Trek- the Next Generation* is effectively the sci-fi wet dream of a Democrat apologist for the United Nations. Instead of gut-heavy crypto-fascist Kirk and his flaky crew, we have an atmosphere akin to a Dukakis seminar on 'good management' and 'political tact'. Rowdy aliens aren't subdued with the old show's mixture of hunches and punches – new Captain Jean-Luc Picard is virtually a practising anthropologist, never deviating from the Federation's 'prime directive' of non-interference in all alien cultures. The resonances this has for American foreign policy are clearly heartening. Methinks a Jesse Jackson adviser has taken control of Gene Roddenberry's brain.

Late at night, there's what amounts to a religious hour for frazzled Manhattaneers. I never liked *The Odd Couple* in Britain – something I couldn't understand my father laughing at ⊢ but it makes complete sense here: Tony Randall and Jack Klugman as two dithering divorcees in a faintly magical late Sixties New York, where racial tension and pavement poverty are just soft, mournful jokes to be batted across the apartment. *The Honeymooners* deals out a similar opium – a one-set sitcom about Ralph the bus driver, Norton the sewer worker, their omniscient wives and their hamster-wheel lives.

Reflecting post-war Brooklyn, it's as accurate a portrayal of shoulder-stooped American working life as Arthur Miller's *Death of a Salesman*. 'Gee Alice,' says Ralph, surveying their matchwood apartment and swelling with hope, 'won't this furniture look great in our Park Avenue apartment?' To all the watching white-collar drones, thrashing themselves to a stretched nerve for corporate plaudits and designer baubles, this early Fifties classic must seem like the dawn of civilization. When Ralph tries to keep Alice sweet by buying her 'one of those new vacuum cleaners' it's like witnessing the first spark in the consumerist forest fire that's been raging round the Western world for the last forty years. No wonder we laugh.

## Low-Rent Mystique

As you've probably gathered by now, this is New York largely from behind a book and through the glass wall of diners. The only mean street me and Gregory ever encountered on our way to work was the welfare hotel on 57th and Broadway, which I always found quite a treat: right in the heart of chromium-covered midtown Manhattan, one-parent families are laying their smalls out on the window-ledge to dry. I'm told that there have been murder sieges there, and drugs, and that it's the epicentre of a recent crime wave. But all that probably happens just as I turn the corner; and anyway, I won't know about it till it's on *Eyewitness News*. As far as my experience goes, urban tact and equilibrium is not unnatural to New York, despite all the cop shows.

And even when we deliberately went where the fabled 'action' was, we found ... well, ordinary angels, winning tiny victories. Joseph our photographer wanted some 'working-class' neighbourhood, and all the suspiciously nasal location-finder could give us were hip private clubs and stupid 'art-neon' fittings ('*Andy* loved this piece', he would honk unsubtly). After being refused use of yet another inexplicably 'hot' dive, we found ourselves in the East Side 'no-go' area of Alphabet City, suddenly realising how many burning wrecks – automotive *and* human – were lying around us. Joseph, with a photographer's typical lack of concern for consequence, suggested we ask the residents behind a particularly fortress-like tenement window (leavened with flowers and a Madonna) if we could set up inside their house.

My conscience-motor started spinning furiously. How would these people react to our use of their home as low-rent mystique? How would their faith and religiosity sit with the secular vision of the songs? Sure enough, their flaking green-walled flat had a virtual tabernacle in the corner, and the mother and son were proud that our photographer was getting so rapturous about it. While Joseph snapped away at these gorgeous colours and forms, I tried to extract some content and context from these people's lives.

Adam had been in the US Marines, and was airlifted out with a cracked wrist three days before the Lebanon strike. 'The developers want this block for $20 000, they won't get it for $200 000,' he asserted. His mother claimed to have cured her second son of leukaemia through supplication to the Lord, but the Santa Barbara she placed us beside stood as the very earthly saint of power and money for Puerto Ricans. 'Stand next to it, it will give you much good fortune,' she insisted.

Relentless yuppifiers at one end of the street, drug merchants and extortionists at the other: how was I going to convince them that what they didn't need was a heaven-sent deity? My idea of an 'ordinary angel' was inspired by a critique of Klee's *The Angel Of History* by German philosopher Walter Benjamin; theirs was a spiritual necessity in the struggle to survive a terrifyingly material situation. This particular piece of opium-for-the-masses looked like it kept the heart and soul from the clutches of the local death chemist.

As we were rushed out of the house by Adam at 6pm – 'you don't want to hang around here with all this equipment, the crack men'll be coming back from work soon' – I realised dimly that we hadn't done something we should have, one shot we didn't try ... 'It's a shame we didn't get a picture of the old Spanish lady,' said our stylist as we scrambled behind the van door. 'She had such a *wonderful* face.'

## It's Only A Movie

I'm writing this in the last days of mixing, and I've just seen the most appropriate button-badge message in a city of screaming lapels: DON'T WORRY – IT'S ONLY A MOVIE. But it gets tiring playing the part of a New Yorker, shedding skyscraper tears, raising Broadway laughter. I want to go home; make home movies.

## ☆ Bloc 'n' roll

(*The Guardian*, 29 August 1991)

Last Thursday, at Poland's biggest ever music business festival, Sopot '91, I was standing in the foyer of Gdansk's Marina Hotel, fizzing with world-historical excitement. Gorbachev's account of his release was playing on a bank of sponsored TV monitors – previously insane with Europop videos – and I struggled to pluck some sense out of a Polish running translation of a Russian press conference. Completely exasperated, I turned to a local festival guide for help. 'Isn't this great news? About Gorbachev?'

She shrugged and said uninterestedly: 'No, no. It's just news.' Then turned to run after a newly arrived Swedish glam rock band, somewhat fazed by their check-in documents.

My trip to Poland – along with a fair slice of the Brit-pop pantheon – was as an audience-building musician; the televised Sopot concerts claim to reach almost 300 million viewers throughout Eastern Europe and beyond. But the luckiness of being so geographically proximate to the second Russian revolution was almost completely negated by the indifference of most Poles I met to these events. Who cares? their shrugs seemed to say. This is a far off country, of which we wish to know very little. Come on, we're all Europeans. Let's do business!

To any saloon-bar socialist who scrawls his Utopia on the back of a beer mat every drinking night in Glasgow – present company included – the new entrepreneurs of Eastern Europe are a fearsome and sobering sight. 'Profitable and successful dealings to all businessmen and women' is the hearty conclusion to the Sopot president's general address. The main festival sponsor is the Polish company Universal – from nuts, bolts and machine goods to frozen peas and carrots – and the festival pamphlet contains ads from every corner of the Polish economy, not just media-related: finance and trade credit, oil importation, food retailing, insurance, cars ... I find we're pictured underneath Danni Minogue on page 24, cowering next to the Rand Corporation's full-page promo.

So the deal is clear. We – meaning the pop alphabet from Bros to Electribe 101, OMD to Roachford – are here to play our part in the glamourisation of resurgent Polish capitalism; in return, we have the chance to capture the hearts and minds of Eastern European pop consumers, hoping that our memory lingers long enough till they have some disposable income to spend on us.

And if you think that's hard-nosed, you should know the 'theme' of Sopot this year. Stamp Out Piracy Our Task. As there is no discernible copyright law for music and video in Poland, the bootleg industry is huge – not just backstreet operators but several major pressing plants, putting blurred Western pop cassettes in every kiosk and newsagent, at 6,000 zlotys (less than 50 pence) each.

'In this situation,' says Mr Ian Haffey, Anti-piracy Co-ordinator of London-based IFPI, 'foreign companies are unwilling to invest … It is impossible to compete with these people.' What, strident international free-market capitalism complains about the *lack* of local economic regulation? Sorry?

Me (and my mortgage) should be arm in sweaty arm with Anti-Piracy co-ordinators from W1 – but Christ, I'm in the New Europe here! Citizens to meet, idealisms to savour, experiences to compare! To bed after a hard day's travel, then rise to meet the dawn of democracy and freedom!

So why does my bedside valve radio Stalinistically switch itself on at 8.45 a.m. – I've checked, no mistakenly set alarm clock – and foul up my ears with Elton John's Song For Guy? Right through that morning and the rest of the day, in taxi, shops and elevators, the same kind of sonic gloop – Lionel, Barry, Julio – clogs up every social space.

If normality is perpetual Radio Two, Desert Storm T-shirts on wee Polish tykes, trade fairs like any other big European city, then what right have we to despise this? We take our blandness for granted – the status quos against which Western artists have had decades to learn how to fastidiously distinguish themselves. For forty years, the cultural norm in Poland was Soviet colonisation and dead ideology. Manilows and game shows in a mad market scramble must be a blessed relief for a while.

But this is not the whole story of Polish popular culture; we haven't got to the pop concert yet! The climax of our night was four British acts flailing away at their mute instruments.

Before us, however, were a selection of Polish acts from a Warsaw production/management/promoting company called Zic Zac. To hear our music as others hear it can be a queasy experience But this Polish reading of the UK Top 40 had more than a passing sociological interest.

It was a bit like a classic fifties-sixties pop revue – everyone with their worked-out gimmick – but using utterly contemporary materials. The first band (no names, no drunken memory) were a kit-car hybrid of Blur and EMF: one audible English lyric went 'our only mission is to have (no?) ambition,' its meaning forever undecidable.

Next, a lumpy white rapper with a walking-stick: a handy translator rendered his Polish rap as being 'like a truthful news-paper ... but poetic.'

After that, some New Kids From The Bloc singing at, not with, a writhing lurex-coated minx; then, a diva in a chainmail dress ('From Vogue, a month ago,' said our drummer), shrieking 'I want you to take me.'

The act on just before us – called Soyka: two acoustic guitars, Meatloaf-eats-Pere-Ubu singer-songwriter, clenched and passionate and rather good – turns out to be a Polish mega-star. 'He sings of love in a bizarre way, of politics as if it were a bad affair,' explains a cadaverous music journalist.

'We love his music in Poland.' Then the director in the headphones waves us on, and we have to ride the subsiding wave of the local hero...

'You know, there is a huge gap in the Polish music market,' says Zic Zac's Marek Koscikiewicz, after the show. 'On the one side, there is the music everyone knows, the big stars – like OMD, la da da da. On the other side, there are types like Soyka – all lyrics, strong poetry, very important to the Polish. But I know there is a middle area – where good music fits to good lyrics; something for Poles to understand but also for the world to hear. Do you know what I mean?'

Marek, you make the perennial pitch of quality popsters throughout the developed world, and I wish you all the very best. See you on the Gdansk record racks, Mitteleuropa, 1999: copyright reserved.

# ☆ Songs for Europe

(*The Scotsman*, 8 June 1991)

'Are you flyin' off to the Gulf or whit?' As a comment on my tear-stained, kiss-blowing street farewell to the loved ones – forever framed in a Partick window – the taxi driver was not being entirely impertinent, or inaccurate. Going on my first serious European rock tour had loomed in my mind as something of a tour of duty – an impression bolstered by the surrounding cloud of music-biz justifications thundering with 'integrated campaigns', 'press launches' and 'market penetrations'.

So as the soldiers are pulling out of Mitteleuropa, we're steaming in – we've even got a gig in Poland this August, satellite-beamed all the way from Munster to Minsk. Maybe if Gorbachev really wants to create his 'common European home', he should reverse a baseball cap over his birthmark and ride some break-beats on MTV.

To continue our military metaphor: this is the Big Push into Europe, an attempt to broaden our audience beyond the psychedelic sauna of the UK music scene, by supporting Joe Jackson on the European leg of his world tour. With our first single going the way of all flesh – that is, rotten after two weeks – we're under no illusions about our audiences' predilections: why should they buy a single, when they'll get it on the album in a month? And why, honestly, should we expect them to?

We congregate in the departure lounge for Hamburg, desperate to forget children's television and mid-week chart positions, and to be immersed in something unprecedented, something requiring new reactions and responses. Rock 'n' roll is a basically narrow lifestyle – plane, train, hotel, interview, sound check, gig, bar, bed and round again – with performances the intense peak of the curve: the hour where the day's tedium is sloughed off like old skin, or burned up like a Roman candle. See how metaphorical pop life makes you?

As for anything existing beyond the ley-lines of rock travel, where national differences are commonly measured by train-seat upholstery patterns and the relative unpleasantness of bureaux des changes, you simply snatch what experiences you can: make your snap social judgments, then test them on your local record company rep.

But I wish I'd kept my peace about East Germans, inquiring delicately of our Virgin rep as to their impact on Hamburg life: 'Ah! The Ossies!' she snapped.

'You can always tell them by their clothes and haircuts – really unfashionable, you know, loud sportswear, shabbily dressed. I really don't like them.'

Her eyes travelled the street, rolling at a knot of broad-shouldered lads with shell-suits on, roaring like bulls. 'And their accents too,' she wrinkled her nose, 'you can always tell.'

I could not help but laugh inwardly: this Hamburger's reaction to the East Germans was comparable to a Morningside resident facing an invasion from Wester Hailes.

The West German bourgeoisie, tediously happy in their consumerist bubble, were now having to share their Deutschmark nationalism with the great unwashed. In conversation, though, they all seemed to agree on the solution: as an East German construction worker told one of our roadies in a late-night bar on the Reeperbahn, bemoaning the duplicity and impoverishment following reunification: 'We need the wall back up, as soon as possible! I'd build it myself!'

The Hamburg train station across from our hotel seemed to be the obvious source for East Germans. A spanking new consumer arcade had just opened in the old station hall the day we arrived and among the well padded commuters streaming through, there were clumps of labourer types, German-speaking but wearing donkey jackets, grimy denims, and permanent scowls.

One shop in the arcade – this was 9.25 a.m – had a large crowd of workies outside. It was a hi-fi and record shop: inside, Walkmans gleamed, stack stereos blinked, and at the back a cut-out of Tina Turner invited all these sons and daughters of the new Fatherland to cough up for some songs.

They might well have done: but what other records are Western or Eastern Germans buying? It's only at the end of the day, flossing my brain with some hotel MTV before the gig, that I discovered what was No 3 in their charts: *Zehn Kleinen Negerlein or Ten Little Niggers* – a centuries-old nursery rhyme about the dissoluteness of black people, updated to include syphilis, mugging and drug abuse.

The *European* reports on the record company EMI Electrola's anxiety that it may lose singers like Tina Turner from their books as a result of the release. 'Liberal-minded Germans' have also been writing threatening letters. For the sake of the comity of the gig, I had to presume that some of them were Joe Jackson fans.

Was I going to harangue an audience about their implication in such cultural atavism via a thick Scottish burr, and more than likely hitting the wrong target? It's hardly the lumpen masses, blindly sentimental about their childhood and unreflective about their national past, who'd be coming to a concert like this anyway, and there was enough politics on a rock 'n' roll level to be overly angst-ridden about finger-wagging. Instead, I smiled sweetly at Jackson's sound men, hoping they'd twiddle enough knobs to make the support band – us – sound more than, well, supportive.

And the gig? Mostly a blur, though I do retain a pleasurable, deep down throb from some moments. Half-an-hour of your best songs does tend to make you feel a bit Nietzschean, but there's a long way to go, and our first real performance for 18 months did have some once-off static electricity, like a new shirt ripped out of its Cellophane.

At the moment, finishing off here, I'm lying in a Rotterdam hotel, hooked up to a cross-channel BBC 1 on Sunday morning; I'm keeping European breakfasts and toilet bowls at bay by ingesting self-help shows, farming omnibuses and especially a Portuguese language primer, stuffed with militant Portuguese academics. Another small nation at the edge of Europe, wanting to negotiate its own terms with European modernisation and development? Lovely. And did you know that German escalators are set in motion only by the pressure of advancing footsteps, thus saving precious energy – the most theatrical piece of eco-ism I've ever seen?

Well, there you are. Europe by fragments, bundled together on a string. Next chunk next fortnight.

# ☆ Nae Luck with the Legion

(*The Scotsman*, 22 June 1991)

There is no doubt that playing the music-halls of Europe is making me feel more European. But when you meet real citizens of the Continent, in cafes or in trains, stretching polite chat into sprawling debates, you realise the shortfall between the ideal of being Scottish/European, and one's own pitiful resources for making it a reality. For the second leg of our Euro-tour, along with some clean boxer shorts, I'll definitely bring some dictionaries and grammars – French, German, Italian, and Spanish.

The German surgeon, crisply grey and fashionably crumpled, made our *en-route* dining-car conversation as easy for me as possible. 'There is no doubt that English will be the language of Europe,' he enunciated smoothly, floating into French for the approaching waitress, who turned out to be a Burgundian exile working for the German railways. Delighted that her Gallic accent had been noted, she began to bat some tri-lingual jokes around the table. The surgeon glowed, chuckled, trilled; and the olive on my plate suddenly became an object of immense interest.

For all that, he turned out to be a high-class travelling salesman, just like me, vending orthopaedic innovations to California, Australia, Austria, and all major points in between. But he was also a definite casualty of '68: anti-Gulf-War, aware of left-wing German philosophy, stridently Green. Unlike the Hamburg bourgeoisie of a fortnight ago, he welcomed the burden of the East Germans: 'It could only be cheaper than if the Cold War had continued or intensified – better no blood, better we just raise taxes.'

The Gulf War reminded him of his Berlin childhood, with the terrible bombs, the shredded families and houses, the numbing human cost. 'We Germans were not chauvinistic about this war – nor could we be; it's in our constitution, the Basic Law, but we always want to be liked, we Germans, forgiven for our sins. Did you know there was a big national debate after we won the World Cup last year? What would other countries think of us – would they resent us winning? Only a country like Germany could be so insecure about its identity.'

Sorry, who's insecure about their identity? The surgeon politely excised himself from my leech-like tourist grip, his eventual boredom reminding me how limited an over-eager mono-lingual Scot would appear to an urbane German professional.

The Polish cameraman was, thankfully, more flawed. But 'Fizz' (our lazy simplification of his name) was no less complex a European; moving across the Continent upon the prevailing media and intellectual trade winds but dragging along a loose anchor of personal and political history. As we sipped coffee in the Galleria in Milan, between pop interviews, he was visibly juddering with the weight of his Polishness.

'You in the West do not understand – we Poles need pain, the pain of unemployment and competition. We must get as far away from the past as possible, by the quickest way.' What, national Catholic masochism meets Thatcherite purity? Fizz was laying into my comments about the centrist drift of British politics – where all parties are accepting that the 'state' is not a dirty word – with the impatience of someone who's had 'society' up to his gills.

'It is in human nature for there to be some imperfection, some unfairness and inequality. Would life be at all interesting in the perfectly planned society? In the East we have had enough', – he sharply surveyed the immense consumer emporium of the Galleria – 'of planning.'

After our shoot, I strolled across the square to enter the great Duomo, the biggest religious edifice I've ever experienced. My thoughts sailed up and around its Cecil B de Mille columns and altars, flying along secular paths of fancy; writing unwritten songs, practising impolite politics, and making connections …

Bump! Or, more accurately, three timber-shivering bangs on a French hotel-room door at 3am in the morning. 'Haw guys, are youse in there? It's me fae the Foreign Legion! I've goat yir taxi money back fae thae thievin' French bastards!' Never mind all this Europhilia: quite the best story of the tour so far concerns a Foreign Legionnaire from Priesthill, encountered by the more nocturnal members of our musical troupe in a bar in the south of France. He made himself known as the band were stuttering over a very late-night taxi booking; initially, his burst of 'Awright guys, whit's goin' on?' was taken as a rural *patois* of a particularly difficult strain. Gradually, through repetition, the startling truth came into focus: this small, perfectly-uniformed, bullet-headed French state mercenary was, in fact, a hard wee Scot abroad, latching on to some home buddies.

It transpired that a Legion barracks was stationed near Orange, where the gig was. This desert-coloured joker took the band through a street of 'Legion bars' to get to their wild-eyed extortioning taxi drivers. The knock at the hotel door revealed the man from Priesthill in a state of severe post-altercation, holding a 200-franc note like a bloodied scalp. The rest of the night's tale – as related to me from four corners of the breakfast table next morning – was utterly believable; for the simple reason that when men express compassion for the constrictions of another man's masculinity, the emotion is so untypical it has to be true.

'Basically a sad wee guy,' was the general view; silent about his past, relishing the violence of his existence, but pathetically desperate to reflect his brutalised cut-off identity in the startled faces of some familiar souls.

What do you do? 'I kill people.' What it's like at the barracks? 'They batter you stupit for the first month, then they give you a new name. You can't use your old one ever again.' Where have you been? 'We were in Iraq, "suppressing the monster", they said. Some monster. Guys wi' nae shoes, cadgin' ciggies aff us. They were tragic. It wisnae a fight, more like a chase.' Where are you off to now? 'Ethiopia. Something t'dae there.'

Then he wanted to sleep overnight in the hotel, and it became fractious; fists at sides, machine-gun expletives, a long cajoling down to reception door. 'Some effin' Scots you are,' he shouted from the night – off to drill his platoon in an hour's time, strafe them with his hobnail-applied French.

An actual Scottish European? Undoubtedly. Though I dearly hope there are easier ways ...

# ☆ Troubles in mind

(*The Scotsman*, 13 April 1991)

Where does one start with Belfast? Our drive in from the airport seems the easiest place. Naomi from BBC Northern Ireland meets us in the glossy arrivals lounge, and up until the traffic jam, this is just like any good British pop TV date: personable researcher; fast, comfortable car; an assiduously cultivated sense of being quite important for a day or two.

'Oh, God, this is really unusual,' says Naomi, as we slow to a halt. 'This road is normally straight through.' Pause. 'There might be some kind of bomb scare or something' – casual and eventoned, banalising such extremes for her quietly nervous visitors.

Looking around us for the first time, we don't see the expected historical murals, but a busy chaos of urban redevelopment – an especially smart design centre to our left, all pink sandstone and blue window frames. It is, however, next to the most smashed-out Victorian warehouse, a vision of stone-throwing delinquency; Belfast Getting It Slightly Wrong.

Naomi hasn't noticed this before – only back six months, four years in London, one in Australia – and her laugh rips out. 'Ho, that's really Irish isn't it?'

Well, you said it, Naomi. Should we try to comprehend this place, with its violent contrasts and inescapable paradoxes, as the urban crucible of fractured Irish identity? Or do we sing the TV songs, smile sweetly to one and all, then get the hell out of here ?

We head for a recommended bar on arrival at the Plaza Hotel – the Crown, a beautiful Victorian pub just over the road, impressively tiled and carved. Joxes, directly across from the reception, bustles with workmen and features a confidently exact apology sign: 'Will Be Open in Three Weeks – Sorry About the Delay'.

A terrorist delay, of course – the bar was bombed ten days ago, no-one would say by what side. And really, you don't want to ask too many exact questions about sides, or specifics, or personal positions; it seems like the worst kind of interested-liberal chatter, insensitive to the deadly consequences of expressing an opinion in this society. There is also an insistent pressure to normalise life, especially among media folk, which it is very difficult to resist. Why not be camp, talk style, trade telly anecdotes? It's only Belfast, after all ...

Our minder, John, somewhat Bushmilled, asks all the wrong questions on the drive to the studio rehearsal. 'Do you want to do a tour of the hot-spots?' says Naomi directly. 'Some bands do, y'know.' We demur, and comment absently on the affluence of the area. Naomi answers as revealingly as could be expected: 'Yes, I live in a nice place like this ... If you come from a middle-class neighbourhood in Belfast you're all right, the Troubles don't even touch you. But if you know the terrorists in the communities, if you've been born among them, then you're always going to be connected, some way or another.'

We hit the gravel-path running, glad hands extended gladly, looking for ebullient thirtysomethings with clipboard and head-mikes. The show is called, well, *The Show*, and comprises live music, satire and celebrity interviews. My favourite radical Country & Western gynaecologist, Hank Wangford, is hosting; the mike sound is wonderful, the director is amenable, the sound check is knee-trembling, all is right for tomorrow.

Stepping out of the hotel crisp and early next morning, I head for the Arts Council Bookshop, and pick up a sheaf of local literary productions – *The H.U.* (Honest Ulsterman), *Circa Arts Magazine*, the Belfast-based Irish political magazine *Fortnight*. This is as expected – the international community of cosy lefties, tremulous aesthetes and typeface utopians has its outpost here – and I note a small ad for Just Books, 'radical anarchist booksellers', in Winetavern Road. Radical anarchists? Everybody must hate them!

Belfast town centre is exactly like Glasgow – generous pedestrian precincts, grid-iron street patterns, plush big shopping centres like Castle Court. 'That gets bombed every other week', said the chambermaid. 'The Provisionals hit all the British-owned shops. I was in there the other Saturday, had to run out 'cause of a bomb scare. Really annoying.' She brightens inexplicably.

'But I'd love to work there, y'know; it's a beautiful place.'

Indeed it is – but the wee metal table forcing the entrants into a queue and the avuncular security guards glancing into your bag make it both saddening and worrying. Could they find anything? Do anything? In time? I chew croissants, read books, watch the promenade, like everyone else.

Just Books has a bell entry – the third of the day, the others a flyblown newsagent's, and a furniture shop. Once inside, I can guess why; a complete rack of Republican journals at the back, like an ideological weapons cache. Snatching some non-Irish leftie print, I make my polite purchase and get out. The map's told me the Falls Road is up ahead, and I'm not succumbing to all the normalisations.

A jokeshop sits next door, window full of lurid masks of Turtles and assorted cartoon characters; small irony noted. But it's not until late that night, absorbing local poet Ciaran Carson's brilliant volume *Belfast Confetti* (Gallery Press), that I come across these lines, connecting Disney and death, carnival hire and carnage:

> When a bunch of hoods pulls up
> in a Ford Sierra and jumps out
> with the sawn-off
> shotguns, plastic masks they must
> have got in Elliot's – Mickey
> Mouse, Donald Duck
> and Pluto – too much watching
> TV, if you ask me, so of course
> the Brits
> *let go with everything* ...

'Belfast confetti' refers strictly to the rain of half-bricks landed on British soldiery in the schemes; but Carson reworks it as a Baudelairian tableau of urban fragments, pieces of a strange, terrible city.

I've gathered my own, minor scraps. The local radio station called Downtown is in the middle of a rural nowhere, beaming the sounds of the street from a grotty agricultural enclosure. Why? 'Well, Pat, if it was city centre, all sorts of trouble could happen – you know, the revolutionaries taking over the radio station and all that Saddam Hussein stuff ...'

I saw ponies tethered on a grass verge in front of a new brick row of terraced houses; most of the front doors were wide open, a rag-and-bone cart beside one of them, as the main road to the city centre thundered by. I saw two women – one receptionist, one TV floor manager – almost jump out of their skins at sharp, unpredicated noises; I heard of one Belfast man breaking down hysterically at the exhaust bang of an armoured jeep passing by in the city centre: I looked into the eyes of a British soldier outside the main courthouse, and saw a petrified young man among the holiday shoppers.

So what if I saw all this? We sang and played well, drove back knackered, flew home the next morning: goodbye Belfast. Rarely have I felt so utterly irrelevant to the real forces and struggles of a place, so unable to comment or judge: never have I felt so sad for the people living there.

Will normality finally win out and gently crush Northern Irish sectarianism, weighed down by democracy, equality of opportunity, a desire for the quiet life? I can only quote an overhead summation from a philosophising satirist in his BBC dressing-room. 'It's us, isn't it: Ulster – half-read newspapers, scripts abandoned ... Ah Tom, I like yer white socks though!'

Belfast: we'll be back.

# ☆ I had a dream

(*The Scotsman*, 8 July 1989)

Every time I open my mouth to sing I'm American. This is not a matter of choice. My psyche has a long-standing contract with my lips, teeth, tongue and diaphragm; whenever this man wishes to rend the heavens asunder with the sound of angels, he must do so in an accent lost somewhere between Hoboken and Minneapolis.

I know where it all started – on a living-room floor in Hamilton, Christmas 1967, with my father's finger prodding me into performance for the assembled relatives. Out came the number dad had been drilling through me for days: 'I left my heart … in Fransan-cisco …' The reaction was a comforting aunties' chorus of ooh and awws, but one behind-the-hand comment has always stuck. 'God, John, he's like a wee Tony Bennett, a wee American.'

Ever since, a small cornerstone of my identity has remained profoundly American; the tougher the outside world got, the more Fourth and Broadway my fantasies became. Adolescence was most memorably spent mouthing Bobby Darin and Frank Sinatra in a stuffy summer bedroom, kids gratingly cheerful outside; or stomach-down in front of BBC2 on a Saturday afternoon, soaking in *The Sweet Smell of Success* with Tony Curtis and Burt Lancaster.

You'll notice that these are decidedly mid-Fifties American obsessions, which could only further alienate a Seventies youth from his peers; who'd bother with a doughball who preferred his parents' party classics to punk or pomp rock? Discovering soul – Stevie Wonder, Marvin Gaye – brought on even more commonroom abuse, a faintly racist and sexist snobbery about black American music that characterised the serious rock fan of the time. 'See all that stuff – it's jist disco crap, fur *lassies*.'

When I moved from the bedroom mirror to the TV monitor, a lonely dreamer in Coatbridge to a video-making popster in Los Angeles, the image that flickered back at me was stunningly ideal: three-buttoned Tony Rome black suit, sky-blue *Guys n' Dolls* tie, perfectly miming a Motownesque first single. The food was Mexican, the behaviour was effortlessly Californian, and I was in Transatlantic Paradise.

But when you arrive in Utopia, an unexpected weirdness creeps over you. To be materially in a place which has only ever been immaterial to you; to find the symbols of your American dreams almost knocking you down in the street, or purchasable for a dollar 50 ... reality just doesn't feel, well, real in these situations.

Living in Manhattan for a few months, making music by day and hanging out at night, it all becomes a little too cinematic to be true. You find yourself sounding like a reject Woody Allen script, constantly making wisecracks and snap judgments, just to stay ahead in the conversation.

So eventually the American dreams of my private imaginings were deflated by the public reality of the American Dream. A hundred disillusions a day – the suppurating beggars with their shaming sales pitches ('War veteran – diabetes – family of five – No Small Change Please'); the insane TV discussion shows, where the dependent and different get ripped apart by raving fascist hosts; the essential brittleness of professional New-Yorkers, insulating themselves from the terror of their own city with culture and cuisine, keeping all social contacts south of Harlem.

One returns to Scotland with a sense that things are manageable in this country, that life can be under some kind of control. A consensus of values, and therefore effective politics, is a daily possibility in Scottish society. It's almost impossible to think of that in New York and Los Angeles, the two main cities of my American imagination.

Economic inequality is so extreme, yet so problematised by factors like ethnic tension, rampant capitalism, civic corruption, and drugs, that any local politics soon resolves itself into three minimal questions; who takes the cut, who's behind it, and frankly, who cares? The news of school teachers in Brooklyn dealing crack to their pupils, or Uzi-toting youths blowing away static drivers in Los Angeles traffic jams, only confirms the suspicion; the America of my dreams is impossibly strung out between madness and glamour – and that I had better find some richer and more constructive dreams, some alternative to big cities and bright lights.

I find myself becoming more politically active the more America recedes on my emotional horizons. The good life is achievable here, through common discussion and action, rather than tantalisingly *over there*, where all one's satisfactions are derived from a few glittering fragments of life that shatter under close scrutiny.

Yet how those fragments still glitter! The problem for anyone who is given artistic voice by American culture, but can't help being disgusted by the excesses of the system which produced it, is to separate technique from content, even technique from the individual. Sinatra might have gotten to his microphones through a mixture of Mafia patronage, media manipulation and vicious commercial instinct – but once there, every immaculate phrase of his ballads would seem to plead for forgiveness, his vocal splendour an inspiration despite the man and the system.

These days, one can listen to a rap track from Public Enemy or Tone-Löc, and analyse its semantic content down to the most virulent fundamentalist politics, or the least forgiving misogyny. Yet the thrill and artistry of the rap, weaving and tugging its street lexicon through the compressed, compelling beats of hip-hop music, is utterly undeniable. And one could say the same for the narrative power of *Fatal Attraction* (despite its medieval sexual politics) or the psychological sophistication of *Thirtysomething* (despite its political retreat into yuppie private life).

The ultimate distinction in one's approach to American culture is not to be for or against, with or without, but active or passive. Does one simply accept that to love rock'n'roll is to love America – or does one employ irony to enjoyably distance the music from the society, or even use its techniques to convey a critique of both American and British societies?

On Hue and Cry's last national tour, in a song called *Survivors*, I sang in my habitual Hoboken twang, 'Won't pay my poll taxes' – which always raised a cheer in our impeccably aware home audience. But they'd never heard the number before, it hadn't been recorded, so it was up to me to make sure the lyric got across. Never have the clicking consonants and controlled melismas of Frank Sinatra been put to such productive, socialist use! To paraphrase the old cornball's millstone classic, I do him my way.

# ☆ Where the music doesn't take me

(*The Scotsman*, 9 June, 1990)

The last thing I expected to get involved in at the Big Day last week was a tense argument about form, authenticity and intention. Backstage after the night-time gig, I bumped into a member of the Edinburgh chart band, The Chimes, and expressed polite admiration for their cover version of the U2 song, *I Still Haven't Found What I'm Looking For*. 'But I hate you, and I hate your music,' said the gentleman crisply, shaded glasses glinting in the floodlights.

I don't often meet such splendid antipathy – it can be educational, in a purging sort of way. Feeling quite good about myself after having crooned to 175,000 people, I swallowed slightly and asked him to justify his opinions.

The resulting conversation has set my mental wheels spinning again about the relationship between the art you make and the feelings you have when you make it. Are artistic conventions at the service of the passions of the artist, or do their structures actually limit the emotions that go into them and come out of them? Can artists be trapped by their most formative influences as cultural history moves on round and past them?

The man from The Chimes had no doubts about my pop-historical redundancy. The whole cult of musicianship, of song-structure, of dramatic arrangement – all the values he correctly imputed as mine – were dead or dying out. Sound-sampling technology had liberated the pop musician into a whole new unprecedented world of creativity.

'You should be ranging all over the field, bringing together things that don't fit, from everywhere and anywhere.' By now, the theorising was in top gear. 'This is no time to be paying respect to traditions – you should be abusing them, refusing to be content with what you know. Why are you so safe?'

Given that he'd just had a hit single where his vocalist's performance was right in the long-established tradition of soul testifiers like Aretha Franklin and Patti Labelle, it seemed a bit rich to be nailing me down as museum curator of Scottish pop. But his pitch about a new technology-led eclecticism in British-American pop – and me being completely out of touch with it – *does* hit a sore spot.

The neatest example of my distance from current chart activity is Adamski's *Killer*, a recent No. 1. The song's sonic impact on first hearing seems as nihilistic as its title – harshly repeated synth motifs, disinterested vocal, a mix which refuses any hierarchy of sounds, impossible rhythms constructed out of the latest technological mutations.

This discordance and desiccation obviously gives its young teenage consumers the same life-enhancing tingle as Michael Jackson or Elvis Costello gave me when they hit the charts. But I feel as far away from this brutal new wave as I did from punk, even further away in that dance music has always been one of my prime inspirations. Now I apparently no longer know how to dance.

Paradoxically, The Chimes' record – for all the anti-performance, militantly technoid rhetoric of its originator – *does* click with me as a passionate dance number. The beat, hung on a lazily syncopating kick drum, reminds me of a whole heritage of soul rhythm sections, from Marvin Gaye to Allen Toussaint to Washington's Go-Go scene. The American phenomenon of 'swingbeat' contains in its title a counter-argument to machines setting the trends for rhythm – the 'swing' links back to jazz/bop timings, and you can't get more performative than those roots.

So if pop-dance music has to be all about samples and programmes these days, it still depends on which samples and which programmes you choose. And there's no rule which says that real drummers can't be inspired by the punishing new machine rhythms of modern dance, turning them into a dazzling part of their repertoire. Hue And Cry's drummer Mark Forshaw often entertains the rest of us in rehearsal by manually reproducing the latest club grooves, and then flipping them around with a true player's dexterity.

Adamski was supposed to be playing The Big Day, but dropped out on the night: the main excuse going round was that he'd left his backing tapes in his hotel room in London. One is tempted to say that a part of the defence's case is thus proven, at least when it comes to major rock festivals. Skilled musicians can still make music after the technical hitch is fixed, whereas the new sampling popsters rely entirely on the reproduction rather than the performance of music. And when the tape machine dies, they also expire.

But we've all faked it before. Any vocal mime on some nondescript TV slot – whether requested by a producer or by artists who don't trust either their own talent or the expertise of the situation – always feels like a sneaky aesthetic lie, which should be exposed where it isn't clumsily obvious. I once saw a Virgin band at a concert for record retailers go through hell when their tape machine speeded up half-way through the song, shattering what little illusion of sincerity remained with undignified Mickey Mouse squeaking and cartoonish rhythms.

That's the nightmare of the 'performance' band, caught out on its own promotional compromises. But the new club record-makers aren't hung up on authenticity, sincerity, 'live' performance. A string of personal appearances at some rave happenings, shouting over the top of your record with dance routines, is a more effective way to sell that particular product than an honest, gritty tour of the toilet venues of Britain.

So I can understand the new dance but I can't become it for the life of me. There is something about the physical crunch of the live band, the miracle of ten humans playing their separate parts but perfectly fitting into a living musical whole, which for me will always win over the digital accuracy of techno-pop. This is a matter of being deeply formed by music where variation was human and unrepeatable – a unique gradation of sound and emphasis which no complexly programmed machine could ever manage.

But it is entirely conceivable that a section of today's teeny fans will respond to the metallic soundscapes of the charts, and see in all that controlled discordance a new kind of harmony. They might begin to combine the sheer musicianly pleasures of melody and inversion, that glorious infinitude of note permutation, with the expanded vocabulary of sounds that electronics and synthesisers bring. Some of Prince's music, for me, hints at that new sensibility. Could there be a Hendrix of the sampler? A Gadd of the break-beat?

Surely it's silly to set up an antagonism between self-consciously 'authentic' and 'inauthentic' pop. As the 'players' have a lot to learn from the gleeful magpie approach and compulsive repetitions of the 'samplers', so the latter must eventually return to the joys of human interaction and performance in music. If they were allowed to react dialectically, I think you could call it progress.

Unfortunately, this writer has his other foot mired in the most unprogressive attitudes towards sonic hybridisation. My brother and I recently did a recording date with the Edinburgh bebop outfit The John Rae Collective. We've never had as much fun musically: six players dropping gently from a whispered vocal, tightening up hard at an emotional climax in the lyric, following each other in dances of rhythm and melody, collectively responding as if connected by a membrane.

Mr Chimes, you can shovel dirt on my pop coffin from your Top Ten chart position till I'm dead and rotting in the Hades of musical obscurity. But let me spin in my grave, on the 1-2-3-4, with the brushers of drums and the splitters of reeds: dead happy.

## ☆ When protest was a four-letter word

(*The Scotsman*, 15 November 1991)

How could a real Sinatra fan like myself be expected to respond to Sid Vicious's anthrax version of *My Way*? By thanking him for my career in the music business. I've just steamed through Jon Savage's superb history of the Sex Pistols and punk rock, *England's Dreaming* (Faber), and I am forcibly reminded of the convoluted debt I owe to those thirty-six months during the late Seventies in enabling me to make music.

I hated it at the time, of course. To my tender soul-jazz ears, listening to the Pistols, the Damned, the Cortinas or whoever tested the limits of aural endurance. I enjoyed the little moments of institutional chaos bursting all around me. But the style and the sounds of early punk barred me from participating – far too disjunct from my own pre-formed fantasies of flashing horn-sections and sharp suits.

But it's the small moments of genuine liberation I remember about punk that have always made me concede its case. At school, during the young male bear-pit that was the free period, there was one fevered music discussion that stays with me, concerning the Tom Robinson Band. A peer-group leader – footballer, romancer, the works – hesitantly expressed his allegiance, and was barracked instantly. 'But Tom Robinson's a total poof! *Sing if you're glad to be gay* and all that shite!'

As the general lisping increased, the lad – to his eternal credit – stood his ground. 'All that stuff doesn't matter. So what if he's gay? That's OK, it's not that important. He's got good songs.'

This was the last guy to be accused of secret poofery, so the issue dispersed and moved on – but I was silently shocked. I suffered 'homo-fairy' abuse from this male élite – day in, day out – simply because of some perceived difference, yet here was a top dog in the pack expressing solidarity with a gay punk rock star?

Punk's role in bringing marginal experiences and communities into the centre of music is well documented and verified. As Savage describes it, however, punk's aftermath was even more productive than its initial, two-fingered assault on sclerotic late-Seventies

Britain: 'If it had been the project of the Sex Pistols to destroy the music industry, then they had failed; but as they gave it new life, they allowed a myriad of new forms to become possible.'

This 'myriad of new forms' is commonly known as post-punk, which is where my musical tastes began to link up with, and be transformed by, the pop avant-garde. Early punk was musically explosive, but structurally conventional: bass, drums, guitar, vocals, 1-2-3-4 ... Post-punk began to soften this very white male musical clench. Groups like Scritti Politti, Ian Dury and the Blockheads, the Au Pairs, Magazine and the Gang of Four brought reggae, funk and soul into their music, albeit in a radically and thrillingly off-centred fashion.

It was this explicit, strategic use of the musics which had shaped me since early childhood that excited me about post-punk. To put it bluntly, you could sing about the tawdry spectacle of Western late-capitalism and still sound a wee bit like the Ohio Players; a lyrical perspective that took in anything but romance and relationships could be practised in a musical context which had syncopation and harmony. A music that wanted to change the world didn't have to sound like the end of the world.

For me, the two bands that immediately realised this potential in post-punk were Heaven 17 and ABC; *Penthouse and Pavement* and *Lexicon of Love* were two early-Eighties albums that set the exact precedents for the music I wanted to make – slick-sounding, radical-speaking. In our first Hue and Cry interviews, I returned obsessively to the image of the 'sugared pill' as a metaphorical handle; initially sweet to suck, but with a harsh medicine inside.

Well, the audiences keep taking the pills, and have done so for five years now; but I think my medicine has changed. Reading Savage's book, especially his transcript of the swearing episode with the Pistols on the *Bob Grundy Show*, I realise how much punk's media terrorism affected me.

During our first hits, I gleefully mentioned the phrases 'sexual stereotypes' and 'Socialist Workers Party' on paranoid children's television; I also remember sticking my tongue into Richard Jobson's ear as he prattled to autocue on a midday chat show, 'venerating' Elkie Brooks's lurex trousers on live television, and many other incidents mentally blanked out since. Why?

I recall the theoretical excuse; your audience has to know you're wiser than this promotional bullshit; witty media awareness sells. But apart from genuinely regretting the grief and heartache this strategy caused to those around me, I don't subscribe to that theory now because, quite simply, its time has passed.

What seemed like a radical act, in the grand demystifying

tradition of Malcolm McLaren, is now the very premise of
programmes like C4's *The Word*. The presenters get their abuse of
the icons in first; a theatre of irritation, in which old Grundies
would explode, making for high-rating television. In fact I've been
seeing McLaren recently in a toe-tapping TV advertisement he's
made for some chocolate bar. 'The media was our lover and our
helper' went one of his last Sex Pistols slogans. Never stops in your
case, Malcolm.

So small acts didn't – and won't – shatter the media spectacle;
they can actually strengthen it as this convention-shaking becomes
incorporated into daily programming. My own personal shift has a
lot to do with my increasing faith in organised politics and specific
policies to enact change – and even that only within an initially
Scottish context. My media interventions are now largely intended
to help reconstruct a modern Scottish consciousness, one way or
another.

'Playing the game', I've now come to understand, means
choosing your battles – or even simpler, not ducking a question but
answering as honestly as possible, articulating one's own passions
rather than incessantly scheming to change others. I heard a Radio
One DJ, with whom we've done quite a few wide-ranging
interviews, follow our current single by characterising the status of
Scotland as a 'politically oppressed nation'. Well thank you Ms
Brambles; that must be the reward for perpetrating a reasonably
winsome Sean Connery impersonation on drive-time radio.

'Just sing the song, Pat,' they used to shout from the stalls, and it
would enrage me; shouldn't the pop moment be *everything* – heart
and commitment, performance and information, love and politics?
Sounds like an old post-punk speaking, beating furious waves on
the ineradicable cliffs of the mass media. To have a clear identity, a
Scottish pop musician taps into a narrower stream – but at least it's
going somewhere, however winding the path.

# ☆ Rhythm and bliss

Simon Reynolds. BLISSED OUT: THE RAPTURES OF ROCK. Serpent's Tail, £8.99; Richard Middleton. STUDYING POPULAR MUSIC. Open University Press, £14.99.

(*The Glasgow Herald*, 1 December 1990)

Pop music and high academic theory are not the most predictable partners. Although the status of pop among the broadsheets and supplements has certainly improved in the past few years, the idea of a scholarly approach to this most transient of media still occasions derisory snorts – not least in the official music press itself. A recent review of *Blissed Out* by one of the writer's *Melody Maker* colleagues began: 'Simon Reynolds is a wanker. Discuss.'

This is exactly the rock-critical tone – cynical, seen-it-all, limply abusive – that Reynolds and his comrades wanted to attack when they began writing in the late eighties. But they also had a grouse against the pop activists – those critics for whom pop was 'church high-mindedness,' constantly attending to the music's political and moral 'relevance.' The banal humanism of post-Live-Aid rock, its caring-sharing values and the insipid musical vessels that carried them, drove Reynolds in particular into torrents of articulate rage, the best of which are collected here.

As someone who finds himself a target of Reynolds's critique, in a chapter called 'Smooth Operators.' I'm obviously going to redeem the humanist pop and rock he so abhors. But I'm indebted to him for this intellectual lucidity – no one has expounded the 'rock-as-chaos-and-abandon' position with as much accessible erudition. It behoves the opposition to get its aesthetic act together, and marshall its own theoretical gurus in defence.

For Reynolds justifies his tastes with the most fashionable of references – the full French post-modern line-up: Bataille, Foucault, Baudrillard, Kristeva, and pre-eminently Roland Barthes, whose theory of aesthetic pleasure underpins the writer's approach. All these thinkers, it could easily be said, are theorists of the irrational, the inhuman, the psychologically subversive. For them, coherent and mature individuality is tyrannical, locking the self into a stifling culture of strictures and norms. The best art threatens, or achieves, dissolution of the self; in Barthes's terms, from the safe satisfactions of *plaisir* to the thrilling abandonments of *jouissance*.

How appropriate this schema is to the traditional understanding of rock and pop as tongue-flailing, neo-bestial wig-out need not be spelt out. Reynolds incessantly inveighs against the attention given to the 'text', the lyrics and statements of a band, in favour of purely sonic and physical qualities – 'the grain of the voice, the materiality of sound, the biological effect of rhythm, the fascination of the star's body.'

Who could ever deny that, since Presley was televisually cut off at the waist on the Ed Sullivan Show, there is more to pop communication than well-crafted songs? The physical rhetoric of contemporary artists such as Madonna, Prince, and renegade figures like Morrissey and Nick Cave, is inseparable from their overall significance. Even watching Paul Buchanan of Blue Nile at Glasgow Royal Concert Hall recently, twisting tortuously round his mike-stand as his voice hit the rafters, brought a new component of the band's joyous modernism into view: the struggle to be humane, loving, graceful that is one of their strongest lyrical themes, literally became embodied on stage.

But does this attention to the extra-linguistic elements of pop necessarily lead to the fashionable brutalism of Reynolds – that all pop must be judged by its ability to chew up verbal meaning, deny and destroy the inevitable presence of sung words by every sound technique available? A a lyricist, of course, I would say not – if we didn't want words in our songs, if they didn't gratify some need, we'd be listening to instrumentals all day. But the mechanisms of this need can be explained from a wholly separate set of intellectual co-ordinates than Reynolds's – which if they don't supersede them, at least carry as much scholarly legitimacy.

Richard Middleton's *Studying Popular Music* is comprehensive enough to provide resources for both positions; as the main text book for the Open University's Popular Music course, its ambitions – admirably achieved – are synoptic and pedagogic rather than polemic.

But it does render up an alternative understanding of how psyche and art interact which emphasises not the irrational and the disintegrative, but the rational and integrative power of pop music – the way that its pleasures can be lastingly derived from the inventiveness and appropriateness of words, the intelligent reworkings of recognised musical traditions and forms, the intentions of the artists and the realisation of these in lyrics and music.

Much of this debate depends, quite simply, on what school of psychoanalysis you borrow from – for if you want to theorise why someone likes something, a working model of the unconscious and language is the least that you need. The one that Reynolds and company usually latch on to is the Lacanian one: briefly, language (and thus identity) comes to the child as a traumatic rip from sensual unity with the mother; every intentional use of language thereafter is always shadowed by pain, as we mourn for the rest of our lives the impossibility of returning to that pre-linguistic, pre-individual idyll.

In this way Reynolds legitimates his aesthetics: every failed, failing, contorted expression in pop can be a little taste of this lost mother's paradise, and this indicates authentic human happiness; a brief escape from the prison-house of language and cognition, into a bosomly, brainless bliss.

Fall upon the book of object relations therapy, however, in the school of Melanie Klein and D. W. Winnicott, and an entirely opposed explanation is to hand. Here, the child has an identity and ego at birth – fragile, prone to splitting up and self-loathing, but desperate for confirmation of itself in the outside world. Communication with the carers is pre-verbal, based on contact and responsiveness, not contingent upon language. So the child acquires language in a slow curve, as a part of its increasing mastery of self, not with the explosive trauma of the Lacanian scheme. Language expresses a pre-existing self, for object relations-theorists; it does not exclusively constitute it.

Under this model, the sounds of pop need not necessarily subvert the sense of pop: words can articulate a sensuality accurately in their meanings as well as their sounds; expression of self is possible, because there always is a deep emotional self to express, beyond the churnings of language.

This is probably the reason why love and relationships are so much the content of pop words – those early bonds of caring and nurturing are what pop content tries to recall, and in an oblique way it attempts to propagate their extension throughout social life. 'What the world needs now, is love, sweet love ...'

But there are other emotions than these to express – envy ambition, trust, submission, domination, altruism, individualism, friendship ... And an artist like myself sees no reason why the pop form is not capable of adequately exploring these areas and their combinations, in ways that use the potentiality of pop as public poetry or 'daily philosophy', in Gramsci's words: as a quotidianising of new language and a revitalising of old words, using music to give daily discourse a new affective force.

The topsyturviness of modern experience need not be surrendered to in artistic form, disintegration mirroring disinte-gration; it can be worked through, cast in significant symmetries and oppositions … in verse, choruses, middle-eights and fade-outs, even.

It is the difference, perhaps, between pop enabling us to understand ourselves, the better to engage with (and transform) the world; and pop expressing our psychic disablement, the only salvation being to escape from daily life altogether. I respect the latter approach, but I choose the former: I am at heart a humanist, not a nihilist. And if mere pop criticism can bring us such clear philosophical commitments, then a little metatheory in your messaboogie can surely be no bad thing.

# ☆ In a bell jar with Madonna

(*The Scotsman*, 3 August 1991)

I am obsessed with two women at the moment: Madonna Ciccone, musician, and Sylvia Plath, poet. Madonna, because she is alive, immediate and powerful; Plath, because she is dead, unknowable and disturbing. I really don't know whether I'm fascinated by the arguments these women raise about sexuality and culture, or whether I'm just sexually fascinated, analysis dignifying lust. Either way, writing about such obsessions saves having to bone up on multinational macro-economics.

Not that Madonna isn't about multinational macro-economics. When our paths crossed briefly about four years ago – she was playing Wembley, we were dodging her audience's cold burgers as a warm-up act – the impact of her concert behind the scenes was as great as the showbiz spectacle; teams of worried technocrats, suits trailing accounting sheets, conference rooms filled with visiting dignitaries. And at the centre – only ever visible to my naked eye as a small, poised woman encased in a phalanx of bodyguards, on her way to the catering area – was Madonna herself; totally in control, the only reason for this travelling corporate edifice, both the foundation stone and the executive chair.

Given this brief experience of the absolute authority of Madonna, it has never surprised me that her music and images are so concerned with sexual power – dominant, submissive, alternative. Someone who is so organised on a business and administrative level must feel able to allow her art to explore all the possibilities of sexual and personal identity; secure that no artistic version of herself – however vulnerable or intimidating – will ever affect the basic power structures of her career. Other women, without that level of real underlying control, could never permit themselves to be so publicly fluid in their identities – which is the brunt of some feminist critique of Madonna's art.

Does Madonna, dressed only in the Stars and Stripes and encouraging American viewers to sign on the electoral register – 'or you'll get your bottom spanked' – mean more voters registered, or more bottoms spanked (or just more Madonna records sold)?

When Madonna states in a BBC *Omnibus* interview her basic belief that 'pussy rules the world', is this a witty feminist fundamentalism (phallic patriarchy, move over!), or is it a wholesale concession to male sexism – women's power residing in men's desire for them?

For this man, at least, it's wonderful the way Madonna mixes politics of the most substantive sort – democratic participation, sexual tolerance, pro-abortion, support for people with AIDS – with sexuality of a most polymorphous nature: straight, gay, tough, tender, harsh, smooth

*In Bed With Madonna*, as a title, has the same double resonance: this film teases you to watch on the basis of an obvious wish-fulfilment, but hints that you may also be 'in bed' with the whole range of Madonna's strong moral and political positions – as American citizens earlier in this century have been described as 'in bed' with Soviets, Cubans or some other subversive malignancy. And as for the 'warts-and-all' candour of her rockumentary, however much it may reveal the hypocrisies, inconsistencies and even pathologies of personality that are a by-product of her position, these flaws are at least Madonna's very own; making money out of their copyright, firmly under her media thumb. The avalanche of Madonna interviews, each one more self-obsessed than the last, shows the superstar is as careful in shaping the impact of her policy initiatives – sorry, her new movie – as any government spin-doctor.

It's the sexual economy, the public distribution of good feelings, of which Madonna is currently prime minister, and I can't help thinking that her next move will be into politics proper. In what other area do symbols have so much power; and where else might the consequences of one's artistry with symbols have lasting effect? Pussy rules America, and then the world? We can but hope . . .

Madonna is a woman artist who seems to have a tight grip on her own mythology. Sylvia Plath's art, recently and for many years since her suicide, has been subject to interpretative arguments of a highbrow but increasingly bitter kind, presided over by the executor and editor of her literary estate, her husband (and Poet Laureate) Ted Hughes. Was the writer of *Daddy* ('There's a stake in your fat black heart/And the villagers never liked you ... /Daddy, daddy, you bastard, I'm through') a brilliant poetic subverter of male rationality who was crushed in the process, as feminist critics say; or was Plath a wild talent whose writing was too hysterical and symptomatic, too much a reflection of her own fractured feminity, as non-feminists have claimed?

In her recent study, *The Haunting of Sylvia Plath* (Virago), Jaqueline Rose attempts to lift the poet from her tug-of-war position between these opposed readings. Rose makes Plath more than a feminist heroine or a masculinist victim, and into a player with the very certainties of self and language, self and other, self and history. Plath's poetry taps into the basic psychological mechanisms which actually enable us to speak and act; the violence we have to sublimate, the submissiveness we have to dispel, so that we can function socially. Plath writes of these processes, but is never quite mistress of them, never quite servant to them; neither analyst, nor patient, but an artist of the highest order.

The specific poetic readings in Rose's book are too marvellously subtle to allow any fair paraphrase – I can only direct you to them, and then back to Plath's poetry. But Rose's general argument contrasts interestingly with my Madonna thesis; the most valuable way to consider Plath's art, says Rose, is not to absolve her or blame her, pathologise or eulogise her, but to take 'her' – the idea of a recoverable self called 'Sylvia Plath' – out of the picture altogether, and have her exist only as her remaining writing.

The Plath of the pen has her own logic; her work a nexus of psychological structure and language, and on that level analysable. The Plath beyond that is no more, unable to answer, her personal 'blameworthiness' or 'innocence' (whoever may adjudicate on that: family, friends, feminists, Poet Laureates) quite irrelevant to the present power of her work.

Compare Madonna; a strong reading of her work keeps her at the centre of the picture, calling all the shots and pulling all the levers: no erasing of the acting, thinking self for Ms Ciccone if you wish to understand her work, which is problematic for the semioticians in the gallery.

Madonna is not Monroe, in that her sexual power is not a compensation for career powerlessness: Madonna is not Plath, in that she is the absolute source of her own artistic corpus, herself the editor of her public effect; her story now, in full, on her own terms – not history's judgment. True, Madonna is alive to construct herself, and Plath is dead and her memory embattled – but Madonna has clearly learned from past tragedies. Madonna is Madonna, unprecedented; a rare state these days – and a good excuse for obsession.

# ☆ Remote from you, now

(*Scottish Child*, June/July 1990)

My younger brother Gregory and I are in many ways opposed, in many ways at one. It's taken us over twenty years to accept this fact as simply given – that our fundamental differences aren't eternal antagonism, that our similarities don't mean we aren't separate individuals. Now we just enjoy, respect, work with each other. It wasn't always so peaceful.

Ours was a family of men – my mother was faced with four traditional West-of-Scotland males, which meant a lot of housework for her and a lot of tension for me. From very early on, I had a crude psychological model in my head of what my relationship with my brothers structurally was.

'It's always the problem with three sons,' I remember an unidentified voice of authority saying, stupidly thinking I wouldn't overhear and understand. 'The first and the last are always spoiled – the middle one always has the problems.'

I never knew whether this preconception shaped Gregory's reality, or whether it was a response to his own actions – but it soon became obvious that Gregory was not me, was defining himself almost in direct opposition to his elder brother. I was introverted, bookish, academic, unfriendly; Gregory was outgoing, practical, witty and gregarious.

As 'our Patrick' got the plaudits for exam results and public achievements, Gregory – no less intelligent – decided to drop out of that race. Measured by the working-class aspirations of my parents, Gregory's resistance to achievement – simply, on reflection, an expression of his own autonomy – became a family problem.

Many seeds of future disruption were sown in these judgments-by-education. Each of us could touch each other's open wounds with the delicacy of torturers – Gregory portraying me as unnatural, abnormal, weird; me retaliating with accusations of his stupidity and triviality. Me as all head, Greg as all heart; like other areas of life, the splitting of one from another caused endless misery.

I cannot honestly pass over the more typical aspects of brothers growing up together – the physical violence and intimidation, from myself to Gregory. I can only remember my exercise of power over him as stemming from my perception of his difference – he wouldn't go along with me, do what I did, how dare he!

My problem with socialising got projected onto Gregory, who couldn't possibly work out all my angst, all my moods. And, when he didn't, I hit him. Other male friends have told me of their own fraternal tyranny, so I don't feel so anomalous – but how could this buried memory not have shaped our relationship?

So we progressed through primary and secondary school, passing each other in corridors and muttering hellos, either fighting or competing at home. The struggle was endless, incremental, painful. We both had a love of cars, their shapes and specifications, and would sit for hours on the living-room couch drawing together – or versus each other, more accurately. Sometimes I could never find later the drawing I'd painstakingly done; it was only recently that Gregory confessed he'd ripped up my best ones, in a fit of sheer jealousy.

Music was yet another marker of difference and antagonism between us. I could sing, but he could play four instruments well; his world became one of glowing reports of good or bad gigs, its esoterism infuriating me.

When we eventually conjoined musically – a jam in the living-room to some old Clash songs with a friend – that was the first spark of the joy of our working together. We could be separate yet complementary, each bringing our distinctive selves to a collective endeavour that was literally bigger than the sum of its bickering parts. I felt exhilarated that day, and later that night tried to listen to the tape we'd made of the jam.

It was blank. Gregory had erased the performance, perversely denying me the pleasure of hearing us work together.

Our first years as professional musicians, on a major record label, were crammed with mistakes. We still viewed each other as essentially polar opposites. Somehow we got a hit with our second record, and the spotlight came down on our blatantly obvious antagonism – which I foolishly tried to make capital of – the biblically feuding brothers who make wonderful music from their tension.

Unfortunately the pressure of the press turned something simmering into something explosive. On various public occasions, we two grown men started thumping the life out of each other, a detail of pop policy providing an excuse for both of us to hammer out our brotherly frustrations. Why couldn't he be more radical, less craven? Why couldn't I be less idealistic, more pragmatic?

We finally, climactically, said the worst things in the world to each other – and then everything seemed to be over. Our gulf was unbreachable. We prepared to part, profoundly and forever.

Our manager sat us round a table and told us we were fools – the antipathy that caused this rested on a more permanent empathy. Something must be salvaged. We embarked on a new album, musically together, but personally we enacted a strange formality. Everything had to do with respect – the only way forward was to regard each other as strangers, humans with our rights to individuality rather than as fatally linked brothers.

So followed an odd year of mutual professionalism and politeness; what we were in effect doing was reconstructing our relationship as adults rather than inflated children – aware of our knee-jerk responses to each other and trying to be honest about feeling them. A kind of mutual analysis.

They were uncomfortable times, but necessary. That might have been enough – a kind of existential tolerance of each other; our existence in various situations determining us more than our essence. The song that defined that period was the title track of the second album, *Remote*:

> *'The tension is all that we'll ever have*
> *May as well use it.'*

We took to performing it as piano/vocal only, like a gentle reminder to each other, in front of thousands of people every night, that we had to keep persevering with each other.

But hollow men cannot give themselves substance simply working from the outside in. Something new came along, an unprecedented jolt into humanity. After I announced that my wife and I were going to have a baby, I saw Gregory acting in a new way, and felt myself responding too.

Surely we must let warmth and love and acceptance flow freely, without inhibition, when we have a far more delicate problem of life to deal with than our own ossified complexities? Brother Pat becomes Pat the father; Brother Gregory becomes Uncle Gregory. My child not only allows us to become new selves – she forces the change on us.

So we find ourselves sitting as a foursome, my wife, baby Grace, myself and Gregory out in the sun on the back green, happy to be together, relaxed, non-performing, non-evaluating. If I never write another song with him, I'm thankful we can be so civilised together. Such normality is enough.

And my other, youngest brother? He has watched us tear one

another apart, struggle for common ground, fail again, and has quite rightly decided that he'll improve on both of us. None of this 'intellectual-versus-noble-savage' rubbish – our Gary gives a percentage of his weekly British Rail telephone engineer's wage to the ANC, which is as neat a blend of his brothers' oppositional traits as you could imagine. He is inches taller than both of us, which entirely fits his largeness of character. I love him dearly and simply, as I now love Gregory.

To be able to say that is a triumph; to be able to maintain it is our challenge. Brothers in arms; remote no more.

## ☆ Pop Life

'... ev'ry body got a space to fill'   Prince

1.

If anything's a tinsel show, it's pop music. Robert Burns's 'fools in silks' and 'knaves with wine' is the usual critical perspective that the 'honest' man and woman has on pop performers and celebrity culture in general. They're not wrong. I look back on the last seven years of contractual relations with the London music business as a mixture of genuine creation, dispiriting pragmatism, and hard education in the realities of the capitalist media. But it has also been a time of excess – silk, wine, vast recording budgets, unnecessary expenditure of all kinds in all areas.

As a pop artist, I can point to transcendent moments and lush achievements; as a socialist, I'm also rather ashamed of how much it all cost. To have spent well over a million pounds on producing and promoting three studio albums doesn't seem to relate to what was actually done in the name of this total, activities which at the time felt utterly normal. The Concorde trip to mix our New York album appeared the only practical solution; the £55,000 video budget, for three and half minutes of dream imagery, was regarded as perfectly adequate; and how *could* Top of the Pops be done without purchasing a full designer wardrobe for the rest of the band, as well as my brother and I?

Writing in mid-1992 – parted from our London record company in the dip of the recession, slowly (and with extreme prudence) starting up our own label – these splashes of cash look reckless, truly the acts of fools and knaves. But to inhabit the tinsel show of chart pop, however much one strains to apply alternative values and standards, is to exist in a world where money determines art – not as a constraint, but as a constant encouragement to spend. As long as the records are selling, the budgets can in theory increase indefinitely; the more the autonomy of the artist is confirmed by statistical success, the more he or she can demand from the company that their music-and-media wishes be turned into reality.

Hue and Cry never rode the heights of that escalator – one single

too many staggering to a halt just outside the Top Forty has
stopped our major-label ascent. But there were times when, seated
before the cream of American East Coast session players in the
same studio that Steely Dan, Madonna and Whitney Houston cut
their most successful albums, one felt what could be called the
Coppola effect; all these expensive talents and techniques at our
service, there to facilitate our sequences of chords and strings of
words, originated in damp Glasgow rehearsal rooms six months
earlier. Never could an artist experience such a sense of control and
self-possession; yet as the percussion pattered and the horns soared,
the budget meter clicked right next to our ears, from that
mysterious nether world of business strategy, projected sales and
horizontal accounting. But who could hear such an ominous noise
in the midst of all this aural luxury, this realisation of long-
nurtured musical dreams?

Not us; and our music-making at this moment is conducted
according to the steady beat of self-generated finance – a tight,
exact rhythm, demanding optimum efficiency and maximised
effort. We're as satisfied with our new songs as any we've done,
even though the time and resources spent on them are drastically
reduced; but unless we'd gone through this million-pound
apprenticeship in the finest musical technology, skills, composition,
I don't think we'd have produced music this well, this quickly. The
very least that our part as a minor high-kicker in the electronic
cabaret of the late eighties has given us, is a highly-developed
musical sensibility. No one can take that away from me or
Gregory; we are on the inside of a symbolic domain which may be
liked or disliked, but which is complex, historic and ours. Our
London record label may have calculated us as a financial loss; we
have used them to gain an artistry, viable in any circumstance.

So something substantial can be braided out of the strands of
pop music's tinsel – song-writing as a vocation, a life-long
exploration of a particular art-form. Yet the metaphor I'm
employing to characterise the thinness of the pop spectacle comes
from the lines of a popular song itself; its savage critique of the
strutting and staring élites of this world takes its power from
rhyme, melody and poetic artifice, as much as it does from
argument or analysis. 'For a'that and a'that' is radical humanism,
but it's also entertainment – and Robert Burns was certainly an
entertainer, and highly conscious of the uses of celebrity in the
salons and literary societies of eighteenth-century Edinburgh.

Are we radical humanist entertainers? Using light entertainment
media contexts to purvey our songs, and hoping – despite the tacky
sets, the dry ice, the whole tinsel show – that the sheer force and

complexity of our compositions goes straight from artist to audience? Like Burns, it seems a waste of an attention span not to craft popular art with as much resonance and worldliness as you can manage. There is an easily calculable trade-off between élite and popular art's effects. The former may be challenging, disruptive, cerebral, and reach possibly a thousand dispassionate gallerygoers. The latter may be white-soul-tinged, have a hook you could go shark fishing with, possess a radio-friendly brilliantine, and lightly brush hundreds of thousands of consciousnesses over a period of weeks – but there may be the chance of a verbal pattern, a performer's surge, a combination of sound and sense, that cuts through and articulates something many people are feeling about these times, in a way they'll never forget. A momentary, singular, irreducible entry in the memory of an entire society, or a total art statement addressing a handful of experts? C'mon! There's no choice.

We're dithering over two choices for our first single on our own label – decision tomorrow – and both of them, listened to on the trusted collapsing stereo, sound like the music we've always made, will always make. 'Baby let me write these words down, I'm "profoundly yours"/Cause everything that makes us fight and fuss maybe means much more'... I have my subtextual explanations of its banality brewing away inside me – anything from the classicism of a 'letter-writing' pop song, to the pertinence of Anthony Giddens's conception of identity and modernity. But for all my considered justifications, I am, of course, trembling behind the tassles; nothing matters in the content of a pop song if you don't grab the public's attention and make 'em hear it. For a' that and a' that, the tinsel show *is* all that there is in pop music. But tinsel is real, material, it has effects; flies into your mouth or your face, shimmers in the breeze or scatters under blows, traduces or glorifies by its presence the world that surrounds it. The show is worth its serious review – from the stage as well as the stalls.


2.

Playing live is the best and scariest part of pop music.

18 July 1987: I am sliding inexorably down a rain-lubricated catwalk on Madonna Ciccone's stage, a supporting artist at one of her sellout Wembley Stadium concerts, singing lead with Hue and Cry. My shoes are new Doc Martens – A&R man flexed his card earlier today – and I'm standing as rigidly as possible, so that their robust tread may find some grip on this murderous plastic sheeting.

But the end seems nigh. In a few moments, I am going to topple over the edge – radio mike in hand, next chorus unsung, a career-shattering pratfall in front of 70,000 people.

Seven hours earlier, in a Bayswater hotel room, I have written this note on the title page of *Rebel Rock: the politics of popular music*, by John Street:

> I'm fed up, depressed, deeply terrified. In 7 hrs time *I'm* supporting Madonna (supporting! *we* need the crutches) – yes, it seems like me alone. 70,000 individuals all there to watch a live video double album called Madonna's Hits. We have one hit record; that's when their bodies will move, and not before. I have to make them into a community: any verbal contact has to be clear + well explained. There can be no 10 second mumbling. It's the mechanics of show-business I'm learning here. I don't know if I can do it. But we musn't blow our reputation, can't seem like stuttering naifs. To work...

The slide appears to have stopped; by themselves, my tongue, teeth and diaphragm have belted out the last chorus. As the smattering of applause for yet another obtuse album-track blows over the stadium rooftops, I find myself frozen in front of this absurd human mass: shaking legs splayed in classic cock-rock fashion – the only way I can keep my balance – and a conclusion or two away from either a political tirade, or a nihilistic leap into the Wannabes below. Who cares? I read rock sociology. I could justify it to the scribes.

The solution arrives like a calling: This is what you must do. This will deliver you. 'OK, I'm sure you all know this next PRINCE number... I want the WHOLE STADIUM to do a MEXICAN WAVE when you hear the chorus, OK? Let's practise...Left side first... and back again... Good, good!' My brother Gregory – hidden behind keyboard stacks and a taciturn practicality – registers a rare surprise, as we thud into the first chorus. The stadium ripples, stupefyingly, like some vast coral organism. And again. And again.

A dull, tradesman's triumph rises in me. With tacky fluorescent t-shirts from the local Top Man (worn in a last-minute realization that, otherwise, no one would see us), only a third of the output of the PA, and a judiciously chosen cover song, we have effectively 'rocked a stadium', however briefly, and stupidly. But it would be the worst kind of rock laziness, I tell myself sternly, to enjoy this cultural totalitarianism; Hue and Cry must incite active consumption, spark off debate between and amongst hearts and minds. Semi-fascist arm-raising to chart hits, others' or our own, is not on the agenda. We troop off the stage twenty minutes later, and (as usual) I blow it with Gregory, muttering 'Well, we're never going to do this kind of bullshit ourselves.' His comeback is withering: Do I have no ambition? Do I have to waste it every time? Weird bastard!

The portacabin door slams, and I am left with my *Rebel Rock* : a frustrated Scottish scholar floating somewhere near the heart of 1987's major musical moneyspinner. I skim through until I find the most self-lacerating quote, picked up from Elvis Costello. 'The first rule of subversive pop is: Don't say it's subversive.'

☆ ☆ ☆

I'm railing at a Brighton club audience, Christmas '87, subverting like mad. 'You've paid to hear the "hit", chuckle to some bonhomie, tap your feet to some live video? Well, too fucking bad! Why did you people vote that monster in again? Don't you know that all the words of these songs are anti-Tory to their core? Are you paying not to listen to us? Fuck, what is the point… OK, next song…'

In the midst of this blind rage my sight clears, and I see a group of extraordinarily injured souls – Sussex students, young workers – at the left-hand side of the stage. Their faces are cautioned, admonished, tingling with my abuse of my position. We begin the ballad, and I know what they've come here for. Instead of scrunching my eyes shut to dig down for a reason to sing well, I keep them open and trained on my victims, as I croon out – testing the melody, confirming my existence. They soften, bar by bar, from frowns to relief to balmy grins, as I curl out the song, giving me the same pleasure as they're getting.

And it's all I can do to stop myself throwing the mike down and storming off, such is my self-loathing. I want to be an ideological nightmare, but I find myself singing as if I were in a dream. I want to radicalize people, but the hurt in the eyes of individuals kills me. What is pop music for? Hang onto the chorus, follow it up and along, let beautiful form save you: no answers as yet.

☆ ☆ ☆

Pop music is for this kind of communion. It is our second gig at the Scottish Exhibition Centre, Glasgow, January 1990 – the one after Christmas 1989, when my voice failed after two songs in front of 9,000 people. Even more are back this time, after meekly leaving the SECC a month and a half ago, ticket stubs in hand, by all reports incredibly understanding.

The gig is going well and we're readying ourselves for the concert master-stroke: dashing off stage while our nine-piece band extemporises, and then running through the crowd to a small stage in the middle of the arena. Once we find ourselves there, it is the oddest sensation – to be in the midst of that field of faces at which you usually project your arrogances, insecurities, talents and deficiencies, only ever getting an occasional sense of what their real collective mood is, perhaps catching an expression that boosts your confidence or crashes you down. I see that part of our audience – the greatest part – who don't wish to relive teenybop ecstasies by cramming against the crash barriers at the big stage; who are adult and want to hear properly, who wish to take our grand spectacle on slightly distanced terms.

We're very happy to meet each other; there are misshapen students staring into space, bearded fathers with children on shoulders, lusty Saturday-sharp girls in writhing knots of three or four: 'every shape face in the book' as Don DeLillo says. As Gregory strokes a ballad into existence (Kate Bush's 'Man with the child in his eyes', as I remember), I am suddenly back on the Christmas party carpet, a late-teenager – when they couldn't stop me from doing my repertoire, no matter the warm familial abuse, the 'we-"hate"-you-because-we-*love*-you' envelopment. I am sure my singing at this moment is a throwback to these times; if not, then why is everybody smiling like aunts, uncles, cousins, brothers, mothers, fathers?

☆ ☆ ☆

Time for some bathos. 'The peak of our performing career', I think, as we walk on stage in front of 200,000 Glaswegians, in the closing concert of the Big Day, the main Culture Capital event of 1990. Piano-vocal, guitar, sensitive ballads, night sky: perfect. Where we felt like a juggling act with Madonna at Wembley three years ago, now we performed to a mass audience many of whom would know our music, understand the dimensions of what we do, and respond with amplitude.

Not so. We strum, tinkle, croon, troop off, completely inadequate to the moment. What this mass wants – as they should do after a day trailing round Glasgow – is big beats and treasured chart melodies, windmill arm gestures and grand unifying statements. Why should a festival crowd this size – even of compatriots – act any different to any other, in their basic requirements of a mega-rock gig?

I hear Ricky Ross, on after us with Deacon Blue, railing against

the Labour Party in Scotland for 'selling us down the river', and I'm
ideologically delighted – he's abusing the occasion as it should be
done, speaking the unspeakable in a context of heightened emotion
and collective fervour. So many Nationalist politicians have
buttonholed me in subsequent years as they weighed up the roaring
response to Ross's invective: Listen, the disaffection was there, we
can replace Labour in Scotland, that was the first big Nineties
spark for independence.

I've assured them it was. But wouldn't *any* rock'n'roll declam-
ation have done at that hour, on that day? The spotlights played on
the crowds like tracer beams in a prison camp; the stage spectacle
disgorged fireworks, spouted dry ice, slammed chords. Audiences
can be voids as well as a communality: you can shout into their
abyss, and the abyss can shout back. But what are we doing, other
than what we are supposed to do in these circumstances? Nope: the
Scottish democratic revolution didn't start here. Just another big
gig.

☆ ☆ ☆

But sometimes performing is like the creation of your own
contained world for an hour or so; a utopia of sounds, movements
and responses that plans itself as it progresses. Supporting Joe
Jackson on a gruelling 22-date European tour, without a tour bus
and using trains, would not seem conducive to moments of
perfection. Yet our thirty-five minutes in front of a three-quarters
full Palais De La Música in Barcelona, on a cooling summer's
evening in 1991, felt to me like an unrepeatable moment; ourselves
and our audience illuminated by the departing sunlight through the
stained-glass roof, every detail of the *modernisme* architecture clear
to us all, and every note of our music completely within our
control. We streamed delight at the Barcelonians; three weeks into
our tour, our band performed with the innocence that every new
audience demands of us, and with the experience of growing with
songs, making successes or failures of them night after night. Never
got as good as that in the rest of the tour; didn't need to.

☆ ☆ ☆

And after half a decade of technically-tooled-up rock performance,
my brother and I are sitting by ourselves on a small stage in May
1992, mini-grand piano and high stool, starting off the Glasgow
arts festival Mayfest in the Moir Hall, Mitchell Library. Suddenly, I
am riddled with fear. How can I be shitting myself, halfway

through this opening number? C'mon, how many times have I done this? In the midst of my panic, I grab a little mental shelter from what I'm doing, and try to source the disturbance. Piano – I can *hear* the piano making its noises, its hammers sending vibrations of wires through a wooden frame: usually Greg's keyboards are electronic, even his piano sound, and I am alarmed by how *material* a real piano is, how percussive; it's thrumming away like a small car, a dominating presence at my elbow.

OK, that's placed – I'll have to work this clang and clamour into my surroundings, make it function for the mood of the gig. But there's something else shooting into me, unsettling me like toothache or a cold day. When I find it, it's lucky we're in a middle eight, or I might have coughed or cracked a line, grief catching my tongue. Like a metal scrape along the bottom of an empty fuel tank, what's jangling my nerves is: how can I presume we're worth listening to?

It's a shaft of insecurity that can slice through you at any time in a performance – caused by bad reviews, a musical contemporary being intimidatingly good on television, an unsteady start where technique is leant on and doesn't support you, a general fuzziness as to one's direction in the music business, feeling fat, thinning, unlovely... And as I manage to ease this self-inflicted weapon out of my system – phrase by phrase, melisma by melisma – I realise that its wound will never close, has never closed; in fact, so painfully pleasurable is the process of making this gig happen out of my sourceless depression, that I have to admit to myself that doubt-about-ability is one of my major energies in performance. I sing in my mind, and the flawed version that comes out impels me to try again; but as every actual try improves what my physical voice can do, my mental voice keeps getting more ambitious, and I have to try once more to match myself up to the ideal – and so on in a circle, hopefully virtuous... But only hopefully; because I then open my eyes and remember that people have *paid to watch me*. But watch *me* do this? How can something this private and internal be a reward for cash spent?

Money in your throat; self-expression as part of someone else's fun night out; pop music, like anything else in mass culture, is a struggle between commerce and art. But I have found that in public singing, these polarities are most explosively crunched together, and strike me most intimately. My Americanisms, my soulster role-playing; does this simply mean that my psychic core is colonised by US capitalist culture? That the reason people enjoy my voice is because it is soaked in the status-quo, its grain in harmony with the textures of commodified life? My harmony, melody, skill being a false mirror image of social consensus and order? Is my voice the sound of money?

Can you believe it – some of this is spinning in my head as I rock and sway on a high stool in a late-night Mayfest gig. Occasionally during gigs I just can't open my eyes for twenty, thirty minutes, as my whole identity spins on its axis, like a toy gyroscope; this is one such occasion. Should I leave the stage, stop the show, change the singing to express my chaos? *What-should-I-do?*

Ah, Gregory: senses the crash of glass and metal, my inner turmoil breaking me apart, and smiles like a child over his playing. *You're a singer, brother. Just sing.*

This is what I do.


3.


Rock'n'roll can often present you with the sharp end of masculinity. Some scrapings from the bottom of the misogynist barrel:

A Stardes tour bus, rolling from the North to the Middle of England; it's the tail-end of the Eighties and we are travelling heavy – an eleven-piece band, seething with power struggles and emotionally demarcated with invisible laser alarms. From my ivory tower at the front of the bus, walled in with books and papers, I sense a disturbing lull behind me. No competitions for Worst Regional Accents, no whooping at another Schwarzenegger limbfest on the video, no involved discussion over arcane amplifier specifications; just a kind of schoolboys-in-lab-period murmur, along with the whizz-bleep-groan of something computerized.

I sense my chance to build some bridges here – a little pre-show blow-out last night about, well, getting the 'blow' out of our set-up, has left me socially stranded (again). Our stellar saxophonist is holding court with a hay-bale sized Apple Mac; a ring of normally rictal faces are intent and blue-shaded in the light of the screen. What's this then? Parabolas, stocks and shares, remand school homework?

'OK, let's open this babe up', says the Transatlantic saxman, flicking his computer mouse. On the monitor is a cartoonish image of a naked woman, lying face up as if on an operating table – which, as it turns out, she is. A mouse-line is drawn from her right breast to her left hip; the mouse clicks to the menu and selects: scalpel. Saxman peels the flesh back with a slow drag on his gadget; the screen shows a monochrome tangle of intestines, bones, beating hearts. The wan smile of the victim – patient – is unchanged. 'We'll go for the ... liver', says the operator, aware of my gathering outrage, my rising anger. Click in for close-up: snip, slash, snip,

suction. 'Right, we better stitch 'er up now. Whadya reckon –
butterfly or catgut?'

THIS IS ABSOLUTELY DISGUSTING. They're only slightly crisping in
my heat, composing their own polite defences. DO YOU GUYS RE-
ALLY HATE WOMEN THAT MUCH? 'Hey, we don't hate women, Pat',
comes a comment from the ensemble. '*We* really like 'em.' I'm
about to launch off a never-used rocket – I'm your employer,
you're my employees, there are certain fucking *conditions*, you
animals. But, as ever, there is a gulf of miscomprehension on both
sides that missile fire would only accentuate. The crisis dissolves
and I know from the shrugs and baffled anger their exact thinking:
what is this hung-up monk doing On The Road in the first place?
Aren't there certain principles of excess – humpem dumpem, roister
doister – which make this life desirable in the first place?

As I crawl back into my eyrie, for a minute I cannot see the lines
of *Minima Moralia* for broken female bodies. Ah, those old tumours
of masculinity! Can't keep 'em at bay forever. Thanks guys.

☆ ☆ ☆

Sexual politics are not easily practised in an upholstered tank full
of youngish men, with daily access to a certain amount of
musician-struck young women in each of Britain's major con-
urbations. In the early, violent days, I threw myself against the
sexist norm like some kind of masochistic saint, feminist scriptures
in one hand, monogamist piety in the other. Admittedly the norm
was objectively loathsome at times: one incident involving an open
van door, some leering at schoolgirls waiting for a bus, and an 'if
rape was legal' comment, is burned into my memory.

Any men-only situation where the mores of schoolyard masculinity come into play, no matter the actual age of the participants, is
a situation which I leave as quickly as possible. But pop life is not
like the engineer's bothy or the construction site, when the compensation for being so explicitly proletarian, and thus powerless, is to
exaggerate your powers over women. A lot of male musicians have
fled from precisely those limiting conditions because their sense of
self needs to be expressed in ways that exceed the practical and the
wage-earning. Making pretty noises and prancing around under
spotlights presumes a level of self-regard, even self-obsession, that
would quickly get your head thrust down the lavvie in any labouring context; there are pathways to even the hardest rockers' hearts
which a gentle consistency of manner can discover.

So I have worked for years to construct a kind of common
ground of sexual and emotional assumptions with the men around

me in rock 'n' roll. If I've civilised to some extent the frightening extremities of cock-rockism, I think I've also been educated in the many ways men can talk about themselves as men. Tough-nut, rampant manhood is as exhausting for most men as it is repellent to most women; the trick is to catch a man when his armour is laid down for a moment, and make him realise how light and easy life is without it.

☆ ☆ ☆

'Whit d'ye need girl singers fur? Ye've already got wan in the band.' The grizzled old roadie – call him Tam, for tact's sake – chucks his dart at me over the dining table; the laughter is half-mechanical (it's Humour Hour at the moment, anything will do), and half-appreciatory: he's hit the big target, and they're waiting for a legendary po-faced retort. I say a truism that keeps the chuckle-kettle on the boil, and also lands my returning punch: weakly enough so that everyone knows how little I enjoy these ritual circulations of laddishness, but just enough so that I don't seem like the Alien Observer from Planet Feminista. *Ach ye know what Pat's like – but he can take the crack. Don't know whether he gets his gash, though...*

But look into Tam's eyes: soft, Disney-wide and cartoon-blue, dropped into a drunkard's face like a bad holiday oil-painting. And his general manner: he must be a father, the way he tells the 'boys' round the bar or table what grimy kinks in the weave of the rock tapestry awaits them, with a blustery, not-fucken-kiddin', I've-been-there authority. He knows he's not tripping any of my sociable switches, that I don't have a Spinal Tap to turn on. But I know he's an adult, with responsibilities somewhere. And he knows I know. It's a matter of time, place, and subject.

A week later, sitting in an auditorium watching a support band tune up, and we're talking via the expected mutual entry point to the heart: weans. We've had to play an extra gig, to juggle a TV schedule around: Tam therefore misses his 'boys' playing in their school team semi-finals, by one sodding day. They are, of course, 'great wee laddies – right into their Da. Ach but, fuck, I miss them'; and I'm hearing all this because he expects that I won't shift in embarrassment in my seat at this show of parental pain. He also expects – and this is where about four years of training and observation on my part come in – that I won't overdo it, or camp it up, or expand this quiet sharing into some 'personal-is-political' confrontation. And I don't; it's enough to listen to Tam the Bam in this open mood, probing me as to how I cope with leaving my wife when touring, what I say to children who haven't seen me for months, whether I justify the travelling pleasures of rock with the need to bring money home: piping resources into a household, perpetually offshore.

I'm with him on some points, against him on others; and a direct question about his notorious red-light sojourns meets with a cockerel's head jerk – 'Wissa matter wi' that? That's just the rules of the game, man' – and terminates our session. But not savagely, at least; and the last few dates of this 1991 tour go almost cheerily with Tam and me. We've released each other from the need to joust, joke, compete with phallic wit – but we no longer regard courteous interaction as a sign of difference, a stiffness caused by my rejection of the masculine rules. We're dads, we're householders, we have fixed points to return to; we can be male and domestic, and not worry about it. All of which would mean, if we talked to others about each other: *aye, he's alright, basically, no problem* – classic male shorthand, blunt scrawls referring to secret emotional correspondances. We can't say we've had a 'heart-to-heart', but we can indicate we've been in that region, made those explorations – and kept our manhood intact.

☆ ☆ ☆

And the biggest joke of all, as far as my rockist reservations are concerned? It's another late-eighties tour, and we're using a female keyboard player for the first time as a part of this white soul orchestra. Lesley is angular, highly competent and mistily middle-class. She's about as skilled as I am in the slap of rubber rapiers that passes for wit on the tour bus – but she keeps me at a proper distance; no point allying yourself too closely with the oddball in a caravan of men. That would only confirm her distance from the rest of the 'backing band' in a double sense – female *and* strange. Best to be female and laddish; even if she's been like a spare nun in a tribe of pricks during the after-show club trails, at least she can share last night's events with the boys the next morning. Served her time on bender duty; bought her ticket of male inclusion.

But the joke is that Lesley flipped my anti-sexist ideology over on its back like a tortoise, and has left me flailing wildly ever since. Picking over a recent gig, somewhere between Futtock and Grimesdale, she interrupted my scholarship with a genuinely wondering enquiry. 'You look like a supply teacher... But when you're on stage, you are totally mad, totally *male*. Do you realise how you act on stage?'

Command, control, lead the band, take the gig by the scruff of

its neck – *frontman*... There is too much tedious psychological
history behind my stamping and swaggering on stage, and my
dormouse demeanour offstage. But I am probably allowing myself
to be male, in a way that schooldays never allowed; this
masculinity dances, sings, shimmies, shakes, exaggerates itself both
in its bravado and its vulnerability. 'Your eyes are mad', says
Lesley, 'you're a completely different person'. I realise I must be
acting out my manhood, projecting it as a confident performer
rather than protecting it as an assailed teenager.

Yet it's weird: I cannot remember a single performance, out of
hundreds, where I have felt sexually stirred in any way. The
'frontman' makes his maleness a front, lets a fantasy of himself
flicker over his body, jerk his limbs and wrench out his voice. But I
go back to the hotel room every night, and ask myself: who was
that? Who is that man? What is a 'man', anyway?

Rock'n'roll keeps posing that last question and for my purposes,
long may it continue to do so.


4.


Retrospectively, I've been heading for the tinsel show since birth;
my pop consciousness feels almost co-terminous with consciousness itself. When was life *not* about performance? Who needed
reviewers, when you'd been reviewing yourself for decades?

I have never known a time when the world wasn't second-hand
to me. Objects, faces, TV shows, conversations – I've always been
able to step back from their immediacy, and observe how things
function, how people put their fronts together. This has meant a
great deal of loneliness. Most of human exchange is conducted
automatically, and I've kept dropping screwdrivers in the machinery, or watched at a distance when it snarled up.

But when I came across theories of communication in university,
it was almost like finding a long-lost friend of the mind. All the
moments I'd been giggling at and revelling in for years – Daffy
Duck screaming at the auditorium to 'Shaddap!', a Foster Grant
sunglasses ad that deliberately didn't make sense, Spike Milligan
turning normal TV upside down and inside out – became more
than my own secret joys in the twists and turns of the media. Being
excessively aware of how the world constructed itself didn't feel so
strange, when academia put its arms around your shoulders and
murmured sweet names and phrases in your ear: 'Semiotics,
textuality, deconstruction, discourse... Foucault, Barthes, Derrida,
Eagleton...'

These noises told me the world was *meant* to be shabby and forced, was always a circus tent of pitches and performances. The words we spoke were part of a system of language which was ultimately out of our control; the reality of television news was inherently biased, as a selection of meanings and symbols; the unconscious mind vandalized every conscious act of meaning, our desires and fears tripping up our reasons and intentions any chance they got. Like any reader who finds their novelist at the right emotional moment, and devours the entire author's list until the therapy is complete, I gorged myself on this stuff, academic term after term.

It explained completely my life experience thus far; miserable over-sensitivity about the cliched, manipulated nature of existence wasn't just a personal problem, but a general social condition. Guy Debord said we lived in a 'society of the spectacle', where daily life was increasingly being conducted according to the logic of advertising. (... I remember the time when a close adult relative brought me into his orbit, showing me off as a paragon of the family, and hissed at me side-hand that this was the boss, be a good kid, it's important...). Michel Foucault outlined how subtly oppressive institutions were, comparing the school to the prison to the workplace, and seeing the same 'discursive structures' of surveillance, discipline and punishment in each. (... We played in a secondary school yard where the staff room perched above us in a glass watchtower; their casual monitoring prickled the backs of our necks. I remember the rap on the glass during some prohibited game – or worse, the side-door swoop: sudden, arbitrary, fatally embarrassing...). Roland Barthes asked us to revel in the 'pleasure of the text', which meant reading according to one's own, self-indulgent agenda, not worrying about the author's intentions. (... Studying for highers, I couldn't get beyond that line in *Tender Is The Night*, where Dick Diver describes himself as 'existing in performance alone' – nor did I want to; the book had served its purpose, rendered up its chunk of insight. Too much to know, too little time...).

Nothing that remarkable about theories of alienation and estrangement appealing to a strange, alienated young man. There is something quietly sadistic about sitting in a literature or media seminar and denying, against all the weight of evidence and tradition, the intention of the author in his or her artwork. Our student 'interrogations' of the text were, in retrospect, exactly that – a torturing of 'John Ford' or 'Charles Dickens' with the instruments of psychoanalysis and semiotics, the 'death of the author' our aim. (This practice cannot be disconnected from the times: 1981 to 1985, my university years, spanned the early terms of Thatcher, her Falklands war and its popular support, her election victory and consolidation. Of course we had to dissolve the human subject, the intending actor; of course we had to describe the self as putty to be shaped by ideologies, discourses, media forms of all kinds. How else to account for the masses outwith these groves of academe voting jingo Tory every four years? It can't actually be their fault! Something must be making them do it!)

I should have been temperamentally satisfied by this framework of ideas. How better to justify your personal inability to emote, reciprocate, be friendly, than by holding to a model of subjectivity and language which claimed that communication was always a failure, that words were slippery and treacherous, that we could never fully say what we mean. But there was another part of my life in those years which brought this anti-authorial, anti-intentional approach to culture into sharp relief. Critically, I'd always found convincing the argument that artforms are combinations of codes, genres and styles that pre-exist the artist; and that a valid analysis of any artwork – literary, visual, musical – would proceed by recognising these conventions, enabling us to determine the meaning of the work more effectively than trying to mind-read the author's 'real' purpose and intent, whether alive or dead.

Yeah, yeah, yeah: but what should I think of myself when I sang with my brother's punk-jazz band? When my voice sounded like my dad, like Stevie Wonder or Frank Sinatra, or even like myself, and made me surge inside – should I put this feeling down to some interesting combination of 'soul' vocal conventions, circulating in the culture like hooks on an automated meat rack, onto which I threw myself every time I summoned up a singing breath? How could I be academically killing the author in the afternoons, then lustily roaring out my new songs in a Mount Ellen church hall in the evening?

It would have been easier to divide these two activities completely, and do a head-heart split. Rock as the escape from reason, the release from cursed consistency; my theoretical self observing this part of me with a field-worker's wry objectivity. So *that's* what his swamp unconscious really wants to do; that's how he uses his body out of the library chair! But my dissatisfactions with the idea of rock as a farewell to reason, and with post-structuralism's subordination of rationality and intention to the unconscious, began to meld together. Could one start to challenge a whole range of modish theories about the workings of contemporary mass culture – its irrationalism, amorality, pulverisation of the indivi-dual –

on the basis of making some culture of your own, justifiable from opposing intellectual coordinates?

Thus began my eight-year long debate about the very grounds of rock criticism which has noised up no small number of metropolitan critics in their attitudes to our music. Why should we ever take some consumptive speed-freak's analysis of our music seriously, when we can give a better account of the motives and structures behind the sounds we make than any scrivener working out of W1, London? But it's time to stop skirmishing with the paracritical enemy, and engage in one last conclusive bloodbath of defined terms. What is an adequate theory of pop? Where do I stand on what pop music does to people? How should pop criticism stand in relation to pop practice? I will ascend from Brendan Behan's quote about critics – that they are like 'eunuchs in a harem: they've seen it done every day, they know how to do it, but they can never do it themselves' – for the simple reason that there has to be a more balanced account of a musician's relation to pop criticism than this sexist, phallocentric axiom.

However absolutely bloody correct it feels after every bad album review.

☆ ☆ ☆

Everybody has a theory of pop – not least those who make it. Even the least self-conscious of artists can be jolted into an extended analysis of 'what's good about rock'n'roll', if you trade the wrong reference with them. There is a real evaluative disdain when two musicians react opposingly to the same source. 'How can you love/hate Van Morrison/Lou Reed/Springsteen/Stevie Wonder/ Kraftwerk? These people are/are not 'great popular music'. How can you say otherwise?' I have suffered (and inflicted) the worst aesthetic hauteur, as my opponent and I push each other to our fundamentalist positions. You are a rocker, I am a soulboy; you find solace in raw-throated guitar release, I am consoled by the bubbling symmetry of a Muscle Shoals rhythm section. Different planets, kiddo.

A chasm of disrespect, even antipathy, can open up between the parties at this point; so bound into the musician's identity is his or her hierarchy of quality in pop, rock and soul, that we find ourselves with the necessity of being tolerant liberals, facing an incomprehensible difference as calmly as possible. If I simply *don't understand* why you like that noise, I either have to attack you – through fear of my own preferences being patronised – or agree to disagree. The latter strategy is boring, but peaceful; the former,

particularly if fuelled by stimulants in a hotel bar, can spiral
excitingly downwards. But when you hit rock bottom, it gets ugly;
you start swinging at the actual music your opponent makes, as an
exemplification of their taste. (I've only done this once, and managed
to avoid a rather violent 'OK-*you*-hit-top-C' singing competition
around the hotel's baby grand by feigning nausea.)

Serious music scholars like Simon Frith have commented on
musicians' own working theories of pop; one, that they exist – pop
music is more than instinctual, foaming irrationalism – and two,
that they occupy a space somewhere between simple like or dislike,
and the jargon machines rolling out from academia or high critique.
Whether musicians, entrepreneurs, or fans, people 'need to bring
some sort of order and justification to the continuing process of
musical evaluation, choice and commitment...The practice of pop
involves, in short, the practice of theorising'. Perhaps we should
call this 'low theory', says Frith – 'confused, inconsistent, full of
hyperbole and silence, but still theory, and theory which is
compelled by necessity to draw key terms and assumptions from
high theory, from the more systematic accounts of art, commerce,
pleasure and class that are available' (p. 21, Frith, 1987).

Pick any early nineties pop publication at random – a copy of
IPC's *Vox* at my side – and the pages are full of Frith's low
theorising. 'The original freak-scene space cadet ultra-kitsch
"mushroom band" from designer hell are back! But hey – wanna
try some of their new LP? It's *Good Stuff*...', spurts a standfirst for
an article on the American group the B-52s. Now it would be the
worst kind of walnut-and-sledgehammer academicism to base any
great treatise on the references skidding through such a hastily
written piece of ephemera. But even this blurb draws on 'the more
systematic accounts' of high theory that Frith talks about, even if
only sardonically, 'full of hyperbole and silence'. Whether it's art
('ultra-kitsch', 'designer hell'); commerce (the B-52s are indeed
'back!' – back in the markets, back in the charts, back for their turn
on the conveyor belt again); pleasure (the clear cross reference to
music-as-drugs: 'hey – wanna try some?'); and class (the 'freak-
scene', referring to the band's post-punk lineage as part of the
college-bohemian cultures of the West and East Coast).

Even to proceed step-by-step through this reflex of a pop paper
sub-editor feels ponderous. The essence of practical theorising in
pop, from either critic or musician, is that it should be light and
quick – grabbing at terms like 'genre', 'sensibility', 'shock effect',
'radical', 'subversive', but never expecting (or expected) to pursue
these terms to their definitional ends.

I'll never forget the giddiness I once felt when reading the teeny-pop rag *Smash Hits* in the late eighties, privately up to my intellectual oxters in theoretical debates between French post-structuralists and German neo-Kantians, and coming across the phrase 'post-modern pop' in a wacky 'next week's issue' blurb. Of course they didn't know what it 'really' meant, what the significance for an understanding of contemporary politics, ethics and aesthetics the 'post-modern' debate actually was. The word had perhaps floated down from a *Face* piece, an overheard Channel 4 arts feature, the posey corner of a media party – and become another adjectival mark of pop difference for the *Smash Hits* reader, like 'Goth', or 'rockist', or 'moodsome'. Could there have been a pre-post-modern pop? Could pop only ever be post-modern? The questions could beg till they died of starvation if the addressee was a *Smash Hits* journalist, reader or featured musician.

It surely won't be long before 'Gaia pop', 'fin-de-siecle pop', 'chaos theory pop' will occupy the same outsider's space in the grammar of *Smash Hits* or *Vox* – with the same absolute indifference to the vast fields of debate around these terms, the same lack of willingness to properly explore their intellectual dimensions. Pop is a *real* marketplace of ideas – entire methodologies reduced to a quickly chewed sound-bite, sandwiched between gory tales of touring and record-company bitching.

But why use these 'high theory' terms in the first place? What kind of sense are they intended to make with their interlocuters, the fans? I've worked in the milieu of rock and pop journalists as a critic, and no matter the degree of seriousness of the writer, media phrases run through this community like new bait through a shoal of starved sharks. Some engage in a battle to master them vigorously, others pick up the fragments that fly out from the fight. Yet there has to be a faith on the part of the writer and musician that the reader and audience will, if not completely grasp the references, then at least tolerate their esoterisms and abstractions.

The way pop music, and its cloud of words and discourse, works in popular culture is almost like a lightning rod for the meanings of the times. Pop makes you abnormally sensitive to the entire reach of contemporary cultural concerns – from the ways that sexuality and the unconscious is shifting priorities within our minds and bodies, through the news-and-magazine agenda of hypes and booms, up towards the most specialized academic discussions of society and culture.

Music is classically understood as the artform which is least representational of the world; its pure form incites a grasping after meanings as much as it delivers a definite content. Pop music shakes up our aesthetic senses with its extraordinary variety and barrage of sounds and rhythms and melodies. In the midst of that shaking up, a singer steps forward with some words – usually romantic or sexual, channeling the emotional and mental energies released in an immediately sympathetic language. But the singer also has the opportunity of riding this swell of sound-and-sensuality on different kinds of board – whether it's Black 'edu-tainer' rappers delivering a revised historiography of global civilisation, or indie-dance acts invoking film history in their lyrics, or rogue pop songwriters bemoaning that 'nothing ever happens' or that they 'ain't gonna work for you no more'...

Lyrics and images which plug into the 'more systematic accounts' of high theory, directly or indirectly, can be given a strange new charge by the music, the sonic sumptuousness, of pop. Such 'literate' lyrics will work either as stubborn, ugly, utilitarian objects in its stream (and thus fail as pop lyrics), or will spin like waterwheels in its flow, generating a power for the words that they would never possess as blocks of conceptual or descriptive prose (and thus succeed as pop lyrics). So to be a pop theorist is not an imposition on an essentially irrational, Dionysian art-form. It's an *option to be taken up*, on all sides of the communicational divide – as artist, critic or audience. Whether it's a theory of love, sex, romance; power, class, violence; art, iconicity, doubt – pop makes its claims to be intelligible through its lyrics, its artists' justifications, its critics' qualifications.

What most elements in the chain of semi-aware pop theorists will make of my words here – I'm trying to make more permanent connections with high theory from within my pop practice, puffing up my low working theories of creation – is anyone's guess. Pop likes its incoherence about coherence, its theoretical looseness about the theories it uses. For the aware pop artist, this openness is both exciting and frustrating in equal measures; a chance to inject new linguistic force into old banalities, or to make higher-level concepts part of the daily argot.

But you only know if it's worked when you do it, sing it, play it; pop theory is always only an ingredient in the creative fusion, or an aid to retrospective analysis – it can never predict results, success, a Number 1. In the light of this, the lower theorist may well say: 'fuck analysis – let's dance!' But they will be inescapably theoretical in that very utterance; there's nothing more clearly a conceptual preference than choosing to deny theory.

5.

In pop life, everybody got a space to fill. Was Prince 'aware' that this lyric could support a towering scaffold of the sternest critical theory? Pop music could be regarded as the vanguard, or the advance shock militia, of capitalist culture: pop as the ultimate means of inciting unrequit-able desires amongst the masses, leaving everybody with 'a space to fill'. With what? With all the other commodities that might reap the benefit from the constant psychic and sensual unsettlement of the music fan – clothes, cars, choc ices, career pension plans, corporate identities... Everything they do – to paraphrase Brian May's particularly noisome example of rock'n'industry – is driven by the state of you, the always-edging-towards-blissed-out consumer; made psychologically mushy by pop, readied for the hard-product pitch, the febrile target of a whim-propelled late capitalism.

This is the harshest kind of Left analysis of how pop music functions in our modern times, traceable all the way back to the Marxist critic Theodor Adorno's disdain for the formulaic, passivity-inducing and deliberately unsatisfying nature of Tin Pan Alley songs in the 1940s. Adorno attacked their status as 'products', delivering controlled repetitions and variations of sounds and structures; never so predictable as to lose attention, never so divergent as to be beyond the current musical 'consensus'. The slowly evolving musical consensus of the pop charts directly paralleled – and supported – the dull normality of the capitalist status quo, in politics, society and economy. Adorno spoke from an absolutely avant-gardist position, elevating Schoenberg and other orchestral modernists as the only effective musical reponse to the weight of the status quo, the 'totally administered society'.

The left-of-centre pop practitioner, reading these arguments, can almost physically feel his or her will to make beautiful noises ebb away. Making music feels like such an assertion of self, such an affirmation of individuality, such an act of tangible agency in the world. It's almost like being mentally robbed when you're told that what you do is only 'an effect' of wider systems, or ultimately contributes to the destruction of individuality in general, through the consumerist frenzy that is pop music.

So if what fuels me to make pop music is the false consciousness of what Simon Frith would call a 'Romantic ideology' (that is, the primacy of self-expression), rather than a market- or sociologically-informed strategy to achieve a particular presence in the pop charts, by whatever means necessary ... then let me be 'ideological', let me be wilfully mistaken. What use would this particular kind of pop analysis be, if all it did was to dissolve the creative intentions of individuals into particles and energies, comprehensible only through the analyst's schema?

I'm painfully aware of the contradictions of pop life: but how is the pain of each contradiction measured, if not against some treasured ideal of music-making, and symbolic creation in general? The most intense pleasures that making pop music has given me – full use of my human capacities, in a reciprocal relation with others – are pleasures which I am convinced can be *universalized,* can be made into a general social condition. Having a great time as a pop musician doesn't remove you from politics – for me, it makes the need to be politically engaged even more urgent.

In this hi-tech age, where the technological means to liberate humans from unnecessary labour objectively exists – there is a politics which can address the fundamental shape of societies in the world, from the position of life-as-art. Under such a reorganisation of society, human activity can be exerted fundamentally for its own, sensuous, creative sake – that is, like an artist's – and not for the benefit of systems of power and money. This is the 'good stuff' the popster steals from the corporations, the distributors, the marketeers: using all their technologies, facilities and resources *as if they were purely at your service, a free technology,* rather than tied to profit and loss. You realise your dreams of sound, image and gesture: and in realising it, taste utopia. It's a fine taste. It should be – and could be – on everyone's tongue. But only a radically restructured social system will put it there. So if you get the chance – *make a hue-and-cry about it...* Anyway, everyway you can... Mike, pen, screen, autocue, book...

# ☆ Politics

Knowledge is power

> Francis Bacon

# ☆ All's fair in love and the class war

(*The Scotsman*, 3 March 1990)

Love is blooming at the moment and not just in the rhyming dictionaries of Stock, Aitken and Waterman. Those of us who take respite from daily barbarism in big safe volumes of left theory have recently discovered that our austere heroes are getting gooey and sentimental in their old age. Take this passage from Marxist literary critic Terry Eagleton's new book, *The Ideology of the Aesthetic*:

'We give each other our desire, which is to say exactly that which neither of us can fulfil in the other. To say "I love you" thus becomes equivalent to saying "It's you who can satisfy me!" How privileged and unique I must be, to remind you that it isn't me you want ... '

With a little stretch of the imagination, can't you imagine Jason Donovan intoning these words over the middle-eight of his next slushy ballad? This from an academic who in the mid-seventies would slam verbal embroiderers like himself for being uncommitted to 'revolutionary armed struggle against the state'. Nowadays Eagleton sounds more like a time-warped hippy than a lieutenant in the Red Army (Oxbridge branch).

'The fullest instance of free, reciprocal self-fulfilment is traditionally known as love ... Radical politics addresses the question of what this love would mean at the level of a whole society.' Terry has dedicated his last few books to the same Scandinavian feminist literary critic, so we may reasonably deduce that some of his love propaganda comes from a profoundly cuddly private life.

But not all of it. There has been a very distinct resurgence of 'humanist' values like love, truth, justice, kindness in recent Left theory, for so long dominated by the anti-humanist severities of structuralism and post-structuralism, and their concomitant politics of post-modernism.

In his scathing new book *Against Postmodernism* (Polity), Alex Callinicos argues that the reign of socialist anti-humanism in the Seventies and Eighties was very much a response by Western intellectuals to the failure of the great social movement of the Sixties. If you thought in May '68 that revolution was at hand – from Prague to Paris to the US ghettos – then the next fifteen years would be nothing but a series of depressing reversals; Reagan, Thatcher, Afghanistan, a Mitterrand socialism with monetarist policies, with no sign of the Great Transformation in sight.

The Western academic Left's responses were twofold; a detour into theory, and a lapse into cynicism, all bound up with anti-humanism. If the proles were incapable of seizing the time, then intellectuals must theorise the roots of their incapacity. 'Discourse theory' arose as the crowning explanation. People's self-consciousness was seen as purely a composite of ideology and culture – how could they let the atrocities of the New Right happen, if they weren't just hollow men and women, empty vessels for the most powerful propaganda?

So politics for the academic Left became much more cultural than economic; if a million, two million, three million unemployed wasn't enough to make workers realise the 'objective reality of capitalist exploitation', then better set about what distracts them from seeing their 'real conditions' – the whole range of consumer and popular culture.

But anyone who's engaged in a cultural politics of this kind – myself included – can testify to the faint sense of hopelessness in using culture as a substitute for political involvement and understanding. So much rhetoric, so much style and form, so many relatively plausible ways to say what you thought you wanted to say ...

That's where the cynicism comes in – too much attention to the form of your message makes you begin to doubt the basic content; your solid political grip on the world loosens as your vision clouds over with an awareness of cliche, stereotype, of tailoring your style to a particular audience.

The shift from excessively theorising political struggle to being wearily pessimistic about it is what is meant by the term 'postmodern'; despairing intellectuals and the image-manipulators of the current Labour Party all agree that media, not economic reality, is where the real terrain of politics is these days. But how do you count the show of hands in the television audience of a party political broadcast ?

This 'bottomless' political relativism has recently hit its floor with the Eastern European revolutions. As nation after nation rose up against their Communist ruler, distinctly old-fashioned notions of truth, justice and love came flying from the mouths of leaders like Vaclav Havel and the students of Romania. 'We want a society of honesty,' said Havel in his New Year speech.

Reading between the lines of Left-inclined commentators like Neal Ascherson, there is a tangible hope amongst the intellectual left that 'people power' might revitalise political culture in the West too, based on the old humanist essentials. That is, people might be able to see the world as it really is, and change it according to their true desires, instead of their innermost motivations being endlessly shaped by the ideology merchants of official politics or commercial culture.

Even before the last twelve months in Eastern Europe, intellectual trends amongst the thinking Left have been shifting away from the bare-bones options of discourse theory or post-modern pessimism. The rise of the German philosopher Jurgen Habermas to the position of pre-eminent European intellectual is as much to do with the essential optimism of his work as its undoubted conceptual brilliance.

As Eagleton says in the *Ideology of the Aesthetic*, Habermas's belief that 'what it is to live well is somehow already secretly embedded in that which makes us most distinctively what we are: language', is a fundamentally 'sentimental' belief. Habermas puts an almost *a priori* trust in the willingness of people to work out their common destiny, as long as they keep communicating: 'the good life shadows our every discursive gesture, running beneath our wranglings like a silent, unbroken sub-text' (Eagleton).

Andre Gorz in his recent *Critique of Economic Reason* goes even further than Eagleton and Habermas in his humanist grounding. To understand society from the perspective of social theory is not enough, even if that social theory – like Habermas's – grants members of society much more credit for their intelligence and autonomy than previous theories.

One must instead begin from the premise, says Gorz, that love is the basic social bond – pre-verbal, sometimes inexpressible, founded on such relationships as mother and child, lovers and friends, where people value each other unconditionally. The best critique of economic reason is the fact that people love each other without any good reason; how does one calculate the benefits and debits of caring for a newborn child?

This promotion of maternal love as a grounding for the good society hints at another reason why all these middle-aged male theorists have recently rediscovered humanist values. Feminism forced many male leftists to re-evaluate their entire politics, confronting them with the reality that patriarchy had being doing down half of humanity far longer than the mercantile capitalists.

I can't help seeing the responses of Eagleton, Habermas and Gorz to feminism as typically male; we know that every detail of our male emancipatory theory is now bogus – so can we just agree to love each other, be nice and friendly and caring and sharing, before it gets too complicated? Whether this idealisation of love is any less tendentious than the latest Jason Donovan epic is a moot point. At least Kylie hasn't had to burn her Maoist felt cap.

## ☆ Obscuring the show of evil[*]

(*The Scotsman*, 16 September 1989)

Los Angeles, 1989. The centenarian Adolf Hitler is giving poolside interviews, discoursing on a new turn to his career – rock promotion. 'Always I have loved spectacle ... I know this business, I can give the kids what they want'. (He's handling Bros for the West Coast.) Hitler's Bel Air residence is done in red-and-black 'bunker nouveau' style, with its own private cinema showing home movies of Poland, the Ukraine, Eva and Adolf in Paris ...

How are you reacting by now? Apoplectic horror? Cognisant chuckle? Whatever you feel, don't blame me – I'm only quoting from *Punch* magazine's '39–89 'Conflict Special', in their Imaginary Interview slot. Of note is the accompanying cartoon; Hitler wears RayBans, earring and a Hawaian shirt, subtly patterned with bamboo swastikas.

I can't think of another twentieth-century figure whose appearance in any cultural context is so charged with moral meanings, so nervously evaluated. The *Punch* parody is as good an example as any of the critical quandaries raised by the symbolic use of Hitler – something we've been bombarded with recently, on the various anniversary commemorations. It invites at least two opposing reactions – quite typical of the reception of Hitler-art – both based on how we regard the impact of the past on the present.

One view is that Hitler as a rock promoter shows up the latent fascism of the modern entertainment industry – the orchestrated spectacle, the technology of illusion, the mute mass audiences, and the unreasoning worship of the Führer-superstar.

By establishing such a firm connection between aspects of these 'civilised' times and those 'barbaric' times, we are thus warning against complacency – against the assumption that fascism is a

---

*These pieces (Obscuring the show of evil/Disquiet on the comics front) were written as both a direct and indirect response to the appearance of the Grant Morrison comic strip 'The New Adventures of Hitler' in the Scottish music magazine CUT, during the summer of 1989. I was writing a column for CUT at the time, and left on the basis of Morrison's strip. The first piece is one of my opening columns when I moved to the *Scotsman*; the second is my final column in CUT.

thing of the past, that all its structures and techniques have been planned out of existence, when they might indeed still persist. The throw-away humour of the piece only makes the insight more disturbingly effective; we are shocked at being amused by such a chilling continuity.

The other view would regard such humour, and such speculative parallels, as a dangerous obscuring of the real historical lessons of Hitler. The past should not be a tool of the present but a corrective to the present; not something that can be reinterpreted to serve contemporary art and politics, but something that should always be retold accurately, in all its precise horror and shamefulness, so that art and politics can avoid making the same mistakes again.

So Hitler-art should stick to the facts of the Third Reich, on their own – the genocide, the totalitarianism, the mass culpability. They are moving enough. Any art which distracts from remembering the full tragedy of Nazi Germany – any art which uses Hitler unhistorically – creates a distancing from fascism's terrible actions, and is therefore pernicious.

According to this view, a Californian Adolf Hitler who escapes from Germany disguised as an ENSA performer, and plans his comeback from Paraguay – 'I figured, hell, if Frank Sinatra can do it, why not me?' – is an offensive creation.

For years now I've been vacillating between both views – whether to artistically re-read or accurately remember Hitler, the better to prevent his kind's return. But perhaps this approach is all too intellectual, too much concerned with the subtleties of intention and reception, the burdens and debts of history.

Why not just ridicule the man? Giggle at his stubby moustache, deride his maniac militarism; in essence, simply deny his own claims to legitimacy and authority by showing how ludicrous he was? From Bertolt Brecht through Charlie Chaplin to Mel Brooks, this has been the working assumption; that the powerful have no power over us if we do not take them seriously. In this light, our *Punch* piece justifies itself by making us laugh; perhaps satire is the best security against the return of the dictators.

Yet the political era which directly preceded Nazi Germany, the Weimar Republic of the Twenties and Thirties, could not have been more virulently satirical of the rich and the right-wing. The vicious caricatures of George Grosz, the public subversions of the Dadaists, the whole range of proletarian theatres, clubs, newspapers, all this constituted what German critic Peter Sloterdijk has called 'the most self-aware epoch of history'.

The Nazis still got in, despite all this satire and societal self-awareness, the pen patently no mightier than the jackboot. Why?

Solely because of Hitler? Is it possible that one man's charisma, cleverness and cruelty could completely dupe such an eminently cultured and highly informed society?

I believe that artists who claim to be criticising fascism by exploring Hitler as an individual – whether through satire, realism, extrapolation or whatever – are misguided. German fascism was sustained more by the weakness of millions of wills and consciences, than by the strength of will of a single dictator.

In fact, to consider Hitler's motivations and psychology as the key to fascism implicitly colludes with the whole Führer myth – that one figure sums up the complexity of a society – is primarily responsible for shaping its general consciousness. This lets German society – and social explanations – off the hook; the editor of *Die Zeit*, writing in the *Observer* a fortnight ago blithely put Germany's tragedy down to 'the crazed vision of one man'.

On the contrary, Nazism was permitted by the everyday actions of everyday Germans. Two recent books show this conclusively. *In Hitler's Germany*, by former Resistance worker Bernt Engelmann, is a numbing account of how people's scruples disintegrated under the regime of violence and compulsory ideology instituted by the Nazis.

Englemann's own involvement in smuggling Jews out of the country is proof that not all German citizens wore the swastika lapel badge when expedient, that some placed morality over conformity. But the cumulative message is depressing; fear erodes the ordinary conscience.

Nowhere is this more evident than in the depth of popular complicity in the extermination of the Jews, examined by Zygmunt Bauman's *Modernity and the Holocaust*. Bauman concludes that it is not the evil of Hitler and his Nazi policies which is the true horror; it is that modern society's structures could be so unresilient to it – indeed that they could so efficiently carry it out, as proved by the massive bureaucracy and organisation of the death factories.

Modernity itself – the governance of society by reason and plan – made the Holocaust possible. As shown by the more extreme political reactions to the AIDS crisis, such as calls for the quarantining and branding of people with AIDS, the same structures of rationalised inhumanity and amorality still exist. The potential for genocide is still there.

But was not Hitler well before his dictatorship a nondescript modern citizen like the rest of us? Then surely the ultimate artistic question, say the creators of Hitler-art, is this: what made him want to move from playing a part in an ordered society to directing that social order for his own evil ends? What might speculation on

Hitler's emotions and early life reveal about the potential fascist in all of us?

But the point about Hitler is that he wasn't a dully standard citizen, cracking at the seams with evil. He was an artist, a bohemian, deliberately peripheral to society: someone whose visionary purism held in contempt what was workaday, sociable, normal. For artists to be fascinated by Hitler is for them to be fascinated by the terrible results of the artistic stance taken to extremes; the outsider mentality applied to the shape of a whole society, rather than safely on a canvas or page.

So Hitler-art is as much about artists as it is about fascism – yet more creative narcissism to add to the dung heap of culture. A genuinely anti-fascist art would lower its sights from the masterplans of Führer-creators, and look at the entirely more difficult field of daily life under fascism.

Take Claude Lanzmann's *Shoah*, a film documentary recording the testimonies of ordinary Germans working in the death factories; Art Spiegelman's *Maus*, a strip cartoon history of the persecution of Polish Jews; and Primo Levi, with his tales of minimal survival in the concentration camps. These works are exemplary in their evocation of the ordinary reality of fascism – what Hannah Arendt classically termed 'the banality of evil.'

The real argument is not whether Hitler is a legitimate subject for art – of course everything is – but whether his use can be truly effective in warding off fascism. Hitler's fascism is well-known; it is the fascism of the many who let him into power which must be examined. The truth of fascism is not in its self-proclaimed leaders, but in its mundane possibility.

☆ Disquiet on the comics front

(*CUT*, July 1989)

Like most males my age, I first came across German history in war comics. And the German language too: 'Gott in Himmel', 'Donner und Blitzen', and 'Schweinhunt' were easily remembered, by dint of repetition, as bullet after bullet thudded into cruelly scowling Kraut soldiers from the righteous firearm of Johnny Brit.

The brutal xenophobia of their content – all Germans as purely evil and sadistic – matched the simplicity of their form; cramped frames, lazily-drawn figures, and perfunctory narratives rushing to predictable cliff-hangers or climaxes, it certainly wasn't a delicate sensitivity for the art of the graphic story.

That started to develop with a strip called *Charley's War*, written by Pat Mills and drawn by (if I remember right) John Colhoughan. Set in the European trenches in the First World War, the story took the form of a young British foot soldier's daily diary, relating his concerns and confusions.

The art was much more emotionally expressive and accurately detailed than any war strip I'd ever read – and Pat Mills's dialogue dealt with a whole spectrum of warfare emotions (paranoias, self-deception, the nihilism of violence, even pacifism) which simply hadn't entered into the heads of Captain J. Brit and his rabid regiment.

Soon after my militarist sensibilities were being subverted by *Charley's War*, along came *2000AD* – devised and edited by none other than Pat Mills – to turn me into a full-blown comics aesthete. To any sussed 13-year-old, the ironic urban sci-fi of stories like *Judge Dredd* and *Robo-Hunter* was the perfect complement to adolescent self-awareness; we got the genre/contemporary references, we appreciated the unprecedented excellence of art (Bolland, McMahon, Gibson, Gibbons) – in short, we knew this was good, and we should stick with it, no matter the opprobrium in later, adult years.

So no one is more delighted than me that the potential of graphic fiction as a medium is now being recognised throughout British and American media culture, with *Watchmen, Dark Knight,*

*V for Vendetta*, et al. I can now sit on public transport with my fortnightly *Crisis* comic (again, Pat Mills the prime mover here) without feeling like some infantile regressive in the eyes of all Adultkind. (Although the cover design of *Crisis* despite all the anti-capitalist eco-feminism inside, is still a bit boys' own-combat chic for me. Johnny Brit's still hanging in there … )

Even that atomically-precise register of the New and the Now, *The Face*, had six pages of Very Advanced Comic Strip from Dave McKean and Neil Gaiman last month: 'No magazines have taken the (comics) hyperbole one step further by commissioning a story of their own,' crowed their introduction. By this one move, graphic fiction becomes of primary rather than secondary interest to UK–American taste élites; a Feature rather than an Intro, or a Funny; equivalent to short stories, current affairs, celebrity features, whatever counts on the sur-Face of cultural consumption. As a long time comics fan, I welcome this prestige; the art/form deserves it.

I should be pleased, then, that CUT is following suit with their own regular strip. But I'm not. *The New Adventures of Hitler*, by Grant Morrison and Steve Yeowell, fills me with dread and disquiet. Let me try to explain why.

## Safety

In *One Chord Wonders: Power And Meaning In Punk Rock*, Dave Laing has a very interesting chapter on the use of Nazi symbolism in early punk, called *Safety Pins and Swastikas*. The point of punk visually was to get a 'shock-effect' somehow; you didn't care for the recognised meanings of the S&M gear you wore, or the swastika emblazoned on your head, because the point was to show how chaotic and anarchic 'meaning' itself was.

Laing points out the problem with this justification; swastikas can deliberately mean nothing to ex-art students like Siouxsie Sioux, but can mean everything to the victims of racial attacks by swastika-bearing National Fronters. Someone's aesthetic act can be someone else's daily terror – something Rock Against Racism realised, a movement almost exactly contemporaneous with punk, reacting to the late-Seventies rise in NF activity.

Note the difference between the use of the swastika and the safety pin in punk, says Laing. The safety pin didn't stand for anything in public before punk used it, or at least had a radically different meaning; a new symbol was created by punk's inspired re-contextualising. The swastika, as a symbol, already has a long and bloody meaning in the public realm; punks using it aesthetically couldn't avoid being dragged into the world of contemporary racial politics.

I'd like to extend this comparison to comics about Nazism. A year ago, Art Spiegelman's graphic novel *Maus* came out in Britain, to almost universal acclaim. It's the story of Spiegelman's Jewish father, a survivor of the Holocaust, told in a classic cartoon form of cats, mice and pigs, standing for Nazis, Jews and Poles respectively.

Take *Maus* as the 'safety pin' end of Laing's theory, and *The New Adventures of Hitler* as the 'swastika' end. Kiddy-cartoon characterisations of funny animals cannot be further away from the horrors of Nazi genocide; yet the use of the most light-hearted form to express the most profoundly disturbing of events in *Maus* reminds us of the incapacity of art to fully represent such pain and suffering, even as it must try to. A new symbol of the Holocaust is minted; one which remembers, but is conscious of its limitations.

*The New Adventures of Hitler* function not to create new symbols of the horror of Nazism, but merely to brandish one of its most obvious symbols for a 'shock effect'. The face of Hitler is as much of a fascist trade mark as the swastika; it has clear meanings of evilness and tyranny, and is part of the iconography of contemporary neo-Nazi movements in Europe. So the calculation of scandalous effect is obvious; we must now try to deduce the artistic justification of using the Hitler-symbol.

It's clear that Hitler is being used here, in Dick Hebdige's phrase, as an 'empty sign' – but not so much to nihilistically proclaim the pointlessness of meaning (like punk), as to be re-filled with contemporary pop-cultural references. The very title of NAOH connotes a comics, rather than a historical-political context; The New Adventures of Spiderman/Superman/Batman etc, Hitler grammatically occupying the place of a superhero. The title of the first episode, *What Do You Mean, Ideologically Unsound?*, anticipates the response of the current critical establishment, wrenching the strip further away from its specific time and place (Liverpool, 1912).

And most explicitly, the appearance of Morrissey in Hitler's bedroom wardrobe, singing *Heaven Knows I'm Miserable Now*, connects the symbolic meaning of Hitler to Eighties pop music culture. 'Hitler was the first pop star', David Bowie said once; and the dialogue points up the parallel between future Fuhrer and contemporary pop stardom – '*Tomorrow I will be famous ...*' (Echoes of Bros?)

In *The Burden of German History 1919–45* (ed. Michael Laffan), Peter Labyani makes an explicit link between images of fascism and commercial, pop culture; Hitler was (and is) 'the star commodity of Nazism'. All the devices of systematic marketing were crucial for the National Socialists, because 'Nazism was not a coherent ideology at all but a multi-purpose ideological commodity, whose unity lay not in its substance but in its forms; in an immediately recognizable packaging and product-style, whose very uniformity served as an instrument for the symbolic integration of the Reich.'

So is the worth of *The New Adventures of Hitler* a kind of post-Warholian commentary on the similarity between consumer fascination and political fascism through the reworked icon of Hitler? It's a reasonable interpretation; it would be easy to end here.

But some things are beyond interpretation. Labyani makes the point that fascism wasn't just a standard relationship between producers and consumers of cultural commodities; Jews in the death camp were the actual raw materials of such a process, their bodies being shovelled out of the gas chambers and industrially converted into soap, lampshades, toothbrushes. 'Of all the images of fascism this was the one which the Nazis did not dare disseminate,' says Labyani, 'but it must always remain the image by which fascism defines itself.'

*The New Adventures of Hitler* constitutes an image of fascism which fascists, past and present, would quite like to be seen around; the Fuhrer's early life portrayed like J. Alfred Prufrock's, all bourgeois bumble and angst; references to hip pop music and comics culture; surely, then, not such a monstrous man, nor such monstrous times?

But the image hides carnage, and is succour to those who would wreak that carnage again. I want no association with it: this is my last CUT column.

## ☆ Into the psychiatrists' lair

(*The Scotsman*, 20 January 1990)

My disbelief cut through the conversation like a broken whisky glass. 'You actually used an orgone accumulator?' I asked, but my friend was completely serious. 'It's one of the most important stages of Reichian therapy. The machine gathers up all the positive sexual orgones ... and transmits them to you. It's a very positive thing.'

If this was not a classic New York exchange, Woody Allen was a carpenter from Cumnock. The record producer's wife had been telling me about the 'many, many years' she'd been 'in analysis' – which had only ceased, it seemed, since her marriage. Her mind doctors had all been followers of the German renegade psychoanalyst Wilhelm Reich, who apparently believed that an unquenchable sexual energy simmered throughout society – identifiable in the 'orgone', or unit of sexuality. Hence the orgone accumulator, gathering in all this energy to transmit to the willing patient.

As she expounded, I heard the sound of distant quackery. But I regarded Michelle – a lovely, generous, non-abrasive Manhattanite, quite contrary to the norm – and began to look kindly on the American metropolitan obsession with psychoanalysis. Could it be that citizens of the most urbanised, fragmented society in the world needed some kind of arcane language with which they could glue their scattered selves together again?

Might this endless trumpeting of 'positive' over 'negative' feelings be a kind of secular faith, choosing the fundamental truths of psychology over the fundamental truths of God's way? Michelle seemed to be steadied by her belief in the effects of gimcrack machines and sexy microbes; it was not my place to be knocking down carefully constructed mental walls.

But the jargon of psychoanalysis has seeped into daily consciousness on this side of the water too. I remember my father getting very angry when, in the throes of adolescent jousting, I called him 'paranoid' without really knowing what I meant. His reaction made the meaning very clear – to be described as paranoid was to be perceived as not being in full control of yourself, of having some mental flaw of a vaguely clinical nature.

Psycho-speak tends to do that to the uninitiated, reaching round behind them with an impressive-sounding term, and then stealing their personal autonomy away: 'the real reason you're so violently opposed to this is because you're repressing your deep attraction for it ...'

'That's the third time you've called me Mary instead of Margaret – Mary's your mother's name, isn't it? You know that's a definite Oedipal projective identification ...'

The popular term 'shrink' captures the resentment many people have of their unique and precious selves being boiled down into a few philosophical-sounding phrases. Out of all the professional classes, it is the authority of the psychoanalyst and psychospecialist in general that is most readily doubted. Other than the obvious cases of the seriously disturbed, the applicability of psychoanalysis to everyday life often seems forced; if someone points out just one more phallic symbol in the street ...

Some psychoanalysts are trying hard to bring their discipline to bear on real social issues, looking at how problems of the psyche can be collectively experienced, and thus become a matter of politics, instead of only a private exchange between doctor/confessor and patient/confessee.

A new collection of essays, *Crises of the Self* (edited by Barry Richards, Free Association Books, £8.95) covers such diverse topics as the mind doctors in Hollywood films, the psychic gratifications of the expensive hi-fi, and the role of the scapegoat in the AIDS crisis. But the most pertinent essays at this moment, as Norman Tebbit fans the flames of British prejudice over Hong Kong immigration, are those on psychoanalysis and racism.

The most useful concept they render up is the connection of racism with a white individual's sense of fragmentation – that the world is literally going to pieces. If society seems like a buzzing and threatening confusion, almost entirely out of your control – that is, if you are alienated from society – it is easy to blame an alien as the main cause, projecting your own desperation and fear on to some clearly identifiable group.

The most powerful analysis of fascism in the Thirties worked from this model, including Adorno's *The Authoritarian Personality*, and even – before he got into orgones – Reich's *The Mass Psychology of Fascism*.

To see if the theory had any continuing relevance, I watched an edition of *Kilroy,* the BBC mid-morning discussion show, on the Hong Kong immigration issue, to witness a florid, red-headed

Cockney lady – white, of course – providing perfect proof of the fragmentation thesis.

The mainstay of her argument was this: how can we allow hundreds of thousands of Hong Kong Chinese in, 'when our young people are sleeping in cardboard boxes in the street, when we haven't even got enough hospital beds for ourselves?'

The fragmentation and impending social chaos that this lady identifies in the homeless and the health cuts is obviously something that frightens her as a working-class person; perhaps because more vulnerable to such dangers, perhaps because of post-war memories of a more stable and ordered economic environment.

But her anger cannot be directed at the architect of the economic policies that have brought her world to this pass – Margaret Thatcher – because it is Thatcher's great-nation patriotism which has provided some kind of psychic compensation for the collapse of her public sphere.

So she asks her premier to 'listen to her voters, realise how strongly people feel about this immigration'. Unable to perceive the economic cruelty of Thatcherism through the clouds of her proto-imperial nationalism, this woman sees the Hong Kong Chinese as yet another contribution to the bewildering mess of her world. 'We've taken enough,' she cries. It is her blindness to reason which is so saddening, in that she doesn't really know what she's taken enough of – the economics or the immigration – or why she can't take any more.

Freud called psychoanalysis 'the talking cure' – conversations which run and run until they dislodge mental blocks, verbalise the nameless, so that sufferers may know themselves in all their contorted mental histories, the better to control their lives.

I wish that Cockney woman could have attended one of the discussion groups at the Self-Determination and Power conference in Govan; the talk there, free and constructive and patient with prejudice, would cure anyone's damaged perception of reality.

Life as an endless seminar? No, life structured so that the frustrations and fears induced by a rapidly-changing world can be shared with all others concerned, and from that a more sophisticated social order fashioned. Who'll need psychoanalysis when true democratic socialism comes? Maybe I need it now. Doctor, I keep getting these mad delusions of a perfect world ...

# ☆ Heroes of the TV revolution

(*The Scotsman*, 6 January 1990)

The revolution will not be televised, sang black American poet Gil Scott-Heron in the Seventies. This line crisply captures the distrust of a strain of Western Leftists with regard to broadcast media. Any real social transformation, goes the argument, would involve switching off the 24-hour gunk, digging the coach potatoes out of their armchairs, and turning them into an involved, politicised citizenry. For Heron, television – in its mind-numbing American variety – is exactly opposed to revolution; the former implies a politically passive society, the latter a radically active one.

The Romanian revolution turns media theories like that upside down. What have Romanians done other than redefine their nation through television? Rather than the box in the corner stupefying and manipulating us, with fantasy lifestyles and three-minute newsbites, the Romanian screen has been a clear and crucial window on reality.

For someone of the television generation like myself, it is incredibly affecting to see that boring staple of broadcast continuity – the newsreader's desk – being used as the public forum for a revolution. Bodies crowding over the table with urgent missives, army-and-people alliances cemented on air, an angry young poet proclaiming the liberation of the national spirit – to the wrong camera. The calculated technical roughness that many Western youth and political programmes use to convey a sense of street-wise authenticity is conclusively shown up as bogus by the Romanian newscasts; when the armed Securitate are shinning up the lift-shafts, that's when a nervous amateurism is legitimate.

Paul Davies of ITN in the Bucharest studios quoted the revolutionaries' hope that television could provide 'a short-cut to the end of the revolution'; that the civil war between the Securitate and the people could be rendered pointless by an army general and a radical student occupying the same TV screen, or by incontrovertible pictures of the dictator's internment, trial and death.

Television here is fulfilling exactly the function imputed to it by despairing Western intellectuals – television itself taking the place of reality, by showing images of political progress and unity that shape the political situation as much as it shapes them. The moan of the Western critic is that all our many political chat-shows, opinion polls, issue documentaries, all the constant prodding of the body politic by the media, only produces confusion and indifference: why bother with the effort of taking a strong stand when all the options are so plausibly presented?

So the paradox of Western media politics is this: political debate has never been so widely represented, but the popular will has never been so difficult to accurately represent. Jean Baudrillard, *eminence grise* of Western cynics, calls this condition 'the death of the social'.

Ceaucescu had been practising his own version of 'the death of the social' recently, involving some guns, some mass graves and some tens of thousands of executed Romanian citizens. There is nothing fashionably paradoxical about Romanian television being the central point of the revolution, the one inviolable base of democracy. Where the Western media system is a hall of mirrors, fracturing and distorting collective consciousness, Romanian television for these last few weeks has been a clean, uncracked mirror of the people's will; a people who before the revolution had been looking into a dictator's portrait or a blank wall, and found nothing of themselves there.

So the revolution *can* be televised – and not necessarily as an Aaron Spelling four-part mega-mini-series, although that will surely come. But the relationship between television and political and national liberation has a Scottish aspect too; and although the conditions are much less crisis-torn than Romania, the same connections are being made between the use of television, and the political aims of a nation.

Scottish Television over the last few years has devised a number of televisual forums in which a distinctively Scottish perspective is worked out on economic, social and cultural issues. *Scottish Assembly* and *Scottish Women*, both hosted by Sheena McDonald, have a real fetish for the opinion poll as an efficient measure of political attitudes – the audience is not only selected as 'representative' of Scottish society by a polling agency, but the programmes revolve around instant electronic votes on issues arising from each discussion.

The agenda achieved at the end of each programme on whatever topic – national self-determination, abortion, public and private housing – is usually a progressive step or two ahead of the Scottish status quo as averaged in street polls. There is a glimpse here of the representative potential of 'electronic democracy' as promised by community-based info-tech, such as Minitel and cable; if the communities wired up in this way made collective decisions as sophisticated as those in *Scottish Women* and *Scottish Assembly*, daily life would be measurably improved.

But even before we get to the futuristic delights of fibre-optic voting, the spectacle of recognisable Scottish women and men being given the chance to rationally decide on policy issues – even if, in Baudrillardian terms, only through a televisual 'simulacrum' of democracy – is a spectacle that can only reinforce the desire for Scottish self-determination.

Neal Ascherson suggested last week that if 25,000 Scots went and sat outside St Andrews House for a few days, tinkling their house keys, that would be it for Rifkind as it was for Honecker, Zhivkov and Ceaucescu. Maybe so, maybe so. But would Gus Macdonald supply the newsreader's desk? Answers on a moonbeam, please.

# ☆ Notes from America's underground

(*The Scotsman*, 11 November 1989)

American political life, as Gore Vidal has been telling it over the last few weeks, would seem to be nothing more than a puppet show. The main performers have the bands of military manufacturers and big business up their backsides; the political script is written across the corporate walnut table, not the White House; and the audience is an indifferent electorate which can barely be bothered to distinguish between the two major political options – slightly vicious and very vicious capitalism.

In his droll and patrician way, Vidal subverts all the rhetoric about 'democracy' and 'freedom' that justifies American state actions at home and abroad – no more effectively than on Channel Four's French Revolutionary bicentennial celebrations, where his magisterial cynicism was dismissed by Roy Jenkins as 'juvenile conspiracy theorising'.

But Vidal only says from inside the American cultural establishment what tens of thousands of kooks, ranters, ultra-radicals and mega-paranoids have been saying for years, hammering away at their nation's consciousness with a barrage of grubby mimeographs, mysterious handbills, and obscure ads in the classified pages. This is the world of the American Fringe, whose members, in the words of Rev. Ivan Stang of the Church of the Sub-Genius, are involved in a 'daily assault against the values of consensus reality'.

The Rev. Stang has collated a directory of these mad prophets, crackpots and true visionaries, appropriately entitled *High Weirdness by Mail* (Simon and Schuster, US). To leaf through its pages is to take a trip through the murky corners of American national culture – a culture obviously so dominant and homogeneous that it squeezes out the purest obsessiveness through its cracks.

The point about the best of them is that their bug-eyed speculations are only barely implausible. Take his excerpt from 'one of the Robin Hoods of suppressed data', Waves Forest, in his *Further Connections* journal:

'Consider for a moment the economic upheaval that would result from broadly introducing fuelless crash-proof cars that float on cushion fields. The industries producing gasoline, tyres, internal combustion engines, paved roads, and auto insurance policies would all become obsolete. With no more crash victims to patch up, a major source of income for medical industry would be lost. Millions of workers would have to change jobs. Also, population groups are harder to manipulate when they can freely travel anywhere, and can take more control over their own lives.'

This is a queasy mixture of technophilia, rampant paranoia and genuine insight – what if technologies which emancipated the citizen were being suppressed for the sake of maintaining profit, or social control? Most fringe members aren't quite as systematic in their suspicions as Mr Forest: too many believe in CIA-Inspired telepathic mind-control, or secret mass-sterilisation campaigns conducted through water systems, to be regarded in any recognisable way as 'political', rather than just lonely and barmy.

The UFO believers and mystic ranters of the fringe are mapped onto the wilder reaches of the American Left in the journal *Semiotext (e) USA*. It originates from the Philosophy Hall at Colombia University, New York – a smaller enclave of embattled hyper-leftism couldn't be imagined. Much the same ground as *High Weirdness* is covered here – the Patrio-Psychotic Anarcho-Materialist Party, Anti-Authoritarians Anonymous, all the wacko favourites – but it's fenced in with pieces by voguish French intellectuals like Jean Baudrillard and Paul Virilio, along with sympathetic American academics.

This is the most extreme example of that futile tendency within US left culture which Paul Buhle has described as 'American Marxism Takes a PhD, and So What?' Faced with the outright aggression of the exploited American masses towards anything bearing the name 'socialist' or 'communist' since the McCarthy years, the US Left retreated into the academy. They justified their now marginal position to society by espousing a politics of the margins – all that post-modernist stuff about the joys of cultural difference and diversity, where the prison rant of a multiple murderer could occupy the same pages as the erudite musings of a post-Hegelian scholar, and each have equal worth.

The complete emptiness of this kind of relativist egghead Leftism is revealed in a classified ad in *Semiotext (e) USA*. 'Busted! Do not communicate with them!' runs a hasty scribble over a caption for the Lewis Carroll Collectors Guild, featuring a genitally-explicit line drawing of a naked young boy; their 'collecting interests include preteen nudes'. Now who is this supposed to emancipate? Paedophiliacs?

Meanwhile, all the old-style American left-wingers become inverted and confused in their historical redundancy. A recent *Newsweek* article on the American Communist Party portrayed it as an embarrassing relic, its octogenarian leader berating Soviet journalists for 'going wild with untruths about capitalism' in their promotion of glasnost.

At the same time, the party advertised in a trade directory for talk show bookers: 'If you want your airwaves to crackle with the electricity of audience response ... to bring something new and controversial to your broadcast market ... then you need to present real live Communists on your show!' At least *Marxism Today* and their bunch are honest about their compromises with capital.

When I was in New York making music last year, I tried to visit some of these places where the words 'democratic socialism' could be uttered without fear of slack-jawed incomprehension. The International Ladies' Garment Workers Union features a Decostyle frontage in mid-town Broadway; inside it's dingy and airless, with a gnarled old receptionist fearless in her ejection of all confused tourists, including me. I fared better in my search for *Dissent*, the left-liberal quarterly magazine, which I found on a dark floor in a nondescript skyscraper; a gentle old union man chatted to me abut British politics, but wouldn't hear of the Scottish dimension. 'Enough with the nationalism!' he grumbled.

Best of all was the offices of *Telos*, a haughty high-theoretical Marxist journal, buried underneath the rubble-strewn streets of Avenue A in Manhattan's notorious Alphabet City. They seemed genuinely shocked to see a real person – 'you get so many jokers round here' – and happily helped me to their back catalogue. The room was beautifully cool, like a little ice-box of reasoning burrowed away from the uncontrollable urban maelstrom above, physically symbolising the tenuous connection their over-jargonised work would have with the real world.

Walking back to the hotel, I spotted at least two World War Three Bible prophesies pasted on street lamp boxes; a day later, someone slapped a bill into my hand proselytising for 'Jews for Jesus'. Thus the American Fringe that I encountered: strung between the Left, and the left-their-brains-in-a-lunchbox.

# ☆ Marxism today, gone tomorrow

(*The Scotsman*, 12 September 1991)

I took a sad phone call earlier this week. 'Hello, this is Wallis from *Marxism Today* magazine. We're closing down for good in November, with a final bumper issue. Could you make a contribution?'

Genuinely sympathetic. I expressed every willingness to fax them down a few valedictory lines. 'Um, that would be nice,' stammered Wallis, 'but what I meant was ... could you get your record company to take out another full-page ad – like last month? It would just help to tidy up some of our loose ends ...'

Such is the condition of Marxists these days: reduced to begging for advertorial from multinational-backed pop musicians. But *Marxism Today* positively thrived on such ironies for much of its heyday decade. Brandishing its *Financial Times* recommendations like a magic wand, it became essential theoretical reading for a broad English Left dazed by the victories of the New Right throughout the Eighties.

*MT* was the first to name, and systemise, the phenomenon called 'Thatcherism'. This critique reached its high point about two years ago, when it called on the Labour Party to ride the historical wave of the 'new times' – individualism, markets, technology – that Thatcher had mastered over the last ten years.

The Labour Party has made the requisite social/market shifts; Geoff Mulgan, brightest of the white-hot 'new times' theorists, even works as a researcher now for Gordon Brown MP. The current issue in the shops looks more like *Management Today* than *Marxism Today,* with capitalist trouble-shooter Sir John Harvey Jones beaming from the cover and fretting inside about the Loony Left still lurking inside Labour.

Hiving off from the Communist Party of Great Britain as its official journal, the magazine has spent a year trying to hook up some proper print-media capitalists to survive. The failure of an arrangement with the *Guardian* – involving a title-change (*Ag enda*) and editorial influence – seems to have been the nail in the coffin.

I once wrote a cheeky note to them saying that they should never change their name; the deliciousness of being an *MT* reader in public – looking like Tommy Trot on the outside, but luxuriating with Candia McWilliam on the inside – was worth the cover price alone.

'Well, we didn't, couldn't change the name,' said Wallis on the phone. 'Too many compromises to take.' So the final jump from Marx and Engels to Marks and Spencer was just not possible; and one of the British media's most useful oddities disappears. A damned shame.

But how does any radical press survive on these islands these days? When *MT*'s editor already moonlights as a columnist for the *Times*, its head guru Stuart Hall does Caribbean history for Channel 4, and its columnist Suzanne Moore files copy for *Elle*, the process of incorporation is obvious.

Mainstream media is always hungry for new talent – and the stylish critiques of user-friendly Lefties can go into the pot like everything else. But that kind of exposure for *MT*'s writers – often specifically bylined as such – seems to have had no reverse benefit.

There is one tactic that the radical press can employ which can make them viable beyond the latest agonising about accepting advertising from British Nuclear Fuels – and that is to start actively agitating, educating and organising political projects themselves.

*Marxism Today* set itself the task of providing the theoretical resources for Labour's ideological refit; conference after conference drew in Party eminences, converting so effectively that they argued themselves out of existence.

*Radical Scotland* gave up the ghost a few months ago, ostensibly by the same process. In the mind of its editor, Alan Lawson, it succeeded so well in placing issues of Scottish self-determination at the heart of political debate, both among parties and media, that it came to seem ever more supplementary to the thud and crash of missives and polemics that currently play across Scotland's newspapers and screens.

Again, a valuable forum for intensive, rather than bourgeois-reader-friendly, debate was lost; but the self-government issue is thankfully far more integral to editorial policies in the Scottish media than token red columnists in 'quality' metropolitan Sundays.

The 'Charter 88' campaign initiated by the *New Statesman and Society* magazine can be considered virtuously as an honest attempt to mobilise people around a politics of citizens' rights and constitutional change. Or viciously – as a means whereby an ailing Left-liberal magazine can conjure up a political arena for itself at a time when its natural constituency was reeling from a third election gubbing, and some new Big Idea was desperately craved for.

Either way, despite rumours of the magazine's basic economic fragility, NSS has boosted circulation through its candlelight vigils for democracy and full-page ads, listing worthy eminences' support for constitutional change.

All this makes perfect market sense; if your target consumer is a highly politicised person, then pitch some strong, new-sounding, inclusive politics at them.

In a climate where politics is more about bullets with names on them than lists of petitions, another political magazine is trying to wrap some bandages round a raddled body politic. Fortnight magazine, based in Belfast, has just received a £100,000 grant from an unnamed charity to set up an independent commission on Northern Ireland's future, seeking the testimony of all parties concerned; paramilitaries, parties, government, communities and individuals.

This is not some self-justifying spasm of the intelligentsia. Fortnight is an absolutely vital publication for Northern Ireland, its continued existence a sign of the potential of the two communities to address each other clearly and fairly, in a shared forum. If only this peace initiative could maintain half the level of informed discussion and equanimity as its originating magazine displays ... 'I think we have a better than even chance' says Fortnight's editor Robin Wilson.

And below the level of publications as effective political actors, the bubble and churn of the pamphleteers goes on. A walk into Glasgow's Clyde Books reveals a tranche of feminist, ecological, Scottish-left, Irish-republican missives – one concentrating on women's self-defence, another advocating 'ethical consumption', yet another detailing the Labour Party's historical commitment to home rule, one more collecting material written by Republican political prisoners.

All have small, separate, often conflicting truths to them; but what you inescapably feel is the force of views that must be expressed on their own terms. The purpose of shops like this (now few and far between) is similar to the magazines already mentioned; to focus dissent, in the raw, on the shelf or editorially digested.

It is not surprising that the market is unforgiving to those large-scale publications which express at least a sceptical attitude towards it; much easier for a triumphant capitalist press to simply raid your best writers and ideas, than to subsidise and therefore control you through what Marcuse correctly identified as 'repressive tolerance'.

If the UK's left-wing press continues its downward spiral, will we end up in another age of pamphleteering, in which print technology enables the impassioned political analyst to publish fast, cheap, clear and undiluted? Distribution via pub, wine bar, street corners and football matches, sympathetic newsagents? Perhaps dangerous information and views can't come between glossy covers; they certainly shouldn't be supported by pop-soul advertising. Cruelly hoist on its own paradox; goodbye, *Marxism Today*.

# ☆ Flights of fancy on the business class

(*The Scotsman*, 24 November 1990)

I stiffen every time I see them; dumped round the Glasgow Airport departure lounge like rubbish bags from a men's tailors, florid faces squinting at the financial pages or chortling ostentatiously into their portaphones, patent leather slip-ons tapping impatiently at the latest shuttle delay. The time is 7.45 a.m. any week day, and I am about to share an airplane cabin with Scotland's finest – our business class, in all their luncheon-vouchered glory.

The mental plastic gloves go on immediately; please don't let me suffer some impossible-to-ignore conversations about the latest boardroom cat fight or thorny problems of 'labour rationalisation' during breakfast ...

But despite my distaste for these bearers of dandruffed collars and crocodile-skin briefcases, dodgy jowl-concealing beards and pathetic power-play language, I am forced to admit the reality of my situation; I am sitting right among them, sharing their morning sausages and hash browns. Doesn't that make me just another young businessman, doing my metropolitan dealings in jeans and crewneck instead of shirt and tie, songs and artwork ideas instead of flow valves and market reports?

Perhaps my quiet loathing of these people stems from that classic psychological reflex – I hate them because I might be like them. To be selling your piece of culture in the market place, via London, is strictly no different in an economic sense from what any of these men in pink-tinted glasses are doing, in finance or industry or services. The only distinction – and it's one that I hang on to like grim death – is that my artefact is borne out of dreams, hopes, a sensibility for form and affect, Utopian urges and intense passions: in short, it's art before it's a commodity.

So this is what separates me from the rows of middle-aged men I pass to get to my aisle seat; the fastidious contempt of the creative Bohemian – just let them try to engage *me* in their mediocre conversations?

But it is my proximity to these shufflers of pension funds and sub-lieutenants of branch plants that nevertheless sustains my passing interest in business culture – its barrel-chested self-importance, undercut by its stupidity and tunnel-vision in so many areas.

As an experiment, one Sunday I decided to keep all the business supplements of the day's newspapers – the sections I usually chuck unopened into a bin. Upon examination, one discovers what Hans Magnus Enzenberger has described as a 'luxuriant language running riot on barren soil'. Metaphors of movement and force abound – in a few pages of one supplement, there are 'plunges' into phone markets, a company 'stiffens' its defence bid, Tories 'weaken' the stock market, new owners are 'savaged' by subsidiaries.

One can almost hear the inner thoughts of the business class as they react to this lexicon of violence over their toast and jam; yes, it's a jungle out there, survival of the fittest, dog eat dog, blah blah … This Darwinist mentality is not only tediously macho, but also reflects on how business really conceives of itself, beyond any political consensus on how the state should intervene in the market.

Business enjoys its daily dramas and grand struggles, its 'Electricity D-Day for Wakeham' and its 'Knives Out in Burton's Boardroom', basically because of the juvenile and boyish pleasures it brings. Hermetically sealed inside the statistics, graphs and curves of the business world, they are freed from any of the social consequences of their actions – how their wheelings and dealings affect the workforce whose labours, in office or industry, provide the basic resources for those takeover bids and 'boardroom putsches'.

Even the merest measure of social planning to reduce this capitalist chaos would be like mummy pulling the Action Men out of your hands and ordering the household chores to be done. Boys will have their toys, and the business world is a tough game with high stakes – but where would the fun be if some damn government body came in and predicted some of the final results and scores for some boringly 'collective' end?

These are clearly the motives for the 'nanny state' critique of the last decade or so; this is also the eternal strangeness of the woman who has led that critique from the front. Has Thatcher been the 'ideal' nanny for the male business class – never censorious, appealing to their most vigorous natures, yet always reassuringly *there*?

But modern economic thought does not begin and end with Thatcher's enterprise era. A recent volume on Scottish traditions and economics sets out the distinctive contributions of thinkers like Adam Smith, David Hume and John Rae as 'a philosophical or

sociological approach to social issues'. Economic activity cannot be
seen in isolation from ethical considerations, from making moral
assumptions about human behaviour and conducting business
practice accordingly. As Douglas Mair says, 'Scottish political
economists make no claims to a monopoly of the absolute truth' –
meaning that a different set of human values (reciprocity and
communality, rather than individualism and competitiveness)
would produce a different set of economic priorities. To repara-
phrase the dear departing lady, for Scottish political economy there
is such a thing as society.

So business is as humans are conceived. I have long held the
heartfelt view that the energies and innovations so trumpeted as the
byproducts of capitalist entrepreneurship can be achieved without
the viciousness involved in unfettered market competition. This
involves a view on business ethics – as yet an undeveloped area in
business culture generally. But will my in-flight companions ever
listen? I am preparing my samizdat for distribution in the BA in-
flight toilets at this very moment ...

# ☆ Revenge of the cyborg trolls

(*The Scotsman*, 21 July 1990)

In the city I live in, £700 million worth of office space is to be built over the next few years. More conclusively than ever, Glasgow will glow with the green hue of late-night VDUs than the spark and crackle of foundries and manufacture.

OK, then, post-industrial point accepted; so what's to stop the open-plan office becoming the next site of workers' struggle, continuing the grand old tradition of Glaswegian militancy? Mental labour can be just as alienated as manual, just as exploited. What kinds of action can the white-collar classes take to become freer, happier, more self-determining and fulfilled beings?

Before you answer, consider this little technical point. Every computer network installed in any institution – corporation, local government, even national newspapers – has a neat facility for monitoring the performance of the worker at his or her terminal. This could consist of measuring the number of keyboard taps in an hour, or how many electronic mail messages are sent and received – and all this information is available to those in executive positions, providing a statistical profile of a level of workrate.

The wired-up office worker is probably under more surveillance from potentially punitive overseers than his or her industrial predecessor, working increasingly in what American critic Barbara Garson calls 'electronical sweatshops'. No safety in the collective body of the factory shop-floor – the head-toilers are isolated, measured by every finger tip.

In this system, there's no realm in which the worker might claim authority, or that this was the process by which the product could be best made, balancing out company imperatives with personal endurance and understanding. In the information economy, you can easily be judged by how much information you process – and they can tell exactly what you've done. What kind of radicalism can take place when those who might be mobilising others to improve their lot can be pulled up for being a few taps below the norm?

There would seem to be little chance for an information

workers' solidarity to develop, with everybody pummelling away trying to appease the omniscient time-and-money monkeys. Even if they don't say they're monitoring you, they might do; result – fear, paranoia, insecurity, a distinctly unpromising well of emotional resources for collective action. The future Red Glasgow will refer, it seems, to the bloodshot eyes of its office workers rather than the proletariat's ascendancy.

But it ain't necessarily so. *Bad Attitude* (Verso), an anthology of articles from the San Franciscan Processed World magazine, is on the bookshelves to show us that there have been precedents for organized resistance to the alienation and robotisations of the information economy. A lot of disorganised, purely destructive resistance too; the book encompasses a wide range of hi-tech office dissidents, from coffee-in-the-keyboard saboteurs to worried middle-managers wanting to deploy computers for 'real human needs'.

Some resistance is more desperate than others. In Silicon Valley, California, the level of petty sabotage and computer hacking is uncheckably high. Dennis Hayes, in *Bad Attitude*: 'Corporations who condemn the social irresponsibility of hacking but manufacture nuclear missile guidance systems richly deserve what hackers often give them; trashed discs, tapeworms, nightmares and migraine headaches. Hostile technology is breeding a strange rebellion.'

Hayes also makes the point that this is not the 'open, constructive activity that social rebellion can be', but it could create a counter-culture which could give a necessary distance from the 'sterile and dangerous corporate culture' of Silicon Valley. This is perhaps something to hope for, if your daily life as an information worker is loathsome in its implications; but what of more mundane practices, like working in insurance? What kinds of collective action could be likely, never mind taken?

The fanzine *Black Chip*, a critical journal of new technology, tells the story of an American strike by clerks working for Blue Shield insurance in 1980. Via the telephone, the Company was able to transfer data-entry work at the striking Oakland office to non-union offices in Sacramento Valley over 100 miles away.

New technology also makes it easier for a skeleton staff of managers and scab workers to continue processing information even if an entire walkout is arranged. The newspaper industry knows this trick very well ... The *Black Chip* writer, evidently an old-style American Wobbly (International Workers of the World) transported through time to the hi-tech Eighties, suggests occupation as the only solution to the strike-busting qualities of new-tech. To abandon the machinery, and picket entry, is not enough.

And if you think that all this carpet-tiled rebellion has no relation to the traditional assumptions of labour politics – that white-collar work is less arduous and therefore less radicalisable than blue-collar – then consider this story from the *New York Times* of a few weeks ago. Paula Tydryszewski, a VDU operator for nine years in a New Jersey tax office, has had two operations on her left wrist. The first one was to remove a grape-sized ganglionic cyst, that she kept 'pushing back inside' for two years, until it wouldn't go back in. She went to the doctor, dropped a milk bottle, then had surgery.

In May, her supervisor warned her that her tendency to 'excessive errors' had not improved: 'as documented by computer compiled statistics' – the record of every keytap – 'you entered 189 documents with 264 errors.' Management tells the pains-stricken Ms Tydryszewski to take more time, but to do that she'd have to fall below the 8000 keystrokes an hour that is her working requirement. So why do they tell her to slow down, when they know she can't? I think the work has a relation to patrilineal exchange ...

In typically anodyne *New York Times* speak, the physical injuries suffered by this operator and an increasing number of other information workers are seen to be caused by people 'being pressed to work hard – in private industry to keep up with foreign competition, in government to hold down spending.' The more it changes, the more it stays the same: those at the sharp end of capitalist expansion – even in the air-conditioned environs of the office – still find that it damages them, body and mind.

The more that society becomes informational, where manufac-turing robots mutely make things that humans frantically programme them to do, the more that the office will become a contested political area – the place where the real forces of production are, where people will realise they are being collectively coerced to keep ideas and instructions flowing into automated capitalism. They'll want a bigger share of the post-industrial cake, and improved working conditions, the way that workers always have.

The kinds of actions to achieve that are unforeseeable at the moment – hypothetically a mixture of direct actions like occupation, a more international span of labour withdrawal so that work isn't so easily transferred, a workers' 'computer literacy' to match the textual literacy so necessary in early stages of labour resistance and organisation. Will the People's Palace in a hundred years time be exhibiting underground pamphlets written by disaffected Glaswegian information workers? Now there's optimism!

In the meantime, the isolated pranksters lighten the bland binary days of office life. VDU operators in Blue Cross of Northern California were assailed with this brain-shrivelling message when their terminals hummed into life: 'Good morning, happiness is a sunny day!' As the *Bad Attitude* writer says, 'no key entry clerk is in the mood to see that at 7.30 a.m.'

So one day, some alienated cyborg troll re-wrote the morning programme. When 250 terminal workers switched on the next day, they were met with the entirely more accurate phrase. 'Good morning, happiness is a good ...' Modesty forbids completion: but I think the word has a relation to procreational synergy – or something.

## ☆ Reasons to be fearful

(*CUT*, April 1989)

If the Auld Man's taught me anything, it's how to be a cynic. I remember being outraged by my father's armchair pronouncements on the Apollo 14 moon mission, as an eight-year-old space cadet. 'Load of crap', he murmured, watching Buzz or Chuck bounce about on their lunar beach. 'It's all done in Hollywood, y'know. Big studio set, cameras, special effects ... keeps the Yanks quiet.'

John Kane wears his cynicism like a well-cut executive coat, a showy sign of consistency. Anything publicly proclaimed to be ideal, harmonious, respectable, can be tipped on its back and shown to wriggle and squirm with hidden motives, secret tentacles of power and interest. Live Aid? 'Well it never did Bob Geldof any harm, that's for sure.' The miners' strike? 'Thatcher had it planned, Scargill was too thick to see that. Joe Gormley, he was a sharper cookie.' Rangers FC's glorious ascendancy? 'They're only doing with money what the Referees Association have been trying to do for years. You know, at one time Rangers weren't allowed to lose ...'

The last two examples hint at the history bearing on my father's bruised perceptiveness. His neck has always been snapped into a white collar, a long march through British Rail from wages clerk to personnel manager. 35 years of placating irate engine fitters and manipulating distant executives, while keeping your own tail covered, would make anyone's politics machiavellian.

John's cynicism with respect to 'legitimate' power also comes from being the victim, as well as the user, of office strategy. Being a professed Catholic in Fifties' West of Scotland meant picking up an *Evening Times* and reading 'Only Protestants need apply' in the Jobs Vacant page; the inscrutable but effective bigotry my father encountered in his early admin days has left him with a bottomless suspicion of systems, élites, leaders of men. Against all my meticulous justifications for supporting Jim Sillars in Govan, the phonecalls kept repeating the same hard-bitten litany: 'A son of mine supporting the Scottish National *Protestant* Party!'

He's handed in his paper clips and staff reports now, and there are signs of a certain mellowing; delighted with his sons' pop success, he'll now concede that some people 'know what they're talking about' and are to be 'trusted' – in the music business, at least. But when our first comeback single frustratingly tripped at the last fence before the Top 40, my father gravely informed me of a conversation he'd had with a BR marketing man: 'He says it just wasn't your turn, son. The Powers That Be took a decision, and for whatever reason, it wasn't your turn.' I really can't afford to believe him; John Kane, ex-professional cynic, can still make my jaw drop.

## Subtly Shafted

'There is no "what should be", there is only what is' (Lenny Bruce). This is the keynote quote in *The Cynic's Lexicon*, compiled by Jonathan Green, the most useful book I possess. Bruce's quip expresses the basic structure of the cynical intellect perfectly; pure idealism undone by messy realism every time.

Every entry in this collection stings because they're all concerned with power – over woman and under men, over nations and under politicians, over minds and under ideologies. One way that political or sexual authority has traditionally tried to justify its actions is by appealing to notions like 'democracy', 'freedom', 'love'; projected realms of shining fairness and reason, transfixing the individual while he or she is subtly shafted.

At some point, the manipulated must wise up, and the manipulators come clean, producing the spasms of condensed wisdom collated in *The Cynic's Lexicon*. Whether it's Aesop in the 6th century BC ('Any excuse will serve a tyrant') or American ambassador Andrew Young in the late Seventies ('Nothing is illegal if a hundred businessmen decide to do it'), the wisest crack is the shortest one. You don't need a 600-page thesis to describe how easy it is to pull the strings, or how bad it feels to be marionetted.

But you might need a 600-page thesis to start cutting yourself free. Peter Sloterdijk's *Critique Of Cynical Reason* (Verso) is an enormous attack on contemporary cynicism, beginning with ancient Greek philosopher-beggars and ending with the nuclear warhead. His question is straightforward: How could a Western culture of 'Enlightenment', privileged, clear-sighted reason and inquiry, have produced such a dark perversion of intellect as the atom bomb, or the totalitarian state?

For an answer, take a gender count of the sages in *The Cynic's Lexicon*. Out of 772 cynics, less than a tenth are women, and most of them are feminists, journalists or Hollywood starlets moaning about marriage. Those steeped in the real cynicisms of power and knowledge – politicians, industrialists, scientists, despots, philosophers – are all men. Most significant public acts of reason over the last four or five hundred years would seem to have been enacted, if the luminaries in this book are quoted accurately, by a bunch of poisonous old bastards.

So Sloterdijk's cynical reason is basically male reason in practice, and as such is fatally faulty and needs to be corrected. Feminists have been saying this for years: that men in power have an 'objectifying drive towards the domination of things', denying their emotions and sympathies to enforce their authoritative reasoning. 'Hard subjects, hard facts, hard politics, and hard business,' concurs Sloterdijk.

His solution to this is distinctly schoolboyish. He champions the ancient practice of 'kynicism', or 'embodied reason', as exemplified by the beggar-philosopher Diogenes, who used to shit and masturbate outside the philosophers' forum in ancient Greece, shouting pertinent abuse at passing egg-heads. A low, rude scatological satire of the people is claimed as the best way to delegitimise the lofty abstractions of power; laughter as the best subversion.

This struggle of cynicisms – plebeian cheekiness versus political calculation – can be seen every Sunday night at ten on ITV. *Spitting Image* and *The New Statesman* occupy what must be the prime viewing slot for adults in British broadcast programming; and one could not get a more precise exemplification of Sloterdijk's 'kynical' critique than the violently flatulent Rupert Murdoch puppet, the salivations of Roy Hattersley, the chest hair and cigar of Thatcher. The political credibility of the New Right is also satirically reduced to naked lust and cruelty in the figure of Alan B'Stard: he screws everything – principles, property, colleagues, constituents, call girls – with breathtaking amoralism. His recent demise was fittingly physical: graphically riddled with bullet holes by one of his many enemies.

So 'kynicism' does strike a chord somewhere in the British broadcast masses. Whether a fully-fledged 'politics of the body', Sloterdijk-style, would ever effectively mobilise people remains doubtful though – a lager lout's antics and a lesbian's disruption of Parliament are both, technically, 'embodied reason.'

Between outright resistance and deliberate repression, doing reasonable jobs and dreaming minor dreams, that's where most of our minds are – a state which Sloterdijk describes as 'enlightened false consciousness'. If false consciousness, in the Marxist sense, is believing what the Tories tell you as they nail your butt to the ground; then enlightened false consciousness is being in a job where it's in your interest to believe what the Tories tell you – but there's all those old sociology books at home, the Nelson Mandela mug in the kitchen, the local pub radicals ... summarised thus: you don't believe in it, but you do it anyway, and you even get to like it in the end.

## Head Bumps

Muriel Gray and me, we've both got 'enlightened false consciousness': I know, because we compared head bumps a few weeks ago. I'd always wanted to meet her – fellow nippy Scot in bowels of media beast and all that – and our conversation fell exactly into Sloterdijk's model of the daily cynic's mood: 'Hectic and perplexed, enterprising and discouraged, caught in the middle of everything, alienated from history, unaccustomed to any optimism about the future.'

We quickly hunkered down to basic world views. Muriel launched off with the most cynical, paranoid plan for Scottish nationhood I've ever heard. 'Listen, it's the Americans that make things happen, not Govan by-elections. We should get the socialists in down south, then declare ourselves totally pro-nuke. The CIA would make sure we were a separate state. Then we'd say, fuck off! We were lying ...'

I countered with my favourite 'eco-cataclysm' thesis: 'All the problems of the world are to do with Western consumerism – we're greedy, we want too much from nature. So what needs to happen before anyone'll really change is a European Chernobyl – maybe a few thousand dead, before we'll get really ecological ...'

I stopped, aghast at the mass murder coming out of my mouth. 'God you've a cheek to call me cynical!' crowed Muriel. What could we armchair Amins and ski-pant Stalins do to atone for our callous notions, our blood-soaked cynical reason? Be *kynical*: eat, drink coffee, laugh, slag, be merry.

# ☆ Authors who come up with the goods

(*The Scotsman*, 28 April 1990)

Materialism is one of those words I've never quite known where to take a stand on. Is it a bad thing, a grasping coldness exacerbated by Thatcherism, to be opposed by more 'spiritual' 'holistic' values, like the Churches say? Or is it a good thing, in the Marxist sense of 'historical materialism', where the labour of humans to survive is the only substantial reality, and the political basis of all true emancipation?

As neither the Churches nor the Marxists are winning over many hearts and minds these days, my original teenage understanding of the word 'materialism' will have to suffice: an obsession with materials, or material surfaces. Perhaps this had something to do with the fact that I spent most of my adolescence indoors, and I probably first came across the word sprawled indolently over my bedspread, dipping into the books and magazines that were my effective substitutes for decent friends.

The surface and textures of my bedroom or the living-room, in fact all the interior landscapes of our house, were intimately known to me; not only their visible signs, but their inner histories too.

I could go on forever, relating in microscopic detail my materialist memories. The chaotic yet compelling motion of nylon curtains in the wind of a half shut window; or how every graphic aspect of the grocer's across the road – shop sign lettering, shape of their Morris hatchback, face of the proprietor, architecture of his wife's perm – displayed a bulbousness which I have always subsequently connected with a minor, bourgeois affluence; or the inverse relation between the expensiveness of pencil sharpeners and their ability to chew up favourite pencils.

This kind of mind-numbing description of one's memories and experiences of the material world has established the reputation of American novelist Nicholson Baker.

Granta Books, the publishing arm of the successful literary magazine, has established its crucial Sunday-supplement reputation on the basis of Baker's first novel, *The Mezzanine*. His second, *Room Temperature*, has just appeared to similarly gushing London reviews.

I've battled through both books, and find the adulation excruci-
atingly embarrassing; it's so obvious that Baker's work is primarily
aimed at a very limited consciousness – that of the metropolitan
media classes, and their hyper-consumerist excesses. Who else
would be interested in a three-page long disquisition on a shoe-lace
snapping, while working in a plush office? Or the politics of escalator ascension, and the sensual pleasures to be derived from the
vibrations of its rubber handrail? *The Mezzanine* has been described as the ultimate capitalist novel – and if you take it in the
first sense of 'materialism' as 'obsession with worldly things', this is
a correct judgment.

The narrator's 'emotional history' is largely manifested through
the history of his purchases – his array of emotional responses from
childhood to adulthood over such vital matters as the changes in
milk packaging, or the evolutions in coffee cup engineering. The
standard critical point to make might be that this is the final
terminus of alienation – being separated from your own natural
feelings to such an extent that, say, a son's relationship with his
father can only be expressed in a comparison of ties they've
bought.

But this critique would miss the point about Baker's work, and
how it fits into the world view of the reviewers enthusing about
him. The public and private lives of the narrators in *The Mezzanine*
and *Room Temperature* are rock-solid and stable; *Room
Temperature* is a materialist eulogy to the phenomenon of male
baby-caring described in manic detail – even in my own child-care
experience, I haven't found myself dwelling on the shape of my
daughter's nostril that much.

But the novel is suffused with directly-expressed, fatherly joy.
The narrator Mike's job – a part-time technical writer and reviewer
of television adverts – is not only immensely satisfying, but also
flexible enough to allow him to care for his child three days a week.

Baker is clever enough to know the pretensions of the critical
establishment he's found favour with – references to the TLS and
Penguin Classics are carefully studded in his texts – but it
astonishes me that the same critical establishment isn't aware how
symptomatic is its gushing over Baker's work.

This is a safe materialism – a stable personality allowing you to
immerse yourself in objects without fear of objectifying yourself;
which is the kind of commanding mastery-over-self that élites
always like to have. With this kind of personal equilibrium, who
needs religious and ecological types to tell you not to be so
'materialistic'?

But if you slide down the socio-economic scale, and perhaps

away from the white-heat intensities of American capitalist culture, your relationship to the material products that surround you might not be so controlled and benign. Two Scottish writers – James Kelman and Janice Galloway – have recently brought out works which talk about how we negotiate and brood upon our immediate material world, much more politically and less euphorically than Baker.

Kelman offers a more painful materialist fiction than Baker; where the East-Coast American takes each object as an excuse for designer rhapsody, Kelman's West-of-Scotland characters shuffle their objects around ritualistically, staving off boredom or concealing despair by fretting over cigarettes or making meals, the objects themselves recalcitrant and trouble-making. Take this from *A Disaffection*:

'The coffee was cold. He had a whole mugful of it sitting on the edge of the fireplace and it was cold, the entire contents, the exact 100 per cent of all that there was and could conceivably be, there in his mug, cold, with its regalia of the English monarchy, imperialism's holy of holies, leaving aside the f... vatican of course, not forgetting the kremlin, plus of course the f... white house, then again you've got the f... zionists. Patrick sipped the coffee. It was a good idea to sip the coffee. Healthy. The life force.'

In one disquisition on a coffee cup, Kelman gestures at a more problematic relationship with the commodities around us than both Baker's books put together.

Janice Galloway's first novel, *The Trick Is to Keep Breathing* (Polygon), is centred on a character whose psychological disintegration is partly checked by her embracing of domestic trivia – lists of things to do in the evening, 'The Bathing Ritual', women's magazines and their trite advice, the skills of dunking ginger nut biscuits.

What makes Galloway even more radical than Kelman or Baker in her materialist fiction – and what makes her virtually unquotable – is the way the actual text itself becomes a material thing, with its irregular typography and variety of forms (factual prose, theatre-text dialogue, concrete poetry).

Baker's ordered, almost academic textual form in *The Mezzanine* – copious footnotes, obscure descriptive jargon – reflects the basic confidence of his white, male, middle-class, American identity; the object-world is endlessly interesting, but never threatening. Galloway's erupting, unstable pages – which caused more than one unimaginative reviewer to criticise the book for poor typesetting! – embody the struggles of a female, Scottish drama teacher trying to deal with her grief and insecurity. The objects around which this struggle rages are made into objects on the page too – a textual materialism which comes across not, as arid experiment, but as a necessary emotional device.

We might never get beyond 'materialism', as the churches would like, or use it as a basis for clear political understanding, as the Marxists hope. Our world is so strewn and crammed with commodities that there is no way we could conceive of the 'material' as anything other than the consumer objects we have bought and sold and made, that we find around us in such maddening profusion and variety.

Baker's work accepts this state of affairs as given, and attempts to carve out new, microscopic realms of experience, in a hermetically sealed American yuppie-bubble far distant from realities like exploitation and social struggle. Kelman's and Galloway's work exists in a society where money and power haven't entirely won us over yet; here, objects are wrapped in sadness, ultimately ineffective in plugging the wounds inflicted by the damage of late-capitalist life in Scotland.

I know which materialism I prefer.

# ☆ Hitching up to the hype bandwagon

(*The Scotsman*, 5 October 1991)

Advanced consumer capitalism never ceases to amaze me. What do you think couldn't be sold? Well, they're already vending water, and you can buy canned air in Tokyo. So what's left? How about the very awareness that one is constantly being sold to, manipulated, seduced by images – surely they couldn't sell you something as logically subversive as that? Oh yes they could; and its name is *Mao II*, the new novel from American author Don DeLillo, glowing malevolently on a bookshelf near you.

Now part of my complaint about the DeLillo type – a record score of reviews and interviews, from *Time* to the *TLS*, and a heavyweight BBC Omnibus 'collaboration' to boot – is rooted in the classic trendy's lament for his underground favourite becoming everybody's flavour.

But the reason why DeLillo attracted the cultists was precisely because of the attack on celebrity and spectacular culture which early books like *Americana* and *Ratner's Star* sustained – a position supported by the shyness of the writer himself, unwilling to share the couch with Uncle John Updike and all.

It is perhaps not entirely fair that I should begrudge Mr DeLillo his bask in the studio lights, after two decades of feeding the paranoias of twisted young men in campus cafes. The only problem is the logical contradiction involved: how do you make a severe critique of the media spectacle, while waving from its conveyor belt on middle-class television or the daily arts pages?

Either you lessen the severity of the critique – in which case, you concede that perhaps a throwaway *Sunday Times Magazine* interview could help illuminate the modern condition (not a particularly cool admission). Or you suppress this hiccup, get on with the intellectual promo, and hope no one notices.

The fact that the actual content of *Mao II* concerns an elusive author, Bill Gray, coming out into the media and political circus after years in seclusion, makes one's head spin with the giddy self-referentiality of it all. Which is possibly the intended effect of the whole package; one is presented with so many sparkling paradoxes and chuckling contradictions that one feels pleasantly smart, slightly bewildered but basically on top of the zeitgeist, a thoroughly modern reader. Yet more velvet titillation of the information classes; giz yer money now.

A few reviewers have commented on the way that *Mao II* seems to be composed of set pieces – bravura chunks of description and evocation, making for a lumpy, disjointed read. More seem to have realised that this is because DeLillo has been punting these self-same chunks round significant Anglo-American literary outlets in the last year – a piece in *Esquire*, the first chapter in *Granta*, a stretch in *Harper's*. This kind of James Bond-is-back trailer promotion does not sit very well with DeLillo's image as furrowed media sceptic; it does, however, juice up the consumer – that is, myself when I caught them first appearing.

It gets worse. A crucial selling gimmick for 'contemporary fiction' (as W H Smith stacks it) is the lit-star shoulder-slap quote on the cover. On the back flap of *Mao II* are two glowing examples – one from super-venerated New York post-modernist Paul Auster (no surprise there). But the other is, unbelievably, from Thomas Pynchon – another subterranean hero of mine. Yep, Pynchon the notoriously reclusive author, whose novels – *Gravity's Rainbow, The Crying of Lot 49* – dissect the shallow spectacle of American media culture...

'This novel's a beauty ... a vision as bold and a voice as eloquent and morally focused as any in American writing,' he gushes. If they can drag a 'New Improved Sudso' quote out of a literary black hole like Pynchon – and even I was impressed by this – then the spectacle really is taking over.

Did I enjoy *Mao II*? I almost didn't, because of this whole superstructure of hype – which annoys me; the phrase by phrase brilliance of DeLillo's style is still there, however much the plot overly dwells on his own writerly condition. I simply resent the way this book has been turned into a lifestyle object for the super-smart; and if its insights into our image-dominated world have been marketed to tickle the sensibilities of only those who dominate image production – the professional middle classes – rather than those who are subjected to them, then I think less of DeLillo for it, either in his ignorance or his collusion.

The question is: would DeLillo want potential celebrity-obsessives like Roger Chapman – or even Lee Harvey Oswald, the subject of his masterpiece *Libra* – to read his book, and be dissuaded from their activities, or to perpetrate them anyway? Or is his writing just another servicing of the bourgeoisie's voyeuristic urge for those that are out of control, flawed and marginal selves?

It's around these positions that a truly 'morally focused' modern writing should be operating – not flashing around amongst the moneyed and powerful. Sorry Don: you've blown it.

# ☆ Too clever by three-quarters

(*CUT*, May 1989)

If being an intellectual ever becomes trendy in Britain, Michael Ignatieff will be held chiefly responsible. Turn on the TV at any time when you think only you and a few other couch-highbrows are watching, and darling Michael will be there – eyebrows twitching dialectically, buttoned-up black shirt highlighting his GQ-esque bone structure, calmly describing 'the modern malaise' in his car-ad Canadian accent. No, I don't think I fancy him, but I'd certainly be Ignatieff For A Day.

He wasn't always the ultimate designer object on BBC2's new arts bulletin *The Late Show*. I first came across him in the early days of Channel Four, when every other show was like the secret fantasy of a Media Studies teacher – all formal innovation, hidden information and the Politics of Just About Everything.

*Voices* was the wettest small-screen dream of anyone who'd ever got a buzz from ideas. Dry names on a reading list became protagonists in a TV discussion drama, where the body language was as entertaining as the terminology. Even my mum, who is not well up on the post-modern condition or the mind/brain argument, would sit with me into the small hours declaring that 'that wee French fella didn't really convince me'.

Someone who always got the maternal thumbs up was Michael. The re-runs of *Voices*' 'Modernity and its Discontents' on C4 recently showed Ignatieff in a slightly less polished state than his later incarnations; hair almost footballerish, tweedy poly-lecturer attire, a little too indulgent of the more crumbly eminences around the table.

But he performs his role – 'I am an accessible, synthesizing intellectual' – with undeniable brilliance. With a brisk 'Let's summarize', he can drag the wilder ramblings of some near-autistic academic back into the realms of comprehensibility. At the end of an exhilarating *Voices* discussion on the sense of constant crisis in Western society, Ignatieff is genuinely breathless, like a schoolboy who's played lead guitar with his bedroom idols.

'We've talked about the biggest possible words there are', he pipes, brashly claiming that 'this really is the only level at which a full encounter with the difficulty of our times is adequate.' Pub philosophy with the lads and lassies is not, I suspect, Michael's favourite pastime.

Which is where I think, his contradictions start. Ignatieff is on the sceptical Left – he wrote an article for the *New Statesman* recently which was as tough on 'Labour's nanny state' as Her Thatchness has ever been – but he recites the proper loyalties like every other stranded English radical.

Why, then, does Ignatieff only appear in middle-class media? *Late Show, New Statesman, Guardian, Observer,* Channel Four, BBC2 ... Of course, everybody is able to watch or buy the things; but, of course, not everybody does. Ignatieff purrs at American critic Susan Sontag's sophisticated defence of sentimentalism on the *Late Show*, yet writes in an *Observer* book review that 'the Left' (wonder who they are?) cannot allow a 'sentimental indulgence of working-class prejudice' to impede political 'renewal'.

If a merely amateur intellectual like myself may comment, Mr Ignatieff's 'Left' have a very confused theory of the sentimental; they are tolerant with each other about it, but must be tough on the brutish proles.

There is as much 'confrontation with the tragic situations of human beings' in the average mid-morning edition of *Kilroy* as there is in Tolstoy, or any of Ignatieff's favourite thinkers and writers. Ordinary people's daily discourse about what scares, exhilarates, defeats or enables them is not more but certainly no less enlightening than the specialized languages of literature, sociology, psychology or philosophy. The 'sentiment' and strong feeling that drives a young black man to movingly express his alienation in an edition of *Kilroy* is surely as legitimate as the impassioned 'sentiment' which fuels the analyses of Susan Sontag.

Consider also Ben Elton's new novel *Stark*, as an example of how a powerful intellectual critique – impending ecological disaster caused by untrammelled capitalism – can both convince and entertain, rather than exclude and self-congratulate. Sorry, Michael, your halo has slipped, though I'll still enjoy your imperial tele-dignity whenever it appears. Is this masterly quality somehow related to the fact that your grandparents were pre-revolutionary Russian aristocrats ... Michael? Hello?

## Prangings, bangings and humpings

Sneaky move that, going into an intellectual's private history; they don't like it. Sometimes the distance between the intentions in their work and the actions of their lives is horrifying. Paul Johnson's

*Intellectuals* – roasted by Ignatieff in the *Observer* – adopts the ethics of tabloid journalism, to reveal some immovable stains on the largest of reputations.

The general response to this book is: how could he do that? How could he say that? Karl Marx, one of the greatest theorists of emancipation, comes across in Johnson's quotes as a casual racist. Lambasting a hated left-wing rival to his factory-owning chum Friedrich Engels, Marx comes out with this:

'It is now perfectly clear to me that, as the shape of his head and the growth of his hair indicates, he is descended from the Negroes who joined in Moses' flight from Egypt (unless his mother or grandmother on the father's side was crossed with a nigger). This union of Jew and German on a Negro base was bound to produce an extraordinary hybrid.'

How could he say that? I'm sure a thousand Marxist scholars could rush in with armfuls of contrary examples citing Marx's righteous critique of colonial exploitation, his wide notion of human brotherhood, etc. But there it is, free-standing and obscene: mid-nineteenth century bonehead racism.

'So often intellectuals work and weep for humanity in general', say Johnson, 'but ill-treat human beings in particular.' Marx's disgraceful treatment of his unpaid family servant, first by getting her pregnant and then disowning his progeny, is reasonably well known. But Johnson does a depressing dirty-washing job on two other favourites of mine – Bertolt Brecht, radical German playwright, and Jean-Paul Sartre. He subjects them to what he calls the Woman Test: 'The way they treat women is the surest guide to their moral values.'

While committing themselves publicly to general human freedom, Brecht and Sartre kept virtual harems in their private lives. If half the prangings, bangings, humpings and dumpings Johnson relates are true, then the old 'car-as-extention-of-penis' theory becomes the 'theory-as-extension-of-penis' theory; dazzle the college girls with a little dialectical materialism, then prang 'em.

'The attack is always the same', fumes Ignatieff – 'judge what they wrote by how they lived.' We should instead regard intellectuals as trying to create great and glorious visions of humankind that will survive their own pathetic exemplifications of them; the hope that 'the work will outlast the life' is the best reason for being an intellectual.

I think I know what Ignatieff means – but I'd suggest a musical parallel. After I read Kitty Kelley's biography of Frank Sinatra, *His Way*, my initial reaction was to throw out every LP and cassette. What a complete shit he was – thuggish, manipulative, opportunist, with an attitude to 'broads' that could easily be described as pathogically brutal. How could anything of beauty result from this monster?

One last listen to the *Where Are You?* LP was my big mistake. 'I'm a fool to want you/Pity me – I need you ...' Away from the microphone, and even in the process of getting to the microphone, Sinatra was one of the most objectionable artists I've ever read about; but, once there, each phrase is a plea for forgiveness, each swoop and quiver disclosing the desperate need of the heterosexual Fifties' male for the approval of women. If the sensitivity of Sinatra's vocal could be translated into general male behaviour, the world would indeed be a 'swingin' session'.

So perhaps great ideas, like great voices, hint at a better life, in their formal completeness and harmony; there is a utopia of hearts and minds hiding in the folds of Frank Sinatra's vibrato, or behind the analytic clarity of Karl Marx's theory of labour value.

Reading Johnson's *Intellectuals* chapter by chapter, one would dearly hope there *was* some greater potential, beyond all their duplicitous, destructive personal activity. Intellectuals might produce work that temporarily heals the wounds of our damaged daily life; but their *own* wounds, so far as this book describes them, seem perpetually open.

## A *bit of a Marxist*

Best intellectual encounter I ever had was in the fitters' bothy in Motherwell Train Depot. Four months vacation work cleaning the squashed flies and occasional cow off the front of locomotives; Dad said if I did it well enough, I'd create a job for someone when I went back to University. Lucky bugger.

The guys were all right, suffered my student righteousness well enough. But in the midst of every bait-the-boss's-boy-contest, a wee cloud of a man would watch me, a grim smirk across his face. Another time-served cynic, I'd note, and plough hopelessly on with my ideology.

Second last day the wee man drifted over to me as I shook out of my rubbers. 'Bit of a Marxist, eh son?' 'Aye, a bit,' I said, watching him shuffle around. He then handed me an old paperback; the pages were curled round like commas, thumbed back at the edges from regular bothy reading.

It was by late Sixties Black Panther Bobby Seals, entitled *Seize The Time*. The cover was a fist in a leather glove. The wee man smiled slightly as I flicked through the outrageously-titled chapters, then pinched my elbow tightly.

'Mind now,' he hissed, 'pass it on.'

# ☆ Onward Christian Socialists?

(*The Scotsman*, 3 February 1990)

My essential reading over the past few months hasn't been some Booker contender or voguish intellectual tome. The book is rent-book sized, deep red, with creamy yellow pages and string binding; it was printed in 1957, so you can run your fingers over the print and feel the letters. In black modernist type the cover reads: *The Socialist Sunday School Song Book*

I found it on an untidy shelf in Glasgow's Clyde Books, a grimly-determined left-wing bookstore muttering to itself behind the Tron Theatre. Intellectually, it was almost too good to be true: I've been trying to conduct a political salvage-job on my Catholic upbringing for years now, and here was a piece of real Glasgow history which embodied – and perhaps might reconcile – all those tortured contradictions. I went for a long coffee and started reading some of the 116 lyrics, beautifully set out on their tiny pages.

Suddenly I found myself sobbing hard, at some clanky old lines from Song No 81. It seemed to be concerned with the commemoration of the dead; I imagined a recently-bereaved child reading or singing it:

> Look in her face, and lose thy dread of dying;
> Weep not, that rest will come, that toil will cease.
> Is it not well to lie as she is lying
> In utter silence, and in perfect peace?
> What though thy name by no sad lips be spoken,
> And no fond heart shall keep thy memory green?
> Yet thou shalt leave thine own enduring token,
> For earth is not as though thou ne'er hadst been.

I found the intent behind this song almost unbelievable: to try and help a child deal with the enormity of a loved one's death, without recourse to God or Heaven or any kind of transcendence. She has died in the world, has made her mark on the world, and now lies as still as anything in the world: an absolute assertion of the material over the spiritual.

Yet, of course, the paradox of this song, and of all the others, is that this profound materialism is evoked through the most standard religious hymnal techniques; the antique diction of thys and thous, the Biblical imagery of lilies and scented flowers, the communal thud and rhythm of the verse

I have known for a while that the devil doesn't have all the best tunes. We included the Catholic hymn *O Godhead Hid* on our *Bitter Suite* album as a tribute to its power as imagery and music. The way an atheist sings that song is simple; a tortuous faith in absolutes – whether it be the omnipresence of a God, or the irrepressible human urge to resist exploitation and oppression – is common to committed Christian and politico alike. The point is that sometimes that faith lasts only as long as the performance of the song lasts, and no longer.

I've been through every song in the Songbook to see if there's a lyric that could be voiced anew – and only the ones that don't directly propagandise, that allow a little ambiguity or philosophy into their arguments, are in any way attractive. The Socialist Sunday Schools movement was founded in Glasgow at the turn of the century to counter the chauvinist and capitalist teachings of the state system – which resulted in direct political conflict in the First World War with the Socialist schools' pacificism. But for all the alternative value systems, young Socialists still had to be very good little boys and girls, and many of the lyrics are excruciating lessons in good manners – carrying Granny's parcel, helping blind men over roads, never wanting for some helpful labour.

The basic motivation of such songs – that true revolution means kinder, less alienated human beings – can't really be faulted. Unfortunately, there is so much candy-floss militancy in the Songbook – 'We're a band of little Comrades, walking in the path of truth', etc. – that if I was a little Glasgow comrade in 1957, I'd be humming Elvis tunes under my breath and dreaming of capitalist Cadillacs. In all likelihood, it was the increased consumerism of the post-war working-classes which did for the Socialist Sunday schools: no amount of 'lofty words, and 'noble deeds' could dim the allure of pop culture.

But there are several of the Songbook lyrics which are breathtaking, using the language of popular hymn to articulate a deeply-philosophical socialism. No. 49 places the child in a world where there are no barriers to human community, and no inequitable parcelling out of the 'common earth's' resources: 'Unchain the sunlight, loose the breeze, make free all time and space.' No. 32 asks what might be done 'if men were wise', and provides an account of the emotional changes a truly emancipated world might make:

*The meanest wretch that ever trod,*
*The deepest sunk in guilt and sorrow,*
*Might stand erect*
*In self-respect*
*And share the teeming world to-morrow.*

The most striking contradiction of themes throughout the Songbook is between the harsh language of activism – the chants against 'Tyranny' and for 'Freedom', obviously intended to soften up the next generation of militants – and the calls for kinder language, gentler communication among men and women. Song No 16 describes the emotionally destructive effects of the 'harsh word, rashly said', followed by a 'kind word' making 'the hate and anger cease'.

But the third verse raises the simple moral lesson to a much higher psychological level: the harsh word 'leaves a trace the kind word could not quite efface'. The psychic cost to Socialists of their constant protest and opposition, the 'scars that long remain' on the heart, is described here with as much accuracy as Bertolt Brecht's weary phrase at the end of his great poem, 'To Those Born Later': 'Oh, we who wanted to prepare the ground for friendliness/Could not ourselves be friendly.'

And on reflection, it's difficult to place exactly where my public tears over some Socialist doggerel comes from: the beauty of the sentiments, or the impossibility of their realisation. Back to the thrusting post-modern authors and academics-on-the-make – but with a heavy, scarred heart.

# ☆ Banality, Solidarity, Spectacle

## 1. *Politics and the banal*

'Have you ever been wonderin', 'bout the way it all is?/Why we can't get a grip on how we could and should live?'

'But maybe if loving ran the banks, flew the planes/We wouldn't snap at each other, while the world goes insane…'

Pop is splendid at elevating the banal. The above lines from our June '92 single, 'Profoundly Yours', are at a level of political simplicity which pop music can carry lightly. I believe every word I'm singing – not simply as a matter of emotional soul-baring, but as the vernacular conclusions of many years of twilight thinking and scholarship-on-the-run, about 'how we could and should live'. Which boil down to? *Love, practised at the level of a society as well as between individuals, would mean real human emancipation.* Now isn't this the very worst kind of idealist banality – a cracker-barrel creed to justify an intelligent citizen singing silly love songs?

In the May '92 edition of the American current affairs journal *Harper's Magazine*, philosopher Richard Rorty argues 'For A More Banal Politics'. Western 'leftists' can best deal with how the post-Cold War revolutions of 1989 and 1991 have attacked the idea of 'socialism' as a potentially desirable state of existence, by resolving to 'banalize' their political vocabulary. 'I suggest', says Rorty, 'that we start talking about greed and selfishness rather than about bourgeois ideology, about starvation wages and layoffs rather than about the commodification of labour, and about differential per-pupil expenditure on schools and differential access to health care, rather than about the division of society into classes. I suggest that we stop assuming that the function of the intellectual is *radical* criticism that attempts to penetrate down to the realities behind the appearances…'

But surely we can conceive of less banal political arguments than 'People ought to be kinder, more generous, less selfish'? Rorty's own hunch is that 'there may be nothing less banal to say'; that there may be 'no middle ground between that sort of banality and attempts to sketch concrete, workable alternatives to present socio-political arrangements.' So between pop songs trilling moral platitudes, and a better-run Health Service, or a better industrial policy in the EC, there is presently – according to Rorty – no area for new definitions of what kind of humans we should be, or what kinds of fundamentally different societies other than 'bourgeois liberal capitalist' we could construct. As Thatcher once said, following Hayek, there is now deemed to be 'no alternative' to the presumption that you cannot have 'democracy without capitalism'. All that we can do is improve and reform the institutions and systems we have, fuelled by an unverifiable faith that lovers might one day run the World Bank, or could conceivably order F1-11's to turn back...

Strange that one of America's foremost philosophers should be making credible pop's capacity for soft moralising. The little that we can effectively do in records – to 'charge mundanity', as Fred Vermorel says, to 'lift ordinary lives to transcendence' – turns out to be an articulation of what really motivates political change in the very late twentieth century. 'Truth and love will win over lies and hate', said the poster of Vaclav Havel pinned to every window during the Czechs and Slovaks' velvet revolution. If such Ivor Novello banalities were part of the rumbling discourse underlying the people power that brought the end of the Cold War, and given that Havel genuinely found succour in the lyrics of Lou Reed while a political prisoner, then it looks as if rock'n'roll might very well be playing its part in saving the world for liberal democracy.

Rorty claims that Havel may be a fitting 'revolutionary' successor to Lenin because of his 'magnificent honesty' about such verities. Unlike the communist vanguards of the twentieth century, absolutely convinced that their analysis of society's end was correct and historically inevitable, Havel replaced theoretical insight with 'groundless hope and trial and error'. Faced with a regime who debased the Czech word for truth – 'pravda' – in its own propaganda organs, and strove to make reality conform to its 'official' version, the tactics of soft revolutionaries had to be improvisatory, spontaneous, aware and alive to gimmicks, spectacles and symbols: Soviet tank statues painted pink, keys rattled outside government buildings, cafe 'scenes' and under-ground performances. All this 'groundless hope, trial and error', all this creative politics, sounds more like the practical daily ethic of the musician or artist in general, Havel's real vocation, than the hardened cadre activist.

Where I agree with Rorty's 'banal politics' is when he accuses all grand theories and theorists of society – Marxist, capitalist, environmentalist, whatever – of not being honest about the rather mundane moral and ethical preconceptions which underlie their great houses of thought. My personal pantheon of modern critical theorists – Jurgen Habermas, Anthony Giddens, Terry Eagleton, Theodor Adorno, George Davie – are all writers out of whose work rises a vision of the kind of human beings they think is implied by their analysis. Or, to put it banally, they have made a clear evaluation of what is good or bad about being human – a clarity which helps the lay reader, eager to put ideas into practice rather than contemplating them in the seminar room, and wanting to relate such critical theory to questions of 'how we could and should live'.

Here follows a small, defined journey through some of these writings. These works have accompanied my life throughout the wildest pop moments, the most victorious and most frustrating political events, the deepest transformations of personal and cultural identity; in short, all through the 'tinsel show'. My own ways and means to the 'friendly life together', in Brecht's vision of the good society – that is, my politics – are determined by these texts. They act like ropes harnessing a sail, without which the fabric would flap and fly wildly into the clouds.

## 2. *Speech and freedom: Habermas and Scotland*

I'm sitting at a table of political activists one dreary Sunday afternoon, in the long grey descent of the summer of 1992. We are discussing strategies of self-determination for Scotland, expertly and productively. Yet a dull panic is throbbing inside me, as it always tends to do at such meetings. This is such a placid wee space of discourse and mannerly intervention: airborne hypotheses gently brought to ground, realities and constraints faced and dealt with. But it will end, we will go back to daily life, and find our stoutly-built plans running aground in the sands of Scottish inertia. Perhaps politics is practised in its purest, most identifiable state in these kinds of gatherings – where good and true men and women display their interests, let these circles of interest cross each other provisionally, and then build on the points of overlap as a cause in common. My fear is that we are simply a fan convention for political argument: as intense but as marginal as any small, obsessed group of people. We're presuming that what we're doing here is what every citizen, with interests he or she wishes to voice or realise, should be doing throughout the land, if only they had the will and the means to do it.

Popular apathy is the enemy of the political activist. But there must be some source for our groundless hope that our fellow members of society are transformable, can have their passions raised or viewpoints changed by a process of argument and exchange. What faiths and principles about what humans are and could be can activists put in place to motivate themselves?

I know where I source my hope, at least intellectually. Language, in its very structure, is the basis of how we free humans from oppression and degradation. Even when we lie and cheat, or are lied and cheated to, we only abuse the basic premiss of language: to bind us together in communication. Even our foulest imprecations expect to be understood. And it is this presumption of understanding at the core of language that makes society, or social existence, possible in the first place. A human world composed entirely of strategic, scheming beings, wouldn't even get beyond the vulnerability of the first child born, or the arbitration of the first tribal dispute, never mind the bristling modern world we live in. If you counterpose the possibility of an ideal situation of speech and language, where people are genuinely mutual and reciprocal, to the reality of a short-term, power-and-money, rationalising social system – then your political motivation is almost inexhaustible. Try to 'live in truth', as Havel says, and political emancipation will always move closer.

'The truth of statements', says philosopher Jurgen Habermas, 'is linked in the last analysis to the intention of the good and the true life' (McCarthy 1978, p. 273). His point is that you won't get to a truth about morality, society, politics, if the process of communication establishing that truth amongst a community has been fettered or constrained in any way; truth is a freely-achieved consensus of meaning. If powerful interests of administrative power, or financial and industrial capital, have impeded the flow and extent of the discussion; or if participants who will be affected by the result have been excluded from the discourse – then no lasting truth has been arrived at. Full democracy leads to practical truth, and vice versa.

It's not inconceivable that such a communicatively-oriented society – say, Scotland – would come to the fully-agreed consensus that a participatory socialist democracy is the political system that would best enhance human existence. There is already strong support for a socially and economically just Scotland, considered in purely party-political terms; in the 1992 General Election in Scotland, votes for parties standing on manifestos that were, to a greater or lesser degree, 'socialist', amounted to 60% of the total (combining Labour and SNP votes). An effective, fully democratic

Scottish legislature – a Scottish Parliament, devolved or independent – would enable this 'left majority' to translate these party endorsements into real political action and policies. And the democratic process upon which this Parliament would be based – proportional representation – means that large, competing political parties (like Labour and the SNP) would have to fully communicate with each other to govern, and would have to be sensitive to the opinions of those who have voted them into this mutual dependence. The perpetually 'hung parliament' would reflect, at a state level, the constant processes of negotiation and consensus that run through everyday life, in workplace and community.

There may seem to be an inherent anarchism, or even communism, in a communicatively-guided politics. Some would say that a national government is nothing other than a too-large concentration of power and money. The establishment of a democratic Scottish Parliament might only mean a lower and closer level of administrative and financial indifference than Westminster to the real wishes of Scottish citizens. Yet another bluff impedance of the vast complexity of democratic will, of what people really want to bring about in their social lives.

But Habermas, whose 'theories of communicative action' underlie my argument, is no communist, and certainly no anarchist. He is not claiming that humans have an 'instinct for freedom', as Noam Chomsky does, which would be best realised in a society of self-governing communities, in relation to which the state would be subordinate or eventually evaporate. Although Habermas's views of language inspires utopian fantasizing in acolytes like me, he dampens down these flights at many points in his work.

The kind of discussions to be had in activists' meetings, community education workshops, enlightened classrooms, shopfloor bothies at teabreak, the university seminar, the local pub or family gathering are often conducted in the spirit of free and equal exchange. But would these 'ideal speech communities' be able to run a health service? A macro-economic or environmental policy? Demilitarize industrial production? Maintain a nationwide media and information network? The 'ideal speech situation' tends to dim a little when faced with the immensely complex structures of West European society as it stands. The systems of power and money that twist and divert humans' tendency to free communication, have also housed, employed, fed and informed larger and larger amounts of people in the West for the last century. The rational sophistication of these systems cannot be doubted, even if their direction and function may be; they maximise their benefits as well as their debits.

Democratic will in the UK may be peremptorily expressed once every four or five years in the Westminster Parliament, with only the bubble of popular disturbances and the constant fluttering of media debate between terms. But the electors of Scotland, England, Wales and Northern Ireland do at least bind their (statistically minority) Tory government to full claims that they will retain public health, education, and services – that is, the basics of the modern Western welfare state – however much the storm rages about the implications and outcomes of the particular ways they're retained. Even triumphant fourth-term British Tories must make their weekly obeisances to the 'preservation of the National Health Service', however much they drag it into the swamps of 'market efficiency' and 'consumer rights'.

The welfare state institutionalizes the practices and values of caring-and-sharing embodied in community life and communicative action; it takes those practices and values out of our hands and into the possession of expert sharers and professional carers. The great popular endorsement of the British welfare state in 1945 could be seen as a genuine strike of the ethics of community and interdependence – what Habermas calls the 'lifeworld' – against the calculations of the system. The communities which had been hammered materially and mortally in the War, put their faith not in their militarist leaders – the steerers of the war machine of British society – but in social reconstructors, who wanted to point the machine of state in an opposite direction: away from death, destruction and glory, towards health, wealth and happiness. But in this great political movement, the Labour victory of 1945, the highly administered nature of British society was unproblematically assented to: we've won the war with state instruments and institutions, now let's win the peace with them.

So we grant the modern state powers to dispose of money and resources to our social benefit; that's the bottom line the British electorate has voted along for almost fifty years. The implication is that a communicatively 'good and true' social and economic policy – that is, a policy legitimated by the widest possible discussion and consultation – would be almost unachievable, given this deep British (and even deeper Scottish) commitment to administrative systems, unaccountably taking a myriad of decisions on our behalf. Is there a level of responsibility for running our own lives – a daily democracy, which monitored conditions and agreed actions amongst ourselves – that the citizens of these islands, and arguably of the West in general, just do not want to assume?

In a recent essay on the Eastern European revolutions, Habermas lands a kindly but fatal blow on romantic socialists everywhere – this one included – who believed that communal self-management and democratic control over production, the withering away of state and capital, was still a valid way of organising society. These dreams of 'free associations of producers' are simply 'nostalgia' for the victims of the early industrialism of the eighteenth century; a nostalgia for the types of community – family, neighbourhood, guild – that arose from the world of peasants and craftsmen, and were violently broken down by the onset of market competition. This breakdown, experienced as a loss, has thrummed throughout the thought of the Left for the last two centuries: 'the idea of the preservation of these eroded communities', says Habermas, 'has been connected with "socialism" ever since' (Blackburn, 1991, p. 31).

The national liberations of 1989-91 in Europe noisily repudiated this nostalgic dream of the Western (and Eastern) non-Communist Left. Any kind of 'Third Way' between capitalism and socialism that might have opened up in the revolutionary ferment, any possibility of state socialism ever being given a chance to reform itself – this was decisively rejected by the liberated nations, however much stunned Western Leftists (and Eastern reformers like Neues Forum, Charter 77, KOR in Poland) may have advocated it. 'The decision deserves respect', chides Habermas, 'particularly from those who would never have been affected by any negative repercussions.'

The way chosen by East Germany, Czechoslovakia, Hungary, the Baltics, Poland, et al, was constitutional democracy, market economics, and a minimally regulative state as the only valid structures of a modern society. That is why Habermas calls it a '*rectifying* revolution', restoring the norms of Western modernity to nations suppressed by the Soviet bloc. But before those taking the name 'socialist' slide into the trough of the 'triumph of liberal democracy', curling up with our communal fantasies as history comes to an end around us, we have to take a last look at the word. What could it be used for, other than as a historical reference? 'That was socialism – this is the future'?

Habermas's last look salvages something for us; but as it passes through the eye of his conceptual needle, socialism is pared down to a minimum. If Habermas's theories about the communicative, consensus-building, anti-systemic powers of everyday discourse *don't* imply participatory socialist democracy as their full flower, then what kind of social organisation do they imply? With more clarity than all his previous works put together, Habermas spells out in this essay what concrete political stances arise from his theories of communicative action.

It turns out that communicative ethics, 'solidarity', 'mutually supportive coexistence' – call the very stuff of socialism what you will – is now only available to us in the West 'in the form of an *abstract* idea'. Its concrete manifestations in the Soviet bloc have been cautionary enough, and the guild utopias of socialist romance were never likely to be realised. But 'socialism' now serves as the 'legitimate, intersubjectively shared expectation' that the values of community and mutuality will be able to affect the direction of economic and administrative systems – of power and money – through proper democratic processes. A Western socialist would then have the role of asking the liberal democratic state to live up to its rhetoric – that is, asking it to respond to rational arguments from concerned citizens, compose its policies under the constant pressure of democratic will, and devise institutions that will be sensitive to that pressure.

From his German perspective, I can understand why Habermas is so willing to take the intense mutuality of everyday discourse, at work in our lives and communities, and tie it down as a necessary belief that democratic systems work. Germany's system of federal government, elected under proportional representation, and its enshrinement of human rights in the Basic Law, is exemplary in the way it provides conduits for the democratic will of German citizens.

Compare the position of Scotland, its social and economic consensus again ignored by a centralised, undemocratic Westminster government. In these circumstances, it seems necessary to turn 'solidarity' and 'mutually supportive coexistence' into something *concrete* and practically defensive of our left-of-centre consensus, rather than leave them as abstract presuppositions that the system will respond to our needs. This assumed approval legitimates a British first-past-the-post democracy not worthy of the name.

Recent calls in Scotland for an unofficial referendum on our constitutional future are mobilised on the basis of the values of community and mutuality. The result of the referendum would help to establish an effective Parliament, able to implement the values of sharing-and-caring, of democratic input into policy, of harnessing capitalist and administrative imperatives to some measure of popular control, that mark the Scottish national consensus. Scots do not have Habermas's luxury of living in a properly-representative constitutional democracy; and the 'official' steerers of this system, our Tory government, are at this point of writing (summer 1992) refusing to respond in any way to Scottish desires for political and economic autonomy.

When a dominant political system is so blatantly unfair, so unresponsive to the wishes of a national community within it, then popular legitimation of that system – the presumption that it is rational and democratic – *must be withdrawn*. There must be some positive mobilisation around *alternative* structures of democracy, asserting an *alternative* legitimacy – the 'people's ballot', as proposed by the Scottish National Party and pressure group Scotland United in the months after April 9, 1992, resting itself on the internationally-recognised right of peoples and nations to self-determination. If this fails, then a fall into what Habermas calls 'social pathologies' – self-destructive despair, apolitical indifference, an erosion of the very idea of the social bond itself – is more than likely in the next few years in Scotland.

At the end of his relentless stripping-down of the socialist tradition, Habermas makes a moral prediction about the point at which socialism will lose all its force as a political critique – and he does it in terms which will be familiar to any thinking Scot. A 'radical reformist' socialism 'will disappear ... when the society in question has changed its identity so much that it allows the full significance of everything that cannot be expressed as a price to be perceived and taken seriously' (Blackburn, 1991, p. 45). Adam Smith, that much misrepresented political economist, graced his *Wealth of Nations* with a similar sentiment, deploring those who 'know the price of everything but the value of nothing'.

The complex tension between system and lifeworld, affection and calculation, tradition and competition that Habermas proposes for Western society is something which is intuitively understood by most Scots. I have been, and continue to be, inspired by the intellectual depths which Jurgen Habermas has mined, and the 'resources for hope' he has brought back up, as that famous Welsh European Raymond Williams put it. But my struggles have to be practical, in the here-and-now of nineties Scotland; and for me Habermas's ideas are words as weapons, tools to open minds, provisions for a long journey. A private, arcane justification to keep the conversation going across tables...


## 3. *Spectacular Times*

The conversation was shocking, in its quiet way. 'No, I don't think it would be right for me to speak on your show, Pat.' James Kelman's voice was coming through the phone, soft but insistent. 'Although I'm fully behind you – Culture City Glasgow is a hype and a distraction, I agree. But sometimes you can be more effective by *not* appearing on television... by *not* doing the whole spectacle thing. You understand?'

At that moment, barely: I had my six demystificatory slots to fill in a BBC2 Glasgow Cultural Capital review, and couldn't quite stomach the purism and fastidiousness with which our 'New Beckett' (copyright the London criterati) was treating the medium. What was the problem? My editorial brief was to be 'polemical', my line was as libertarian socialist (Kelman's politics) about Glasgow 1990 as it could possibly be, and Kelman's trenchant written critiques could easily have been captured in a few choice soundbites...

Following my own logic brought me to a standstill a few days later. The man was absolutely right. Why should he surrender his long, complex denunciations of the Glasgow culture hype – published in pamphlets and unedited press articles – to the editing decisions of a BBC production crew, where even a sympathetic soul like me would have his intentions subjected to the television skills (and technical bullshit) of others? Was the visibility worth it – providing a few strings of visual argument which would only be part of a more 'balanced' montage, the force of his points lost in the equalizing flow of the 'well-made arts feature'?

As my slots went out, I found I understood Kelman's fears more and more: the hard-hitting only occurred in my pieces-to-camera, which thrust rudely into mutually cancelling series of talking heads. I stepped on screen like the house bore, sternly theorising in the midst of play-safe interview snatches. I hung onto my self-written script, and forced it through each show unamended. But there was one moment of unarguable censorship, which has to be recorded in full. In a slot on Scottish pop and its American obsessions, I wanted to make the point that the growing political nationalism of Scottish musicians (and Scottish culture in general) during the eighties was a reaction to Thatcher's explicit English nationalism – the Falklands, attacks on our 'dependency' culture, impositions of poll tax and denigrations of national institutions and traditions: you know the litany. A well-ventilated thesis amongst the Ascherson's and Ignatieff's of the metropolitan opinion-forming élite. Hardly pushing the Scottish liberationist boat out.

'We'll have to change "Thatcher's English nationalism" to "That-cherism",' relayed my timorous director/producer. 'Orders from the series producer. Thinks that your phrasing will annoy them down in Wimbledon'. What if I refuse? 'It may not go out this week.'

My distinction between 'Thatcher's English nationalism' and 'Thatcherism' precisely recognised the growing nationalist explicit-ness of Scottish popular opinion (corroborated by fistfuls of opinion polls at the time). To elide this distinction was to make Scottish musicians' attitudes diffusely anti-Establishment, rather than part of a growing, positive awareness of being socialist-through-Scottishness. Such interference should have resulted in me storming straight up to head office. But my nerve failed – ultimately, I like to be liked – and I made the concession to record both versions for the voice-over edit, with an explanatory note justifying my choice and a motivated director/producer to plead my case.

What appeared in the final, televised edit? No prizes for guessing. It seems, in retrospect, like a small battle lost, in an otherwise respectable TV intervention in the wider argument about Scottish pop'n'politics. But this smallest of repressions is still a concrete reminder to me – that there are managers of the media spectacle; that they can, if necessary, impose sanctions on expression, hiding under a cloak of 'appropriateness' and 'balance'; and that if such exercises of power can happen in an unwatched, minority channel arts programme, what can possibly be going on elsewhere?

☆ ☆ ☆

'The society of the spectacle.' It's a notion that slips easily into vernacular understanding – yeah, it's all showbiz these days, big hype, a tinsel show and a' that, bullshitters and shysters everywhere, life is a cabaret old chum. But the committed subversive who first coined the term – French situationist Guy Debord – did not intend it to merely express our ennui with an over-mediated society; a portentious abstraction of all our indifferent shoulder-shrugs at the latest public scam, scare or spectacle, whether political, economic or cultural. Debord wanted to smash, or at least to muddy, the screens and mirrors of these spectacular times – that total version of reality given back to us by commodity and consumer culture, in all its proliferating forms. Debord wanted to drag our eyes from the stage, pull our bums out of our seats, turn us into actors making our own history – rather than passive recipients of some managing elite's interpretation of our thoughts and desires, even our understanding of 'the real world'.

It's been strange, knowing and appreciating the force of the situationist critique of the media 'spectacle', while attempting to use its many pathways to practise political mobilization. Out of the hundreds of multi-media current affairs and arts slots I've done over the last four years, almost every appearance had some kind of statement referring to the desirability of an independent Scottish state – to a greater or lesser degree, from casual comment in a pop interview to leading the charge in a party political broadcast, but consistently (and deliberately) there. Yet how could you measure the effect of your own, small propaganda trail as it snaked wispily across the spectacle's clouded heavens? How could you gauge what impact these words were having on the silent majorities receiving your transmission?

On an individual level, I know I'm being personally effective through the media – 'aye, we all know what you stand for', comes the street quip, which usually results in a political debate with some direction, if not exactly conversion. And one watched with interest, in the late eighties and early nineties, as other interventions from musicians, writers, actors began to spread the issue of strong Scottish autonomy across different screens and surfaces, putting an unaccustomed nationalist grit into contexts of leisure consumption – TV shows, concerts, newspapers. In so far as polls measured anything, they registered over this period a burgeoning popular sense of the rights of Scotland as a nation, politically, economically and culturally. It seemed natural to assume that this nationalist mood had been partly fuelled by the acts of such Scottish 'cultural-politicians'.

And of course the run-up to the April 1992 General Election saw an intense shake-up of the spectacle, as Guy Debord would understand it – 'the activities of the world's owners' (Debord, 1990, p. 6) – by one of the spectacle's prime activities, an opinion poll: that startling Scotsman /ICM census in mid-January, claiming that fifty per cent of Scots wanted some form of independence, or statehood, for Scotland. How 'the world's owners' – at least, those with their grip on Scottish life – were terrified by that statistic! Industrialists and financial institutions predicted their withdrawal on Day One of independence, political Unionists painted horror-scenarios of European diplomatic resistance and massive job losses. (If only we had a transcription of all the life-or-death calls between corporation boardroom and progamme controller, party head-quarters and editorial chair, during the Scottish election ... But this is the essence of the spectacle: we presume a secret network behind the media, where power and information is as one, as a reaction to its very authority and omniscience.)

Yet the spectacle of Scottish life was rattled a little looser by the poll, both by internal and external pressures, to allow left-nationalist voices much more of a say than ever before. I worked myself into a weekly column with the *Glasgow Herald*, pushing a high-profile line on every aspect of the independence movement: my inevitable dumping soon after the Tory victory on April 9 was no surprise, given the clouds of nationalist psephology on which I floated into the paper. Even something as subversive as militant Scottish nationalism can be used to sell newspapers. But when the scare recedes, and the readers crave their balm ...'Repressive toler-ance', as Marcuse called the supposed pluralism of the media, becomes mere repression.

The 'fifty per cent' statistic also brought the world's media to bear on Scotland. If the media spectacle is to be understood in Debord's malevolent way – as a 'communication of orders' (Debord, ibid.) from the real power holders – then the swarming presence in the country of media functionaries from four conti-nents, in the first four months of '92, was a reflection of the real import of Scotland's possible moves towards statehood. In terms of basic realpolitik, the nation-state is still the fundamental agent and actor in world politics, in at least the formal and legal sense (how-ever much real sovereignty of action is being eroded by multi-national structures). The emergence of a new Western European state – with its territorial claims over resources, its ability to enforce conditions over defence, environment and economy, its capacity for strategic alliance in global councils – is something that 'the world's owners' need to know about, and need their subject populations to know about, in the correct way. The first need often travels under the cloak of the second: several Nationalist figures have told me of long, detailed, strategically precise conversations with grey men from obscure international news agencies during the election run-up, whose need was more obviously for political 'intel-ligence' than journalistic 'information'.

But those who live by the spectacle, die by the spectacle. The hope that a media campaign, a cultural politics, or a battle of slogans would mobilise the silent majority of Scots for indepen-dence as much as grass-roots activism was a forlorn one. A constant Unionist onslaught, from all other political parties and their propaganda, from most tabloids and broadsheets, was some-thing that the SNP was practically and financially incapable of defending itself against, in terms of a battle of public images. Even the endorsement of Hollywood Scots such as Sean Connery, and the market-oriented conversion of the Scottish *Sun* to independence, wasn't enough to counterbalance the entire Estab-lishment weight of the Unionists' disinformation and negative discourse.

Debord claimed that the only way to challenge the spectacle was through 'mass revolt' – active citizens seeing their very actions as making a new history, a new world for themselves, rather than passively accepting their place and their fate according to the orders of the spectacle. The General Election vote in Scotland was calamitous precisely because the electorate expressed their political decision *as an act of passivity to the spectacle*. Scots were told, in opinion poll after opinion poll during the last two weeks of the election, that the Southern English electorate were going to reject the Tories in sufficient numbers to ensure at least some progress towards a properly representative Scottish society, through either a Labour victory or a hung Westminster Parliament.

If there had been a genuine *mass movement* for independence, where citizens had been encouraged to connect the deprivation and shortfalls of their immediate conditions to the need for national-democratic control, then there might well have been an autonomous vote for the independence option far in excess of the one actually expressed – genuinely 'independent' of the messages coming from the media. But the actions of a populace passively mesmerised by the spectacle, and taking their orders from it, are as predictable as a lab rat: the hype windfalls of the televised Great Consitutional Debate, Sean Connery and the *Sun* effected the fifty per cent independence poll; the Unionist attack eroded that poll support; the last few UK polls showing some kind of end to Tory rule on April 9 halved the Scottish poll results for independence, boosting Labour fortunes ... We know the rest.

The post-election organisations for Scottish self-determination have all had, as their prime objective, the refocussing of Scottish politics on 'people power' and community mobilisation. Although groups like Scotland United have shown a continuing interest in the politics of spectacle – either through mass rallies with ensured media coverage, or a variety of visual and physical 'stunts' to keep the issue of Scottish democracy in the news agenda – their real strength lies in the network of local chapters and meetings of Scotland United supporters: aiming their activities towards referendum fund-raising or cross-party protests on Tory policy, and trying to create a truly 'activist' movement for Scottish self-government.

For me, the election signalled the end of my over-estimation of the powers of cultural politics, and of attempts to use the media to bind together collectivities for radical change in Scotland. The 'imaginary community' of Scottish nationhood – that consensus of values which gives a majority endorsement to left-of-centre policies in Scotland – is not enough on its own; either as something expressed infrequently and abstractly through parliamentary democracy, or as the background to our daily dealings with each other in Scottish life. We must begin to put our imaginings and ideals into some kind of practice – organising and holding a referendum, non-cooperation with Westminster laws and edicts, acting as if we were prepared to defend our values – rather than remain happy with these imaginings, reflected back to us from talking heads on screen, newspaper platitudes, 'television forums' or favourite fictions.

I'll still be seizing my opportunities to make opposing voices heard in the corners of the spectacle, amidst the tinsel of its show. But I'll only be striking poses in the face of the unknown void of the media audience: only if my symbolic acts crystallize what is happening in the daily world of solidarities and communities, might they have any real political effect. And those effects I'll never really know, from *my* end of the camera, microphone, or word-processor. The spectacle must be *surprised* by the democratic revolution in Scotland – from the dark perimeters beyond the fall of its light, from those who will not sit still in the glow of its transmissions. The spectacle is intrinsically incapable of initiating or fomenting real change; only in moments of social revolution (as in the Romanian revolution of 1990) or faced with overwhelming mass disturbance, will its transmitted orders waver. Any desired democratization of the media – that is, understanding the spectacle as a reformable media structure – will never happen by itself.

# ☆ Scotland

He canna Scotland see wha yet
Canna see the infinite
And Scotland in true scale to it.

Hugh MacDiarmid

# ☆ Unashamed of kitsch and kin

(*The Independent on Sunday*, 13 May 1990)

The first time I knew I had working-class taste was as a gawky 18-year-old student visiting new friends at their dishevelled flat in Glasgow's bohemian West End.

On the old tiled fireplace was a collection of what I regarded as familiar domestic trinkets – wally dugs (china dogs), tartan holiday mementoes, swooning figurines with rosy cheeks and lips. It was the kind of stuff that crowded on top of our Baird telly at home, relics from deceased grannies or all-weather friends of the family.

Each time I came back to Coatbridge after a baffling day's lectures – a major proportion of Glasgow University students live at the family home – these objects would be waiting; part of the comforting surround of shapes, shades and textures that I had known since infancy. I could say nothing about them, make no judgment of them: I only noticed when they were moved, and felt a strange absence where a seaside ashtray from Whitley Bay had been. To see such things in my friends' flat was strange. Surely they were too relentlessly avant-garde for such cosiness, or perhaps a mature student was living here? 'No,' they airily pronounced, 'we call this our kitsch corner. So bad it's brilliant, you know?'

No, I didn't – and a minor panic stirred in me that has not really died down since. In the dictionary, I found that 'kitsch' meant 'tawdry, vulgarised, or pretentious art, literature, etc, usually with popular sentimental appeal'. So the rotating tube on the family display shelf – printed with scenes from the Fire of London which flickered with internal flames when you switched it on – this was 'tawdry'? The clockwork musical Spanish guitar with pearl inlays that I once played with till it snapped – 'vulgar'? My parents' favourite flamenco lady picture with the unnaturally long legs – this was now 'pretentious art ... with popular sentimental appeal'?

Until that moment, I simply had no idea of what could be called my parents' aesthetics, and certainly not of the lower-class inferiority implied by kitsch. Desperate for peer-group acceptance. I knuckled down to the complicated business of developing an appropriate 'taste' for my new position in society. This taste had to reflect the fact that, as a lucky beneficiary of higher education, I was now able to know everything worth knowing. All aspects of my life – principles, footwear, lampshades – were now cursed with intellectual awareness.

These days, as a fully certificated member of the information classes, I buy posters for rooms that pretend to be art galleries, sofas that make sophisticated references to the Viennese Secessionists, lamps that are spatio-temporal statements. Oh, and we have our 'so bad it's good' item: a plaster-cast, inter-war skiing girl, hair bobbed and cheeks blazing, frozen in mid-slalom.

The only problem with my re-fitted sensibility lies with this wally snow queen. When I look at her, in all her 1930s', glazed innocence, she makes me feel warm and happy, not superior and post-modern. Her 'popular sentimental appeal' is indeed 'pretentious', aspiring beyond its station: an image of alpine joy and grace which would have no foundation in the crushed tenement lives of Glasgow half a century ago. But the distance between proletarian reality and plaster fantasy incites sadness in me rather than snickering irony. Not many skiing excursions from the Gorbals in those years; not many more now, I imagine. And there is something honest about the aspirations expressed in the skier – glamorous leisure. unabashed hedonism and physicality.

I am tired of media-fed middle-class restraint and discrimination, tired of the simplest act of consumption generating a thousand lifestyle connotations. My new information class has got where it has by the accumulation and exploitation of cultural capital. When these people return home from their ideas factories, frazzled by conceptual competition, they want their intellectual edge to be confirmed by the manifest intelligence of their decor. Nobody can argue with their decisions here, no office politics interfere with their information processing. The media person's home, to paraphrase the famous Englishman, is a fortified castle of taste.

But all this has to stop somewhere. The fatal step from hanging a Picasso print favoured in adolescence to semi-exhibiting a lovely wee original from last year's Glasgow School of Art Degree Show – 'ectually an investment in the next New Wave, Alasdair' – is one I shall now not be making. Real bourgeois taste means the sincere pursuit of 'quality' and 'culture', instead of a self-loathing unease about the very authority of these terms. I have been saved from élitism by two things: a father's birthday card from a Bridgeton gift shop, and the return of revolving ornaments to my life.

Bridgeton is the kind of place the Saatchis would find hard to market for Glasgow, European City of Culture: poor, sectarian, territorial. In Bridgeton Cross on this last afternoon there were drunks lying in the pavement dust, alienated young men flailing away on the corner, the occasional Sierra stampeding through the traffic lights.

The only basis of warmth was the gift shop, staffed by two girls in cardigans deep in local analysis. It was the 'For a Special Dad' card that clinched it, one of several A4-sized extravaganzas in the window, all dealing with weddings, births, illnesses and anniversaries in the same way: a fluffy animal with Disney eyelashes acting out a corny scenario. The 'Dad' card showed a cutesy tiger in jungle wear grilling sausages at a campside; the message was 'Fun and surprises will be yours to explore'. Gold inlay, a big badge saying 'VIP' and a fuzzy photo insert of a mountain range: jarring techniques, screaming sentimentality.

Yet I'd guarantee the Bridgeton dad – any dad – who got that card would really feel 'special': the conventionality of the symbols means that they are already well understood, the emotion immediate and happy. None of the art-history-on-display graphics of the average birthday card I give to relatives; quite rightly, its postcard size is seen as a mark of cheapness. 'What's that on the front? A Man Ray? Oh, aye ...'

Conventions in mass culture exist because people sometimes like to have the same feelings about an event as everyone else. The working-class birthday card wants to generate a reciprocal warmth, quickly and unequivocally; the middle-class card respects only the ego of the giver, still trying to score reference points. On someone's birthday?

Begetting a child has for me nailed all this taste-politics stone dead anyway. No matter if it is kitsch, functional or designer, the domestic object seized by my daughter goes straight into her mouth, or is thumped off walls. The more 'garish' it is, the more loved it is; two Fifties rubber swans from our *dreck* shelf are now in active service, drenched in infant saliva.

So my mother comes at Christmas and sits this plastic dome on the mantelpiece. 'It's a lovely thing, isn't it?' My de-education in taste almost goes into reverse – this is a revolting battery-powered snow scene, in which a flashing house vies with a 400 revs-per-minute windmill, which flurries up white flakes like an antarctic blizzard. Part of me produces the thought: this is irredeemably ghastly; but I hate myself for this feeling, hate every line of my education that separates me from the insane Santa-dome and its good intent. Thankfully, I have no choice in the matter: the kid sees it, roars mightily, and is transfixed for a blissful forty-five minutes, cocking her head to catch the thin twinkle of 'Walking in a Winter Wonderland' rising from its innards.

It would be marvellous if my child could grow up in a world where no one felt ashamed of their cultural education because everyone would have the same chance to be educated culturally. After all, aesthetes like myself exist only because of others' exploited sweat and toil. My four years at university doing nothing but reading books have left me with a sense not only of privilege and distance, but also of political loyalty and debt. The kind of society I want is one where all its members have the opportunity to enjoy their lives making fine cultural discriminations instead of some specialising in them and others brutally excluded from them. So if we end exploitation, might not the inequalities of taste also come crashing down? That would finally bring the bulldozers in on Kitsch Corner.

## ☆ A hitch on the bandwagon*

(*The Scotsman*, 24 June 1989)

That's *two* epochal moments of modern Scottish politics I've been involved in now – one win, one loss: such is life. And my crucial position in this great clash of party machines, of ideologies and demagogues? Hanging out the back of a wobbly van, grinning manically at harassed mums and placid pensioners, doing rent-a-celeb for the SNP.

It doesn't feel as futile as it seems – although everything takes on a somewhat theatrical aspect from the Wee Snappy Bus. Being politically active in these situations means making good eye contact with pedestrians, timing your performance to the rasping loud-speaker.

'PAT KANE OF HUE AND CRY' – slow dawn of recognition on hapless passer-by's face – 'WON'T BE PAYING HIS POLL TAX' – either a happy beam and a wave or a frown and a pair of fingers. Sometimes, with particularly campaign-literate citizens, you get the first cruelly followed by the second.

Even the autograph is a potential battleground for hearts and minds. In normal situations, one accepts the request with as much humility as musterable. A precisely-constructed illusion of intimacy with the star is part of what compels people to consume my art in the first place – so I can't blame them for wanting a piece of the real thing when they see it.

One can never expect too much from these everyday encounters: the only knowledge usually generated is a statement of my love and three Xs for Elaine or Andrew on the back of a Thursday pay slip. Anything more substantial – biography, philosophy, let alone politics – becomes embarrassing or inconvenient for us both.

Waving one's party cutlass from the Wee Snappy Bus, however, means a pushier approach. Love my celebrity, love my ideology –

---

*This was my first *Scotsman* column: the two 'epochal moments of modern Scottish politics' referred to are Jim Sillars' Glasgow Govan by-election victory for the SNP in November 1988 – the beginning of the 'nationalist bandwagon' in Scotland – and the following defeat of his cohort, Alex Neil, in the Glasgow Central by-election in June 1989. I campaigned extensively for both candidates; my explicit commitment to political nationalism began here.

admittedly, a crude equation. But when the election's on Thursday and the polls are fluttering, there's no time to be pondering over the aesthetics of reception.

'Hello! Are you going to be voting for the party next week?"

'Och, I don't know, son ... sign this one for my daughter-in-law Cheryl ... Well, I might give them a try this time." Mission accomplished: next punter please.

If this seems a rather instrumental way to help bring about a 'democratic revolution' (Alex Neil), consider the problems of fomenting radical rebellion in a high-rise flat. I had wondered why the SNP's bus had a 90-degree cheese slice on its roof, with the words 'Do It Again' pointing inaccessibly to the heavens. I figured it out at the Roystonhill flats, looking up at the hundreds of windows and balconies, peppered with faces and forearms.

To top floor residents, today's intellectually unassailable pitch from the SNP would be a tiny yellow square and a megaphone buzz. 'Move the van round,' Jim would bark, 'the wind's blowing the words the wrong way.' In the spirit of the day, dark Labourite conspiracy theories crammed my head: they deliberately built these things in the Sixties to destroy street politics, abolish the public spaces like Glasgow Green or George Square where ideas might clash and convince. Who would brave the piss-ridden, unreliable lifts down to the howling concrete concourse, just to argue with some MP? Would listening to another speech sort out the fungus on the walls?

The only crowds mobbing our bus in these areas were teams of Saturday kids, plastered with every available sticker from RCP to SLD, drawn like magnets to the distinctive eight-eyed profile of Charlie and Craig Reid from the Proclaimers. Maybe later the weans would proudly display their autographs to Ma and Da; maybe Ma and Da would be faintly moved by such celebrity largesse, and let a little chink of Independence-in-Europe into their hearts. Or maybe not. Who could tell?

But this is cynicism based on a few afternoons being cosseted and flattered on a campaign bus. I'm sure there are hundreds of feet-blistered and throat-ragged canvassers who would testify to the struggle of ideas on doorsteps, the difficulty of changing old loyalties and renewed optimism, the surprise conversions and immovable diehards.

Whatever the differing results of Govan or Central, my contribution on the streets was more like a charitable royal than a folk hero; by the time I hitched on the wagon, the work had all been done. So I did what I do best: waved and smiled, smiled and waved, over and over again.

I got much more involved in the Central campaign than in Govan – tremendously confidence-boosting, I'm sure you'll agree, given the final outcome this time round. Being thrown into the full *melée* of political promotion is tough on one's ideological consistency; instead of lazily regurgitating chunks of *Radical Scotland* or Tom Nairn to clueless metropolitan media types, you have to convince fellow Scots that you're worth listening to.

First press conference, I was like a rabbit before the headlights; and when I was asked out of the blue by the SNP's PR man to 'tell the journalists why you support Alex Neil for Central', I thought I was facing the Madonna crowd at Wembley Stadium again.

What came out of my mouth would probably confirm all the Labourist stereotypes of Scottish nationalism as 'essentially petty-bourgeois'. I'd become a nationalist by being able to visit other European and American cultures in my pop career, appreciating their distinctiveness by recognising the distinctiveness of my own – thus proving Neil Gunn's phrase (always a handy saw, this one) 'every real nationalism is also an internationalism'.

A quick look up from my lap to catch those tell-tale tics of journalistic boredom (well-suppressed in this crowd); and then onward. I suggested that the Independence-In-Europe policy outlined a modern, intellectual, progressive nationalism, which simultaneously maintained our sense of nationhood and connected it with other European cultures. I then started to sound like a Euro careers officer, wittering on about Scottish talent and native skills, and quickly shut up.

Charlie and Craig Reid raised the level of politicing suspiciously high – I knew they'd been party members, but this concept-perfect exposition of Left-wing nationalism made Alex Neil sound like a passionate publican. Charlie revealed his secret at the end: 'Takes me back to the old national executive days,' he reassured me. 'Get three strong headlines, then stick 'em out – never mind the question.'

My personal highlight of the whole campaign had to be the party political broadcast. I'd just done a Manchester arts TV show, and become autocue-literate. I kid you not; widespread knowledge of the utter dependency of broadcasters on this machine would cause more media subversion than a bus-load of Malcolm McLarens. This is the ultimate tool in creating not only an illusion of intimacy, but also articulacy; you deliver your soulful intellect into the camera, and the camera sneakily reflects back your script. The easiest gig I've ever done.

I could handle the form of TV sincerity; Sillars and Neil gave me a free hand to fill in with political content. And although I was using every stage technique and small-screen skill I had, timing every breath and shrugging as meticulously as I could to get the maximum effect, I still believed every single word I'd written.

But to say it as passionately as I believed it would have been a spectacle of halting sentences, emphatic blind alleys, inaccuracies and exaggerations. So, like camp, pop'n'politics is the lie that tells the truth. It don't bother me if it don't bother you.

## ☆ Down but not out in London

(*The Scotsman*, 14 October 1989)

Who can avoid London? The place determines my life far more than it should – both oppressing me and enabling me, making things and stopping things happen.

Perhaps I should get out of the music business, to get rid of this love-hate for London. When the resources for your innermost expressions of Scottish sensibility hang on a corporate whim in West Ken, London becomes a structural fault in your imagination: it's there, deal with it, do the work anyway.

But London is much more than an economic problem for me. London as metropolis, as the power-centre of British-nation state, means cultural and intellectual power as well as political and financial.

Until quite recently, I've been unaware of just how much my perspectives have been shaped by metropolitan culture. In fact, I'd go as far as saying that I couldn't write this without London sitting on my shoulder, checking my text for concentrated wittiness. For that's where I learned this dubious art of turning my intuitions into passable prose, presuming that anyone would find them interesting in the first place. It's an arrogance which initially develops out of necessity – that is, you need to have some self-esteem if all you are is a portable typewriter, a Tufnell Park one-up, and a few indifferent contacts in the music press.

I went down the line in 1985, half-propelled by adolescence, half by a buried anger at the power of the London critics I'd been reading every week since my O-levels. What gave them the right to opine so authoritatively on music, television, film or literature? I had all the education, the verbal style, understood all the delicately-layered references and was a clear-headed unhypeable Scot to boot. Would they take to me? I'd be irresistible.

As it turned out, I was eminently resistible – my clippings from those days would barely crease the cardboard of the standard folder. The people I dealt with in the few rags that would have me – a declining monthly called *Jamming*, and the *New Musical Express* – were like me as I would be if I spent four years in the place.

Almost all were from the regions, their roots either pulled out or suppressed to leave a gaping hole in their personalities around which flickered the darkest cynicism and nihilism.

I remember the most pointless evenings, in Camden pubs choking with plastic plants or rooftop record promotion parties, where my colleagues would bitch, rant, devise flaccid psychological traps for worthless subjects, suck up to more powerful journalists and attack the weaker ones. Their emptiness was like a self-willed response to the vast indifference of London: why retain any fixed identity if survival means flowing with the media currents, tailoring your character to suit those with power and influence, your only commodity being the ability to turn a vitriolic phrase or two? I realised that to be a critic in London at that level – to apply one's intelligence solely to the latest press office hype – couldn't be the basis of a working life. Better to make the symbols than react to them: still on an economic chain, I broke out of the metropolis, my lyric sheets and chord progressions in hand.

I can't even say that my experiences as a London critic helped me in my pop career. I conducted every early interview under storm clouds, brutally second-guessing each pause and duplicitous phrase of each interview. Even now there are broad swathes of the music press – sprinkled with former colleagues and interview victims – who fiercely avow never to allow my product to stain their pages.

But London's not all hype and revenge, power and money. The main areas where I socialised when I lived there, Camden and Brixton, were relative paradises of plurality but also full of hellish social problems. Their streets were like open-air laboratories for experiments and personal lifestyle, not much cash around, but plenty of dreams. Stray beyond these oases, however, and insignificance beckoned: the android commuters on the Tube, the pedestrian madness of W1, the intimidating office blocks with their even more intimidating occupants ... And the one lesson I learned in all these London adventures: if you need London, you can't be cleverer than it, still less understand how it really thinks. Better instead to value a different way of thinking than London's altogether, taking solace in the distinct traditions of Scottish intellectual culture. To challenge the metropolitan mind-set is perforce to challenge the dominant culture of the British nation-state; the break-up of Britain can be pursued at the level of review prose as well as at the ballot-box or warrant sale.

Again, London forces a paradox here; there is much metropolitan intellectual work which cannot be ignored by the thinking Scot. *New Left Review, New Statesman*, and *Marxism Today* all provide lucid analyses of national and international politics and culture which obviously benefit from the proximity to the main power centres of the British capital. Yet even their most authoritative thesis can be seen to be more a product of long sessions in comfortable cafés than a full historical and social understanding.

*MT*'s silicon chips-with-everything 'New Times' manifesto, as its upcoming conference I'm sure will prove, is much more a justification of Labour revisionism that a real understanding of the problems of hi-tech capitalism, specifically as it affects peripheral economies like Scotland's. I'm down as a guest speaker, but I'm dreading it – lots of Oxbridge-educated Filo-radicals, brimming with opinion poll confidence about Westminster finally falling into their hands. But if I don't turn up on the day at City University, London, I'll feel as if I'm letting the Delicate Left down again. Oh the contradictions of UK Socialism!

Many of my arguments down there will be drawn from the flourishing intellectual work on Scottish culture and society conducted by magazines like the *Edinburgh Review, Radical Scotland* and *Cencrastus*, and publishers like Polygon, with their splendid 'Determinations' series. Certainly the most useful book in that series had been Beveridge and Turnbull's *The Eclipse of Scottish Culture* – contemptuously reviewed in Scotland, regarded as the work of academic savages in London – which establishes for me anyway some kind of distance from the intellectual dominance of the metropolis.

The writers accuse Scottish intellectuals of 'inferiorism' – anti-colonialist Frantz Fanon's theory that a subject nation is more easily dominated if it believes its own culture is backwards and crude, and greatly in need of the civilisation of the coloniser. The mediators of Scottish culture, its intellectual class of writers and academics, are shown by Beveridge and Turnbull to be conditioned almost entirely by metropolitan condescension, their arguments resting on unexamined metaphors of English 'enlightenment' dispelling Scottish 'darkness'.

This dynamic duo have had their sources unpicked and their arguments qualified in many reviews but I find their book useful for the connections it makes. It is not a reasonable assumption that the centrality of religious institutions to Scottish culture has resulted in questions of morality and ethics being at the core of Scottish traditions of thought, from John Anderson to Alastair MacIntyre? And might not this sedimented religiosity also relate to the seriousness of Scottish citizens when matters of public welfare and common good arise, evident in the long-term adherence to broadly communitarian politics?

I haven't the time nor the energy to explore fully Turnbull and

Beveridge's conjectures, but they conform an intuition about Scottish culture which I feel everytime I leave the country, everytime I enter the hall of mirrors that is media London.

But if you're going to admit to sustaining myths, best make your own ones if you have to. Even if all you want them for is some intellectual ammunition to throw over the record-company table, to get some money, to comprehensively justify doing your own thing – it's true, you can't avoid London: sometimes the best you can do is to use your Scottishness to make sure it doesn't avoid you.

# ☆ Something to write home about

(*The Scotsman*, 28 October 1989)

If the metropolis is evil but unavoidable, the home town is benign yet ambiguous. In a sense, you know exactly where you are in a big city – fundamentally alone, surviving through goal-attainment, emotional injuries compensated for by the giddy speed of city existence. In the home town, by contrast, one need never feel lonely or empty – every conversation strives for consensus, every action takes place against a background of shared knowledge or a common plight.

Although this willingness to communicate and relate can be wonderfully comforting, it can in an instant stink like dead fish: the consensus can settle on the wrong values, a pinched etiquette or unexamined prejudice. And then you suddenly feel estranged from, even repulsed by this community, its cramped pettiness twisting your principles like a hair-braid.

I've lived in two home towns now. The first, Coatbridge, is unclear in my sights – it's the place I put behind me to go to London, and I still regard it dimly as the cornerstone I had to kick away to rebuild myself. Any comments I could make on it would be obscured by a film of adolescent anger, so best I spare you.

The second, Gourock stretching into Greenock, I chose as an adult to make my home, so I can see it far more clearly, as an interested stranger rather than a prodigal son, learning the rules of this place rather than being forged by them.

And the rules of this place are that the most parochial thing can turn into the most global thing, and vice versa. Gourock and Greenock are unassuming West of Scotland towns which exist on the edge of immense absolutes – environmental, geopolitical, economic.

The River Clyde flows eternally by the two towns, having swept them into being over thousands of years; the hills beyond are so breathtaking they make you feel deliciously small, put you in your natural place. The US navy submarine depot at Holy Loch twinkles dangerously in the distance, filling the river and stuffing the hills with enough nuclear violence to wipe out nature itself. The derelict

Scott Lithgow shipyard lies flattened by the winds of world capitalism, blowing impassively towards the cheap labour markets of the
Orient and the Third World; and the dominating presence of the
post-industrial future, IBM and National Semiconductor, hulks
behind the towns like beneficent corporate lairds.

Hedged in by so many powerful forces, the citizens of Gourock
and Greenock take two escape routes: – obsessive conformity and
quiescence as the majority option, and a wild imaginativeness for
the scattered few.

The *Greenock Telegraph* exemplifies the first route – a daily
newspaper which grounds itself in the community minutiae of its
readership's lives. It treats every major industrial or political event
in the area with a certain nervous hopefulness – quite under-
standable, given the battering Greenock and its environs has
endured in such matters.

The charity sales, the schools competitions, the drama nights
and boating clubs, all these activities dominate the pages of 'the
Tilly'; activities which are at least entirely in the control of those
who do them. Too militant a journalistic emphasis on activities the
locals could not possibly control – the fluctuations of micro-
processor markets, the machinations of the SDA, the unaccountable
practices of the US military – would only make the rain even
wetter, the wind cut even sharper than it does already.

George Wyllie, world-infamous sculptor, has taken the other
route to Inverclyde sanity – making joyous art out of the
unpropitious conditions around him. Walk down his street and you
pass by one pebble-dash and wagon-wheel monstrosity after
another, until you come to a garden filled with cast-iron
constructivist chookie burds, and iconic ocean liners majestically
parting the grass lawn; this is George's house.

He will snort and shake when asked about Greenock and
Gourock – 'Small towns, small minds," he'll say, complaining
about the *Telegraph's* ignoring of his work. But despite his moans,
his work can really be understood beyond the context of this place
– his symbolism is drawn from its shipbuilding heritage, his
materials from those old industries and the natural resources which
surround them, his political critique profoundly shaped by the
conditions of this area. Many universal issues and themes arise
from the Firth of Clyde – not such an unusual inspiration therefore
for such a worldly artist.

There is one weekly phenomenon which brings a wholly
separate part of the world bizarrely onto Greenock's and
Gourock's streets: the American military on shore leave. On Saturday afternoons, the tiny shopping centre is like a cross between a

Peter McDougall play and a Spike Lee movie – groups of black guys jostling around in hip-hop day-glow clothing and angle-shave haircuts, peering at the trundling, chip-fed shoppers like a *Star Trek* landing party.

The train leaving Gourock, where the ferry drops the sailors off in Dunoon, can sometimes be transformed into a Brooklyn house-party – the back third of the carriage booms with a preposterously-sized ghetto blaster, and homeboy rhymes are chanted out to the puckering distaste of the Gourock elderly. They come back at night, families bearing several boxes of *Dunkin' Donuts* (the only branch in Europe is in Glasgow), clinging on to cartons of home in a cramped ScotRail train.

So New York, Detroit, Minneapolis comes every weekend afternoon to West Blackhall Street, Greenock; and every Friday evening, on the Cal-Mac ferry to Dunoon, the hardest-working girls on this side of the river return the compliment, their faces and bodies signifying business, their eyes sightless. My heart leaps whenever I hear a 'wassa-madda-wit'choo' in Greenock – but Greenock regards the Americans solemnly, and has its good reasons.

So, as home towns go, Greenock and Gourock touch the wider world in many unexpected ways; time spent there as respite from metropolitan madness has been valuable in its own right, and has taught me many things. One, that old people are on the whole incredibly nice and cherishable; two, that the best ice-creams ever – made with milk additives surely well over the EC limit – came from Gerry's Cafe round the corner, now defunct and boarded up; three; that my new home in the West End of Glasgow will only be an improvement if it matches Greenock and Gourock's blend of the local and the global, the worldly and the friendly. I notice that the dingy quarter-gill pub round the corner from me just happens to be called 'The Manhattan'; a good start.

# ☆ That's why we'll take Manhattan

(*The Scotsman*, 23 June 1990)

In my first eight months living in Partick, Glasgow, I have not yet discovered a more authentic piece of city-culture than the one at the bottom of my road. The Manhattan Bar has not changed one fleck since its inception in 1957 – nor does it ever need to. A few tales are necessary.

I first stepped in to make a panic coin-box call and, peering through the fag smoke, witnessed the bizarre spectacle of about twenty bunneted bauchles sipping away in what seemed to be an off-Broadway bar. A distinctly mid-Forties silhouette skyline of New York behind the bar faced two giant photos of Central Park on the other wall; the whole bar was in streamlined wood and illuminated frosted glass. 'Would make a great location for youth-cult telly piece," I noted mentally, battling through the gloom.

And so it has proved. In the bleary early morning, half a year later, I'm tripping over camera cables in the cabin-like Manhattan Bar, explaining to the unflappable proprietor that this is a 'kind of weekly review of Glasgow culture during Mayfest, you know?' The cameraman is grunting at the director, and I'm overdoing it on the diplomacy.

His long, shadowed face grimaced a little at my media manner. 'Oh, I know, son. I used to use a wind-up camera to capture one whole variety show at the Glasgow Empire. From three angles. Perfectly synchronised. And remember, only one camera. You'd shoot 20 seconds from one corner of the hall till the spring ran down, then take 20 seconds to get to the other side to shoot another 20. In the later matinees you'd time it exactly to get the middle 20 seconds. All the dancing girls had to do was to kick their heels at exactly the same time."

This man was no stranger to show-business, to say the least. He had been a compere of ice-dance spectaculars – in the Barrowland, the Empire, other places long since rubble – and dabbled in a little movie newsreel production at the time.

And much to the annoyance of the media professionals present, he guided them through all the lighting and framing permutations of shooting his bar. Why shouldn't he display his old expertise? The Manhattan was so obviously an extension of his own theatricality – a small piece of West-of-Scotland utopian Ameri-cana forever playing *One For My Baby* – that to capture it was to capture him.

But more revelations came, more evidence that real culture in Glasgow is something which happens for its own sake, not for sale or prestige. On the wall were stunningly crisp caricatures of all the American presidents since the Manhattan opened – Eisenhower, Kennedy, et al, right up to Reagan. Again, the media Hush Puppy rose inexorably to my mouth. 'Some journalists come in here? I see those sketches – very good, very professional.'

'Used to be a postman in the sorting office at Partick, son,' he rumbled sonorously. 'Does it for fun alone. He's been asked by the odd hack' – crushing pause – 'if he'd ever do it for money, but he always says no. Not much pleasure in doing it to a deadline, he'd say. Now he's a janitor in Glasgow University, I believe.'

The politics of this is that the Manhattan's sense of spectacle is intended for its ordinary, quotidian users, not for over-stimulated info-yuppies to briefly chew on in bite-sized TV slots. This might be culture as performance – the empty future for post-industrial Glasgow feared by many of the non-Labour left in the city – but it performs in a community, for a community.

The outlandishness of its aspirations – an island of Midtown cool just off dusty Dumbarton Road – are a damn sight more honest than the motives for using it as yet more TV background. If Partick will never be anything more than Partick, why not reach to Manhattan? Better to mentally span the Atlantic and gently enjoy the impossibility of getting there, than being like the media middle-class and only enjoying culture over which you can show mastery. The Manhattan is not 'camp' or 'kitsch', just a bloody good local; but I was foolish to think that this could come across in broadcast television, hungrily out for new realities to nullify and then slice into quick-thrill pieces. Hopefully this might redress the balance; words on a page are always much more controllable than the audio-visual. The Manhattan Bar deserves a finely drawn portrait.

On a quiet evening in Partick, even as you stagger out of the Manhattan, you can hear the productive racket of the Kvaerner Shipyard in Govan over the Clyde. Ralph Glasser, Oxford anthropologist and Gorbals graduate, turned up in the last of my TV pieces to extol the cultural virtues of free public culture in Glasgow – but also to stick his own spoke in the blurring wheels of Culture City. And he did it with a spanner – talking of the strong self-definitions of Glaswegians in relation to manufacturing work.

'Is there anything intrinsically wrong with getting dirt on your hands?' said Glasser at one point, fastidiously professorial in his bow tie and thick glasses. From any other academic, this would have seemed like the height of idealised prole-love – until one remembers the remarkable autodidacticism of Glasser's youth in the Twenties, soaking up the resources of the Mitchell Library after punishing days at the garment factory.

But what was he saying? That there was an old-fashioned 'dignity' in labour of the hands? 'No! Only that it is wrong to assume that manufacturing should always be separate from living. Glasgow is making that fatal mistake at the moment. Tourism will not replace the strengths of a community that lives where it works.'

In the *Financial Times* a year ago, Glasser made his grouse against current Glaswegian development explicit; the acceleration into services and tourism would destroy Glasgow's sense of itself, turn it into a performing city, not a making city.

But Glasgow is the city-state capital of that country within a country, Strathclyde Region – and the kind of tough state planning in Scotland that would ensure a new manufacturing culture is eschewed by the region's mouthpieces and fellow travellers.

The *Glasgow's Glasgow* exhibition makes its prejudices against a Scottish national solution to Glasgow's uneven economic development quite clear, nothing 'nationalist' or 'parochial' about European Glasgow. As a chirpy video reminds us, Strathclyde gets enormous European grants as a region, which benefits all Glaswegians. It would have to if a third of them live on or below the poverty line.

So we must have jobs at all costs, culture making them possible – the council knowing that service industry jobs are 'the worst paid, least unionised, most seasonal jobs, with the longest hours and the poorest conditions in terms of health and safety.' But we've got to keep the managerial and young professional class who revitalise Glasgow entertained, or they'll go off to more pliant service pastures. Somebody's entertainment is somebody else's long shift.

Now, given half the chance, the Manhattan's fittings would quickly find their way into one of the new city centre theme bars, catching the eye of the Highly Aware and Well Salaried, occasioning witty design comments over Mexican beers. I can't picture the donnish Professor Glasser on the same side of the barricade as the pint-pulling ice-dance compere. But they are together in spirit; both ghosts of an earlier age, part of the struggle to connect Glasgow's complex past to its worrying future.

# ☆ Planning without a concept

(*The Scotsman*, 6 July 1991)

It's a familiar feeling, a bathos one comes to expect: how modest Glasgow looks in the taxi home from the airport. European cityscapes are still on the insides of your eyelids – but the Kingston Bridge flies over a muddy river, ill-assorted office-blocks and empty street grids: a skyline of mediocrity, secondariness. What does it need – an Eiffel Tower, a Duomo, a Brandenburg Gate? An enormous glass-fibre model of a part-eaten haggis supper?

But these are tired half-rationalisations, unfair at best. One of my most violent reactions to a European city over the last month was based on the horrors of exactly this kind of civic triumphalism.

Le Parc de la Villette dominates a corner of suburban Paris, like some architect's casual napkin-doodle constructed to the last scrawl. The adjacent Museum of Science and Technology is megalithic enough – tenement-sized geodesic dome, pastel girders the length of football pitches, and all the glories of French *savoir-faire* within; a sci-fi celebration of the nation's productive cleverness.

But the sculpture park takes the choux pastry for architectural folly on a huge scale. Its 'deconstructive' architect, Bernard Tschumi, prefers the Gallic connotation of *'la folie'* – mad buildings that challenge our senses, our logical understanding of what urban experience is, or could be.

Unfortunately, the edifices at Villette seemed less like an exercise in applied deconstructive philosophy, and are more like half-built hamburger stalls. One is supposed to stroll through these cornea-numbing red hulks and feel a 'subtle urban disorientation': the actual response is to complain about the excessive length of the boulevard, the lack of interactivity of the sculptures, the general pointlessness of the whole exercise.

Which is either the point – a sublime pointlessness – or I don't get it. But the most startling and heart-felt reaction was the obscene waste of money this represented. How could the French government afford to blow zillions of francs on this yuppie strollabout – when across the Channel we have hospital wings closing, schools falling apart, cities made out of cardboard, not concepts?

I felt what could only be described as a kind of Thatcherite astringency. Surely the private sector should be stumping up for this kind of nonsense! Is this what the French pay taxes for?

A child of the Eighties, *sans doute*. But my response does have some bearing on issues of the direction and character of cities like Glasgow. In a brisk feminist overview of urban history, *The Sphinx in the City* (just published by Virago), Elizabeth Wilson cites Glasgow's city centre regeneration as 'not conforming to free market principles at all', being initially financed 'largely by public funds'. Pat Lally as a mini-Mitterrand, then, the most ornate triumphs of his reign Princes Square and the Merchant City?

But Wilson also notes the way this municipal endeavour gives rise to a 'dual city' – 'a prosperous middle-class core, and grimly deprived marginal estates; stylish renovation for the centre, and a (declining) welfare culture for the new urban wastelands on the periphery'.

We've all heard this story – it's the standard brickbat thrown by domestic Glasgow critics, and brutally true as far as it goes; where cities like Paris are putting on new architectural clothes to cover their basic economic strength, Glasgow is painfully polarised and brightly papering over the resultant cracks.

Edinburgh is a political capital in waiting – so its monumentalism has a long and legitimate history, and will be less like a tourist shell and more like a fitting centre of policy and resources when the parliament arrives. But recent calls in Glasgow for some kind of pre-fab city icon like Edinburgh's castle – a massive Ark museum, an arch over the Clyde – would seem to put cart before horse; it's as if a gigantic artificial symbol of civic grandeur would create a vacuum over the city, into which would then rush power, money and tourists.

Again, how would that look from the perspective of those with culture growing on their walls? The Parisians may have erected a pyramid in front of the Louvre, but a Glasgow ark or arch could be closer to the original tradition of Cheops and his toiling masses.

There has to be a mid-point between the neo-imperial constructions of Mitterrand's Paris, public coffers raided to make the city at least the architectural capital of Europe; and the shabby private-led leisure developments that threatened public spaces like Glasgow Green.

There is no intelligent public argument in Scotland about the very nature of city life; as Elizabeth Wilson says, 'We'll never solve the problems of cities unless we like the urban-ness of urban life'.

Planners, she argues, have conceived of cities as villages, machines, works of art, communications networks, but rarely in terms of the very uniqueness of urban experience, in which cities become 'spaces for face-to-face contact of amazing variety and richness'.

In that sense, cities are much more made by citizens than planned by planners. If the Glasgow Barras on a Saturday afternoon isn't the ideal exemplification of Wilson's definition of city experience, I don't know what is. Yet this is not a Glaswegian space that is carved out by battalions of London and Japanese property investors, reflecting back your pedestrian insignificance in their mirrored glass. Nor is it a planned municipal rat-maze, an engineered sociality, of which generations of Glaswegians have quite enough, thank you.

If the Barras is market capitalism, it is of the oldest and most respectable kind – masses of producers meeting masses of consumers, with no victory between the two ever in sight. Can you plan a city for such enriching chaos, or can it only develop historically, as the crowds command a place, make it their own?

Let's leave the policy answers to the opinion-editorials. Perhaps cities are about feet more than flyovers; in any case, next time I'll keep my generalisations until the taxi door opens on to Central Station – and get some Glasgow on my shoes.

## ☆ Why must Bhoys always be Bhoys?

(*The Scotsman*, 14 April 1990)

I went to my first Celtic game for at least ten years last Saturday – and the experience opened a trapdoor of football memories I'd almost forgotten I had. The after-effects are still there: perched in front of this bloody VDU, I feel my right foot involuntarily twitching to make the perfect midfield pass.

Not that the result was in any way inspirational. Trust me to reacquaint myself with the team of my youth when they're playing like a bag of onions being rattled. Struggling to fit unfamiliar names to numbers, I missed the first of St Mirren's three goals scanning through the match programme, and the second trailing up to buy the traditional ashet pie and Bovril. The third went in, appropriately enough, as I stared at the terrace steps in disbelief after yet another banana-boot pass from a hapless Celtic midfielder.

So I missed the actual body blows to the loyalty of the assembled faithful. Seeing their reactions, however, was far more informative as to why football is so much a part of Scottish male life, and was once a part of mine.

'Just look at the faces,' said my brother Gary John; and what a tapestry of punctured hopes and frustrated ideals they made. One middle-aged man in a car coat was literally thudding his head off the terrace railing; fathers perched their three-year-old sons on their shoulders and shouted despairing obscenities; young men pleaded at the top of their voices, almost as if their best friends had profoundly let them down. 'Come on, Celtic! Beat this mob! COME ON ...!' 'Did you hear that?' said our Gary, a season-ticket holder attuned to the mood of the crowd. 'Somebody was shoutin' on Celtic to "Just give us a goal". Reduced to that, man: just give us a goal.'

It's the reduction of Celtic that I find difficult to cope with. When my father took me to matches in the mid-to-late Seventies, the team was still living in the afterglow of the nine-in-a-row League Championship wins, beginning with the winning of the European Cup and ending with the formation of the Premier League.

I saw Kenny Dalglish in a few games, but my main experiences included players like Charlie Nicholas, Bobby Lennox, Davie Provan, and the magisterial Danny McGrain. McGrain in particular gave you the feeling that every time he got the ball, things would eventually work out on the field; it was a shock to hear such an articulate, intelligent player be such a shy mumbler off the park, and that such a graceful powerhouse was also a long-term diabetic.

Watching the game on Saturday, I was also reminded of the compelling physicality of football. Sitting in the stand with my dad, I used to wonder at the absolute disparity between the panting, sprinting, 400-mile-an-hour frenzy of the game before me, and the insect circus of the televised version later that night.

Paradoxically, the distanced spectacle of the TV game always encouraged me to get out and play myself when I was a teenager; the terrifying speed and aggression of the real thing, the leathered slap of boot on ball loud in your ears, always made me feel that professional football was for supermen only.

There were no supermen playing for Celtic last Saturday. Not for lack of will on the part of the crowd; whenever the captain Paul McStay had possession, an excited murmur would briefly rise. The evident elegance of McStay sums up all the glorious possibilities of football, the act of spatial imagination and physical skill that might bust a game wide open.

But nothing like that today: every mistimed pass and panic-striken blooter at goal made the punters feel awkward themselves, screaming individually and futilely at players' ineptitude, denied any moments of communal celebration of excellence. The sullen silence that follows a goal by the opposition at a home game is truly eerie; tens of thousands of men muttering imprecations, feeling even more distanced from a game which exercises their manhood by proxy.

The only way to get out of these troughs is obviously through humour. 'It's called a ball, Grant. A ball. You can hit it with your foot. Football. Understand? This team's goin' to Europe? We'd be lucky to get to Butlin's.' The football fanzine *Not The View* captures this mixture of commitment – while sourcing Celtic's current travails in a very specific quarter:

Who is it stops us in our quest
To play against Europe's best?
Our gate money they're known to hoard,
You'll know them as THE CELTIC BOARD.

My brother Gary rationalises the current decline of Celtic against the only comparison that matters – Rangers – in explicitly

political terms: 'Rangers – huh! Bunch of bloody capitalists!' He
tells me wonderingly of sitting in the Ibrox stand in the recent Old
Firm game, as stewards worked their way up and down the stairs
getting drinks for spectators and guiding people to toilets, and
cannot suppress his admiration for the affluence and organisation
of Rangers plc. 'But Celtic's always been the People's Team,' he
rallies. 'We'll do it even if we're poor.'

This is a consoling modern myth about Celtic which I've often
encountered – an institution intimately connected to an Irish
Catholic immigrant community's struggle to gain acceptability in
Scotland, and therefore almost quasi-socialist by comparison to a
Protestant, Establishment Rangers, which only recently abandoned
sectarianism (goes the lore) to rake in more cash.

It would seem that Rangers are trying to set themselves up as the
top Scottish national club team – what with the Rangers tartan, the
deliberate cosmopolitanism of the team, the bid to make Ibrox the
stadium for the national team's games. For a club whose less open-
minded elements sing of loyalty to the English Windsors, this seems
almost like a football equivalent of the SNP's Independence In
Europe policy – Rangers on a par with the big players in the Euro
Super-League, Scotland as an equal in the Council of Ministers? Is
Jim Sillars's surgery in the Ibrox complex an anti-Unionist cell?

Whatever the economic, political or moral pressures on Rangers
to abandon sectarianism, it has freed them to express a sense of
broad Scottishness as a club side, taking the sting out of their own
distinct Protestant tradition. Celtic should also try to become a
great and specifically Scottish club, spending whatever money it
takes: the reason being that the club's Irish Catholic tradition now
relates to a third and fourth generation of immigrants who are
effectively Scottish. Celtic should express this Scottish identity as
strongly as its Irish connections; not only to be properly
representative of its fans, but for political reasons too.

At a time when Scottish self-determination is reaching such a
crucial stage, supported by a wealth of sophisticated cultural and
political endeavour, we do not need any sense of Scotland's ethnic-
religious identity being anything other than plural: Protestant,
Catholic, Jewish, Hindu, Muslim, whatever you want to profess as
long as you're committed to living here and making it work ...

The best contribution a potent cultural symbol like Celtic
Football Club can make to this process is to properly pick up the
soft-nationalist gauntlet thrown down by Rangers. Why shouldn't
a small nation like Scotland have two world-historical football
teams? And why can't those teams acknowledge the difference of
their traditions without it leading to the evils of sectarianism?

Tims and Huns are all Scottish citizens, desirous of a new Scottish polity that would truly represent the will of the people. And as consumers, Celtic supporters should rightly expect their club to be working as hard for their money as Rangers do for their own crowds. Any kind of 'paupers' nobility' arguments that might lurk in the depths of the terraces or across the boardroom table at Celtic Park are a political as well as commercial disservice to the real interests of the fan-as-citizen. It's not only the terrace die-hards that need Celtic to be great again; Scotland needs it too.

But perhaps an easier way to deal with the convoluted nature of Scottish-Irish football consciousness is for Celtic to keep playing like they did last Saturday. Could even the most ardent Bhoy stick that for long? 'Ach we should boycott them, then they'd sort it out,' said the bunneted father next to me, between goal two and goal three. 'But you couldn't do it. Your heart's in it, y'know?'

No, I don't know – and maybe that's why it took me ten years to return.

# ☆ A Day for Scotland[*]

(*Radical Scotland*, Aug/Sep 1990)

For Scotland, the last decade has been marked by the rise of the Scottish Voice. When the crude 'It's Scotland's Oil' nationalism of the seventies collapsed in confusion and apathy on Devolution Day, March 1st 1979, a decade-long identity crisis began. Why didn't we Scots even want the limited measure of self-determination the British state had offered us? What did it really mean to be 'Scottish' – and was it really worth fighting for?

The result of these ten or so years of cultural angst – expressed in anything from epic theatre to chart pop, the rhetoric of strikers to the rationale of teachers – is a truly modern Scottish consciousness: more confident, flexible and diverse than ever before. If a Day for Scotland is about anything, it is about the raising of this new Scottish Voice to a fever pitch.

This Voice has many intonations, and can contradict itself, but possesses one undoubted value. Every time it speaks, rendering Scotland's past and present on its own terms, it dispels another cloud of Scotch myth – those stereotypes of inarticulacy, Tartanry, and historical sentimentality which have done so much to distort Scot's self-image.

The experiences of the urban working class are a major part of this voicing of Scotland. Presaged in the Seventies by comedians like Billy Connolly and charismatic union leaders like Jimmy Reid, the Eighties saw a flourishing of proletarian and socialist images of Scotland – in the theatre, with Wildcat's propagandist musicals or 7:84's radical history; in literature, with such stylistically diverse writers as William McIlvanney, James Kelman and Liz Lochhead taking working-class experience as their natural subject; and in art, with painters like Ken Currie and Peter Howson simultaneously idealising and analysing the Scottish worker.

---

[*] The Scottish Trades Union Council organized a massive cultural-political event in the summer of 1990 called a 'Day for Scotland', at which artists like Deacon Blue, Runrig and Hue and Cry performed to a crowd of 35,000 people. Many alliances between politicians and pop stars were forged that day... The following is my contribution to the official programme.

Another factor in the growing socialist identity of Scotland is, of course, Thatcherism. The aggressive English nationalism inherent in Thatcher's New Right policies, combined with her use of Scotland as a political testing-ground, has resulted in a strong popular identification of 'Englishness' with 'Toryism' and 'Scottishness' with 'Socialism' – expressed by the quarter to third of the electorate who regularly mandate the SNP's attacks on an 'English Tory Government'.

Institutions like the Scottish Trades Union Congress, and the education system at secondary and graduate level, have both stressed the specificity of their Scottish traditions in the face of Thatcherite assault. 'Consensus', 'egalitarianism', and 'interdependence' (rather than 'dependency', as the Tories would have it) – these are the values held to be a constant weave in the social fabric of Scottish life. The electoral commitment to Labour every four years is as much a commitment to this collective moral self-image as it is to the saving powers of Westminster government.

The Scottish Voice also has a showbusiness inflection. In the last decade, Scots have entered into national and international media networks to an unprecedented degree. TV presenters like Muriel Gray and Kirsty Wark, comedians like Robbie Coltrane, the Funny Farm and Elaine C. Smith, and pop groups like Simple Minds, Deacon Blue and Wet Wet Wet regularly occupy prime time slots in British, European and American broadcast media. All of them are naturally, confidently Scottish in the lightest of entertainment contexts – yet, in the case of pop especially, have also been involved in specific Scottish political events, like the STUC's April Fool's Day anti-poll-tax day.

So a sophisticated sense of Scottishness has been developed over the Eighties: a voice both historical and contemporary, politically forthright and culturally stylish, able to define its current needs and express them powerfully.

But the new Scottish articulacy can seem to be coming from only one place: Glasgow. If Scotland's main products over the last decade have been cultural, then Glasgow has been the first to realise that culture can mean economy these days, if nothing else can be manufactured. Its status as European City of Culture in 1990 might secure Glasgow as a genuinely cosmopolitan centre – yet it might also make it the New York of Scotland, a city-state only tangentially related to the rest of the country loathed for its Lowland arrogance and narcissism by Highland communities. (It's no coincidence that a Day For Scotland takes place in Stirling – attempting to express the unity-in-diversity of Scottish culture; highland and lowland, urban and rural.)

Glasgow is also the locus for an underlying snarl which the Scottish Voice would gladly pass over; sectarianism. The recent furore over Rangers Football Club signing its first Catholic player revealed one of the less valuable traditions of Scottish working class history – the continuing separation between Catholic and Protestant loyalties, institutionalised in the state Catholic schooling system. My own experience – third-generation Irish immigrant, educated at St. Ambrose High, went to Glasgow University – is relevant in understanding the contradictions of Scottish identity; I feel that my background contributes to the diversity and richness of Scottish life. Others, however, do not.

This fracture, between the principles and the practice of Scottish egalitarianism, can also express itself in attitudes to Scotland's large Asian community. Many Asians moved to Scotland in the sixties and seventies because they found the climate a lot less racially hostile indeed, part of the Scottish self-image is that racism has no hold in the culture. Recent reports of a rise in racial attacks on Asians is a real threat to that collective moral sense so constitutive of the modern Scottish Voice. A Day for Scotland has made strenuous efforts to make Asian and other ethnic cultures a natural part of its programme, simply a valuable facet of our nation's culture.

This day is historic for Scotland – both the largest meeting of Scottish artists under a commitment to self-determination, and a vision of what Scotland in control of its own identity could be like. Whatever Scotland's achievements in self-understanding in the Eighties, the Nineties must continue the development of a plural and principled national identity. Whether that is within or without the United Kingdom, is another set of questions altogether.

## ☆ Balkans raise the Scottish question

(*The Scotsman*, 20 July 1991)

*Nationalism deserves a better name,* rumbled a senior columnist's headline in last week's *Independent on Sunday*. Well thanks awfully, Jenkins of City Road EC1; we'd been hanging on for your thunderous validation for some years now. At last, we can unpack those fusty old boxes of Liberation Shortbread!

London pundits may be beginning to accept the inevitability of nationalist aspiration throughout Eastern Europe, the Balkans and the Baltic – but it would still seem like a cataclysm were one of Her Majesty's regions to demand the same degree of self-determination.

The nearest Peter Jenkins got to conceding the existence of Western Europe's own stateless nations was the 'regional nationalism' of Catalonia; this is consistent from a paper which once gave Salman Rushdie the same editorial space to say, 'If Scotland is allowed to become independent, why not Pimlico?'

A handful of writers in Scotland has begun to make much more serious comparisons between the latest gyrations of post-Cold-War nationalism and Scottish self-determination. Tom Gallagher speculates on the SNP's hopes that 'the revival of Balkan nationalism' will be 'strong enough to plunge the European state system into question', but not so blood-soaked as to dampen the popular desire for a Scottish state. Ian Bell substitutes Scots for Slovenes, conservatives for Communists, and London for Belgrade, and finds Tory commentators ignoring obvious parallels to the Scottish situation.

Jim Sillars has said recently that the Labour Party is Scotland's last substantial political link to the UK; we shall have to wait for the votes of the Southern English at the next General Election to see whether that link will be progressively reforged as a devolved Parliament, or whether we'll have to break it ourselves, faced with the intransigence of another Tory Government. If the latter case should transpire, then the Baltic and Balkan parallels will become much more than idle Sunday-morning punditry.

But in the meantime, it would be best to listen as much as possible to the clamour of ideas and perspectives on nationalism arising from the intelligentsia and radicals of post-Communist Europe. Among them the essential 'national questions' are being asked, and Scots would be foolish not to learn from such a test bed for modern national democracy.

Asking some of the toughest questions is Slavoj Zizek, a young philosopher from the University of Ljubljana in Yugoslavia. Zizek is not only the current darling of the Transatlantic academic Left – 'an extraordinary new voice we will hear often in the coming years' blurbs Frederic 'Mr Postmodernism' Jameson – but has also put his theories to the test in the political fray, standing as a Liberal Party candidate for the presidency of the republic of Slovenia in 1990 (unsuccessfully).

Zizek's theoretical understanding of nationalism is shaped by the territorial mess of Yugoslavia and its peoples. He draws widely (and wildly) from psychoanalysis and philosophy, trying to find some strong explanation for the revival of old-style blood-and-soil nationalisms in the Balkans.

The standard anti-totalitarian leftist argument was that countries like Romania and Yugoslavia actively promoted their ethnic tensions; central government's appeal was as the great guarantor of stability. 'So why does this attachment to the ethnic cause *persist*,' writes Zizek in a recent *New Left Review*, 'even after the power structure that produced it has collapsed?'

The answer is to do with a fundamental *imbalance* – the imbalance of the new capitalism sweeping the area, and the imbalance inherent in our very own human psychologies. Capitalism, as someone once said, makes everything solid into air – but in the post-Communist Yugoslavia, the reaction to this chaos has been one of 'national chauvinism'; nationalism as a kind of shock absorber against the unprecedented terrors of capitalist openness and change.

But why, automatically, is the nation the form of defence? In these unbalanced circumstances, 'the demand is for the establishment of a stable and clearly defined social body,' says Zizek, 'that will restrain capitalism's destructive potential'; and that body is the nation.

Medical metaphors abound in Zizek's 'diagnosis'. Capitalism is even described as 'hysterical' in its very essence – it has 'no "normal", balanced state: its "normal" state is the permanent production of an excess – the only way for it to survive is to expand'. It satisfies more needs than other socio-economic systems, but creates even more needs to be satisfied in the process; and this 'vicious circle of desire', Zizek says, is almost clinically hysterical.

So nationalism, in the Balkans, not only internally regulates this hysteria, caused by too-rapid social and economic change; nationalism also copes with the excesses and imbalances by externalising them – the conjured threat of other nations and cultures reinforces the demand for a pure national stability. Xenophobia and chauvinism is just another way to master this excess.

So instead of abstract, constitutional, formal national identities, self-assured and self-composed, there are Slovenes who define themselves primarily against lazy Serbs, Serbs who define themselves primarily against calculating Slovenes, Croats frantically defining against both ...

How much of ourselves could we see in this? Zizek's analysis of nationalism as a response to the threats of economic development echoes that of Tom Nairn, and has the same efficacy. But Zizek's strongly psychologistic rooting of the less virtuous aspects of Balkan nationalisms – fundamentalist itself, in a Freudian way – almost seems like one of our own, weel-kent cliches of Scottish identity. Either on top of the world, or cowering under its weight; supremely self-confident, or profoundly fearful and loathing – of both ourselves and the hated, English (or Serbian) 'other'.

At least we have political open doors in Scotland, routes to national sanity; an active constitutional nationalism, a European polity to share our sovereignty with, and visions of self-determination across the political spectrum which are orientated towards the nations of Europe, not against them.

To watch the trials of Slovenian identity is to appreciate our own political achievements in Scotland over the last ten years. We've been thinking, arguing and creating our way out of this kind of self-lacerating national identity crisis, typical of all small, subordinated nations. In the mirror of thinkers like Slavoj Zizek's desperate account of nationalism, we can regard ourselves more kindly and be kept aware of old pitfalls.

# ☆ Soul brothers under the skin

(*The Scotsman*, 13 October 1991)

What does a Scottish nationalist make of Black nationalism? Or, to make the encounter more mundane to start with: why do I like Spike Lee's films so much?

My recent viewing of Lee's *Jungle Fever* left me with a characteristic mixture of pleasures: an admiration of his visual style, an education about African-American lives, and an obscure sympathy with his ideological aims.

In an essay by Harvard professor Henry Louis Gates Jr, *Jungle Fever* is claimed as a symbolic vehicle for the 'new, young, black, upper middle class: neo-nationalistic, thoroughly bourgeois, unsafe at any speed, and marvellously sexual' (*Five on Five: the films of Spike Lee*, Stewart, Tabori and Chang).

'Neo-nationalistic' refers to the constant emphasis in Lee's work – inspired by the black arts movement of the Sixties and Seventies – on the absolute legitimacy of black perspectives on their own conditions in America; the necessity of some kind of cultural and political solidarity among blacks to effect change, to force genuine equality and justice. 'This good ole US of A has two motherf-ing standards and sets of rules: one white and one black,' says Lee in *Five on Five*. 'I'm gonna say this, and I'll continue to say it until things change'.

Almost uniquely among successful American moviemakers, Lee addresses class issues as directly as ethnic ones. Paulie, a sensitive young Italian selling newspapers in *Jungle Fever*, reads a passage from his book to his racist customers – about five Sicilians in Louisiana owning a factory in 1890, who gave their five black workers equal partnership; when the local white citizens found out, they lynched the Italians. As Professor Gates points out, this highlights the film's implicit theme – 'how very much economics is the foundation on which racism is built'.

Black nationalism, then, is nothing if not economic in foundation. This was brought home to me recently as I watched a black activist on *Newsnight*, commenting from the streets about the recent clashes between blacks and Jewish religious communities in Brooklyn. 'If blacks have no jobs, no decent housing, no welfare, no prospects or future, then what they're gonna do is driven by despair, hopelessness.'

One third living below the poverty line among Brooklyn blacks, an expanding prison population, communities screwed up by internal violence and drug barons; if we replaced 'Brooklyn' with 'Strathclyde', would the statistics and situations have to change that much? The rhetoric is certainly the same as the Scottish socialist response to our own conditions.

So is this the sympathy, as a Scottish nationalist, that I have with black nationalism – that it posits a national community which conceives of its struggle as primarily about money and power: an economic and political nationalism? The imperatives feel the same, at least in the structure of the demands, if not in the actual level of injustice and discrimination.

When Lee dedicates *Jungle Fever* to Yusef Hawkins, a young black who was killed by whites as he went to see a used car in Bensonhurst, NYC, he repeats a regular point in his movies about the physical and mortal danger most American blacks endure daily – a good reason for nationalist solidarity, as the murders and attacks are despairingly internal as well as external and racist.

Part of my own Scottish nationalist ire stems from a kindred fear of mortality – from trucks containing the world's nuclear waste juddering up to Inverness, from leaky reactors in pointless submarines on the Clyde. As a disregarded British region on the periphery of Europe, without an ounce of political clout, we should expect such environmental prejudice; the nationalist response is to protect the people of Scotland through effective independence, with powers of control over defence and environmental policy.

There are familiar objections here. Are black nationalists being insufficiently universal when they demand both an economic and civic defence of their people, even given their terrifyingly high death and murder rates compared to other ethnic groups in the US? Are Scottish nationalists being parochial in wanting to remove nuclear threats from their country, ignoring the transnational effects of catastrophes like Chernobyl?

Black nationalists would argue that a prosperous and secure black population would be an asset to the American nation as a whole – but this will be achieved primarily by black action and pressure. Territorially, the 'black nation' in America *is* America; blacks fighting for their rights from Santa Barbara to Bensonhurst, on the basis of a collective black experience of discrimination.

To their charge, Scottish nationalists would reply that the inability of Germans, French and Russians to dispose of their own

waste, and the idiocy of UK military policy, does not mean that
Scotland should mop up the messes of others. Similarly, an independent Scotland would be able to argue effectively and passionately for European and global nuclear scale-downs in our own
right, improving the collective safety of the planet by our participation in international political councils. The particular can bring us
to the universal; human emancipation has to start *somewhere*.

But there are other parallels between black and Scottish nationalism, which probably structure all nationalist politics – particularly an obsession with the interpretation of history. Martin
Bernal's study, *Black Athena: the Afro-Asiatic roots of Classical
civilization*, has caused a continuing furore, since it came out in
1987, with its exhaustively substantiated claims that the African
contribution to classical Greek culture has been decisively
suppressed by the racism of Western scholars during the eighteenth
and nineteenth centuries.

These findings have been taken up by black nationalists and
used as part of their continuing cultural radicalisation of young
American blacks; rap artists like Public Enemy and Kool Moe Dee
not only reflect the chaos of the streets, but give thumbnail sketches
of black achievement and Afro-centric history.

Scottish nationalism has its own primal historical moment – the
Act of Union – and its own set of debates about the effects that has
had on subsequent Scottish development. Scotland sunk in pre-
Union barbarism and saved by the post-Union Age of Enlightenment, is a classic argument to justify the necessary civilising
influence of England on Scottish life. Recently, this metropolitan
reading of the Scottish past has been challenged in philosophy by
Alexander Brodie in *The Tradition of Scottish Philosophy*, and
Beveridge and Turnbull in *The Eclipse of Scottish Culture*.

It would be impudent to claim that the task of reclaiming
Scottish history was equal to the Afro-centric agenda of intellectually refuting centuries of active racism – but both projects
serve the same nationalist ends; the broadening of the meaning of
one's national community into its true, complex history, out of the
hand of wilful mystifiers.

So is nationalism all good? No. All bad? No. It is a political
response to a world which is as Janus-faced as capitalism or
socialism – and Western liberal democracy currently sprawls across
all three of them, regulating their relationships.

'Nationalists of the world unite!' may never be on many lips; but
at least when I watch a Spike Lee movie, I think I know where he's
coming from.

☆ Exorcising the royal prerogative

(*The Scotsman*, 17 January 1992)

Usually they don't bother me, but occasionally the symbolic mon-strousness of the British Royals consumes me with republican rage. How do we get rid of Diana?

Why her smug smile on the cover of this month's *Vogue* should set my tumbrils rolling more than any other of her media spots is largely obscure to me; something's gotta give, I suppose. The magazine itself is questionable enough. A random flick through finds various Chanel-clad yah-yah models striding *abite* the Serengeti, grinning fastidiously as Masai women clasp their hands in exchange for some convertible currency.

Loathsome – yet it only makes explicit the implicit neo-Aryan élitism of cover-girl Diana. Can't you just hear that 0.1 per cent of the population trill: 'God, doesn't she look wonderful! Really, honest-ly, could anyone else look so absolutely, so *naturally* beautiful ...'

It's this undertone of fash-ism – that Vogueish beauty isn't necessarily a matter of luck, cosmetics and dieting, but can be simply *good* lineage – that has really riled me about the Princess of Wales and about the whole bunch in general.

But if the Princess of Wales's *Vogue* cover reveals the aristocratic susceptibilities of high fashion, she's also endangering that sense of the Royals as tantalisingly other-worldly, recognisable yet distant, which seems to be the root of their hold over the public imagination. You can make it as a fashion model with your own physical raw materials, no matter your social background: and at least structurally, we can posit an exact equivalence between Sarf-London black supermodel Naomi Campbell and the iridescent Princess of Wales – both, now, *Vogue* cover girls.

And the Royals can't afford to get too comparable with their subjects – otherwise people might ask them to do things that ordinary people do ... like pay income tax. *Royalty* magazine's yearly review makes Liberal Democrat MP Simon Hughes's parliamentary bill to that effect its 'most striking event' along with opinion polls showing almost four-fifths of the public agreeing with Hughes.

The Royal biographer, Anthony Holden, is unashamedly strategic in his analysis of the Royals' rotten 1991: the worst portent for the monarchy's future was that resentment of the Royals and their finances was highest in the 18–39 age group – the generation that will be running the country when Charles gets his shot at the throne. He must 'make contact' with that group, and help his mother to 'return the royal roadshow to the straight and narrow path it must travel to survive'.

Prince Philip and Charles shooting grouse while their regiments were puffing off to the gulf, Sarah off skiing and Andrew out golfing as Our Boys strode forth ... this is all, presumably somewhat off the straight and narrow path demanded for Royal survival. 'Royal roadshow' is a remarkably frank admission that the monarchy is a paid-for entertainment, which must be as sensitive to its audience's sensibilities as any satellite channel or publishing house.

This kind of media-sensitive understanding of how the Royal Family function in society sits badly with their role as symbolic embodiments of the United Kingdom; the former is a matter of delicate PR and poll watching, while the latter is supposed to possess the legitimation of ages.

The ludicrous soap-operatics of the Royal family are perversely heartening for Scottish republicans like myself – the more their presence seeps into every corner of ordinary British life, the more prey they become to substantive demands about what they are actually for, other than as a tabloid diversion.

As someone who fervently desires the break-up of Britain, I agree with writers like Tom Nairn and Neal Ascherson that the Royals are the dazzling cloak thrown over the archaism of the UK's political system. To remove them would enable the peoples of this island to understand themselves as truly political animals: legitimised by their own democratic will and actions.

But will any opposition political party be brave enough to chuck the republican half-brick at this enchanted glass? Even Simon Hughes's meek demand for fiscal justice was royally gubbed by all stout parliamentary parties in the vote, including his own Liberal Democrats.

Labour's Brian Wilson did raise a few pertinent questions in the House a few months ago, and then let the issue of Royal finances quietly slip off his agenda. Willie Hamilton quietly spins in his grave, and Tony Benn's recent Commonwealth of Britain Bill – replacing the monarchy with an elected president – found far more consent from readers of the *Guardian*'s back-pages than it did from Parliament.

And it truly puzzles me why the SNP, whose urgency to abandon the creaky British Union for the clear opportunities of European development I fully share, still feels the need to pay its respects to the most potent symbol of that union – the monarchy – in its independence strategy.

I found the SNP's concept of an alternative Queen's Speech to a putative Scottish parliament somewhat risible, to say the least. To expect a High Windsor to glow with inner contentment at no nukes, full employment, effective wealth redistribution and emancipation of the Scottish people is surely going too far.

If we build the future Scotland on bedrock principles like 'bairns not bombs' – as we should – would it be so fearsomely radical to presume that none of our hard-earned national resources goes towards keeping little Harry and William kilting around Balmoral, in the grand manner to which they've been accustomed?

An effectively independent Scottish parliament will be a leap into the world for which our national maturity and political confidence will have been sorely tested; but I can think of nothing less futuristic, and more depressing, than some pointless Royal perched on a high chair in the parliament building, bringing the old lingering stink of the *ancien regime*.

Wouldn't it be better to have a president like Ireland's Mary Robinson as 'PR for the nation' – an elected meritocrat rather than a blooded aristocrat? If we're going to do this thing can't we do it *properly*? Do I hear the distant snarl of a kamikaze killer corgi?

# ☆ Surreal life crisis

(*CUT*, June 1989)

You know the Spitting Image song *I've Never Met A Nice South African*? Well, recently I've met several nice Scots people who have lived, worked or otherwise tried to justify their presence in South Africa. And their niceness worries me.

They've mostly been male minicab drivers, chauffeuring me from Gourock to Glasgow Airport in the early morning. It's almost always a talkative journey: the combination of a decent fare and a night spent wide-awake makes the driver pleasantly, if rather manically garrulous. The soul of post-industrial Scotland is often bared in these half-hour sessions – most of the Greenock taxi drivers are ex-shipyard or heavy industrial workers, the only tool they wield is now a tinny Nissan through the unconscious hours.

So the talk is of 21-week employment contracts at merciless electronics factories, the futility of yet another retail megastore, a bastard policeman slapping points on your licence for 'over-zealous soliciting for trade' at the local Tesco's ...

But there's one opening exchange that always fills me with dread. 'So how long have you been on the taxis then?' 'Oh, a few years, son. I was abroad before that.' 'Where?' I stupidly ask, hoping against hope that this one'll say Australia, or America, or *anywhere* except – 'South Africa, actually.'

The first time this happened I clammed up, visiting on the driver a chilly moral freeze, suffering the remaining minutes silently. Then it occurred to me that I should encourage these men to talk: rather than be angrily embarrassed at how far short they fell of my 'ideal Scot' fixation, better to draw out their reasoning and self-justifications, criticize from the inside rather than the outside.

What results is a disquieting mixture of delusion and guilt, worldliness and prejudice. They maintain they're down there 'just doing a job', plying their trade as head brickies or electrician foremen in the absence of opportunities at home, supervising the building of dams and power-stations like they've dreamed of doing. Yet the surreality of South African daily life always gets to them.

'I couldn't call a forty-five-year-old workman "boy" all the time, like the Afrikaners told me,' said one driver. 'I was only twenty-five at the time myself. And I lost my first job because a white boss complained that I was treating the blacks too well – for example, everybody sittin' down and crackin' into a carry-out, after finishing a job early. No big deal, eh? But I was forced to leave on it.'

The same driver wistfully recalled living in Johannesburg as being 'really fast paced and competitive – it was a rat race, a very demanding lifestyle.' His descriptions of the South African white job market – no unions, six-month contracts, secret incentives, personal negotiation of wage rates and, therefore, constant back-stabbing, head-hunting and suspicion – sounded flesh-crawlingly Thatcherite and familiar.

But even this mini-cab driving free-marketeer had to admit that the South African regime was basically propped up on disparate hourly rates; eight rand for him, 76 cents of a rand for his 'boys'. The final twist: a South African 'lawyer friend' had just vaporised with all his hard-earned savings; he'd left them behind returning to tend his dying mother in Greenock.

Most of them tell the same story – structurally alienated from black culture *and* white culture; labouring with the former and inescapably establishing a connection with them, yet having to instrumentalise this connection under the glare of their native white paymasters – which, in the end, isn't *that* difficult to do.

None are outright white suprematists, but most have their sustaining myths – 'they'll kill each other for a job', 'the tribal problems are as big as any other', the expected post-rationalisation of people who want to live with themselves after having leeched off apartheid.

## Extremely nyaff

To get a critical perspective of these people that doesn't rely on a higher education, my mother's disgusted remarks on a nursing colleague who returned from South Africa should suffice: '*Her!* she came back here talking about her big house, her swimming pool, her maidservant . . . Then she told us that the blacks actually *liked* being subservient, because they didn't know any better! She went over there because she was a wee nyaff, a wee nothing, and she wanted to be a something. Well I'll tell ye, it hasn't worked – 'cause she's *still* a wee nothing!'

Nothing, something, nothing again: this is the structure of feeling that over-arches the five S.A. -tainted cab-drivers I've met in the last year. To go from performing enormous feats of hydro-electric engineering to picking up sick-encrusted partygoers at Port

Glasgow, from sun-drenched patios to damp bedroom walls, this must result in some tortured reflection.

As much reflection, I would hope as a persistent young yuppie on a 6 am call would cause, intrigued to know whether their profitable excursion to a land which treats nine-tenths of its inhabitants like nothing has caused them to question themselves, their involvement, their prejudices; has made them feel something or nothing.

As I write, Scotland's subterranean relationship with South Africa is bursting out all over the front pages, with the Scottish Rugby Union's decision to give the all-clear for individual amateur players to take part in the S.A. rugby centenary celebrations this summer. However it ends up, the very decision itself indicates a deeper connection between the two countries than just the morally flaccid opportunism of taxi-driving tradesmen and labourers.

It's appropriate that such an establishment Scottish institution as Rugby Union should disgrace us. Historically, the Scottish middle and upper classes have done marvelously well out of South Africa, as they did out of the British Empire. Tom Nairn in *Marxism Today* has described educated Scots as virtually 'administering', doing the office work, for the whole colonial system.

The first Governor-General of the non-colonial Union of South Africa in 1910 was a Scot, Lord Gladstone of Lanark, as were several previous colonial governors. The first independent news-paper in S.A. was produced by a Scottish printer and proprietor, Geordie Greig, in 1873; Scottish ministers served in both Presbyterian and Dutch settler churches, and Scottish teachers were in charge of the Cape Colony's initial education system, both until the mid nineteenth century. When South Africa joined up with the British Empire in the first World War, there was even a 'South African Scottish' regiment, by which the chinless ones of the Cape could happily waltz their charges to glory and collective slaughter.

Rugby, like cricket, is a quintessentially imperial sport – witness its successful assimilation by ex-colonies like the West Indies, Australia, India – and rugby, like cricket, has repeatedly run into trouble over its continuing post-colonial association with South Africa.

The Scottish Rugby Union decision reveals the extent to which areas of Scottish ruling class culture are still bathed in the glow of the Sun That Never Set, despite the struggles of liberation and the present horrors of apartheid. No matter that the current scandal has behind it a set of familiar remunerative reasons – i.e. if we don't allow our players to earn a bit on the side as individuals in South Africa, they'll emigrate *en masse* and set up a highly lucrative 'pro-circus' tournament: for in the words of the SRU's own defense, 'South African players have taken part in celebratory matches over here and it is felt right that there should be a reciprocal arrangement.'

## Colour-coded

For all their taste and education, the lawyers and professionals who run Scottish rugby seem to relate to South Africa in values of celebration and reciprocity. This friendliness towards a country which shoots at publicly celebrating crowds, and denies reciprocity between fellow humans on the basis of skin colour? Obviously the colonial roll-call in the clubhouse lounge received more consideration here than murdered Sowetan children.

And what do all these imperial middle-class hangover and lax working-class ethics, all these historical and contemporary sins and faults, say about Scotland now? An answer can be found in Jurgen Habermas, writing about the complexities of post-Second World War German guilt. Habermas says he is a 'constitutional patriot': the past Nazi crimes of German culture can only be atoned for by a commitment to universal values of justice, equality and security, enshrined for the future by the post-War democratic constitution of Federal Germany.

As historical guilt, Scotland's Imperial and emigrant connections to South Africa cannot compare with Nazism. But in the midst of the current passion for Scottish self-determination, we could do well to think of ourselves as constitutional patriots struggling towards a future, fairer Scotland, as well as an ancient, injured nation waving our not-always-spotless historical credentials about. The past is as ethically muddied as the present: one disquieted taxi-driver and one pilloried sports official are two steps into Scotland's future.

# ☆ Nationalism and modernity*

In the last hours before the expiry of the UN deadline for Iraq's withdrawal from Kuwait, I watched a BBC Newsnight roundtable discussion, which included a representative from the Palestine Liberation Organisation. Talking of the unwillingness of Anglo-American leaders to consider a geo-political linkage between Iraq's invasion of Kuwait and Israel's treatment of Arabs in Palestine and the Lebanon, he lamented that 'we had believed the West when they talked of human rights, of democracy – of their *universalism*. Perhaps we have been naive, very naive.'

Interviewed in Frankfurt in April 1989, a few months before the revolutions in Eastern Europe, philosopher Jurgen Habermas answered the question, what does universalism mean today? He said: 'Relativizing one's own form of existence to the legitimate claims of other forms of life, according equal rights to aliens and others with all their idiosyncrasies and unintelligibility, not sticking doggedly to the universalisation of one's own identity, not marginalizing that which deviates from ones' own identity, allowing the sphere of tolerance to become ceaselessly larger than it is today – all this is what moral universalism means today.' (Rassmussen, 1990, p. 210).

Both these quotes illustrate the crucial contemporary relationship between modernity and nationalism. Habermas's quote arises from a discussion of his notion of constitutional patriotism – the way that a particular national identity can give rise to universal norms and values, as in the French and American Revolutions. 'If not in the nation,' says Habermas at the end of the last lecture of his Philosophical Discourse of Modernity, 'in what other soil can universalistic value orientations take root?' (Habermas, 1987, p. 366).

But Habermas derives this universalist notion from his own

---

* A talk delivered to the Glasgow University Philosophy Group, in the first few days after the descent of Operation Desert Storm on the Iraqi people in March 1991. Although its references are time-bound, I believe it still makes interesting points about the functioning of nationhood in contemporary politics.

particular historical identity – as someone profoundly traumatized by his country's Nazi past. Constitutional patriotism in West Germany worked because of the continuing reverberations of the 'moral catastrophe' of Auschwitz – citizens of the Federal Republic, says Habermas, 'took pride in having succeeded, in the long run, in overcoming fascism, in having established a constitutional order and in having anchored it in a halfway liberal political culture' (Rassmussen, 1990, p. 209).

As Habermas has recently admitted, patriotism of a far less abstract and formal – and guilt-ridden – kind was a major determinant of the speed of German unification after the Eastern European revolutions; his formulation of it as 'Deutschmark nationalism' correctly defines the East German voters' desire for affluent Western society as well as democratic constitutionalism. Eastern Europe and the Baltic states in 1990 were something of a vindication for Habermas's view of the universalistic potential of the nation state. Poland, Hungary, Czechoslovakia, Romania, then Lithuania, Latvia and Estonia all emerged from the deep freeze of the Cold War attempting to continue the democratic traditions practised nationally before the arrival of the Red Army.

But that new 'springtime of nations' seems very far away at the moment, a distant time which one commentator has called a 'phoney peace' (Paul Hirst). Indeed, it is the very contraction of the supranational imperialism of the Soviet Union under glasnost and perestroika that has given rise to the resurgence both of bourgeois democracy in Eastern Europe, and of classical nation-state violence in the Gulf. The positive 'liberation-chaos', as Tom Nairn has put it, of Eastern Europe's national cultures released from Soviet influence has to be matched with the present disastrous contestation of Western capitalist hegemony and militant Arab nationalism, again a direct result of the end of the bi-polar Cold War order and its power politics.

It's at this point we should return to our PLO representative, whose people's fate is more complicated, and potentially more tragic, than the mutual demonizers at war in the desert. His disillusion over the universalist value orientations of the West stems from a recent political history of the PLO, where the virtues of moral universalism so eloquently adumbrated by Jurgen Habermas – 'relativizing one's own form of existence to the legitimate claims of other forms of life' in recognising their oppressor Israel's legitimate national identity, abandoning political violence and attempting dialogue and cultural exchange with Israel and its supporters for the partial reclamation of Palestinian territory – all these virtues are now seen to have been fruitlessly pursued. Not just in the light of the actions of the Israeli state, but in the ineffectiveness of such vaunted universalist institutions as the United Nations to effectively condemn such actions according to the strictures of international Law.

When a UN resolution to condemn Israeli military action in Palestine is vetoed by the United States and Britain, while the same category of resolution against Iraq receives full support by both countries in the Security Council, it makes the universalism of the UN as based on international law and human rights seem not only ineffective, but ideological – a moral smokescreen for powerful Western capitalist interest.

While pan-Arab fascists like Saddam Hussein use a rhetoric of 'double standards' to mask the expansionist imperatives of Ba'athist ideology, the Palestinian complaint is truly justified; for having failed in their attempt to pursue their nationalist, or at least nation-state aims according to the classic precepts of Western modernity – democracy, universal law, human rights – they find themselves ridden with pathologies of demonization of the West and valorisation of any attempt at Arab self-determination; driven to choose between an Arab and an American imperial universe, which is no choice, and no universalism.

It is a truism to say that nationalism and modernity are one and the same historical movement. Development, or the general process of industrial and social modernization, creates nationalism: expanding power-centres – be it a British Empire over its dominions, or a Thatcherite government over this island – force the principalities to demand, as Tom Nairn says, 'modernization on different, less disadvantageous terms than those offered by the existing development-controllers.'

So nationalist resistance is not an attempt to escape from modernity: the factors of nationality (what Nairn caustically lists as 'ethnic purity rural bliss, ancestral gemeinschaft or ineffable idiom-truths') are only, as Ernest Gellner has suggested, 'instruments of self-defence', mobilised by nationalists as part of a broader strategy of redefining the relevant development-frontier in more favourable, or less unequal terms.

Who could deny that the assertion of Scottishness over the last decade has implied a resistant attitude to the processes of New Right social and economic modernization? Consider the Claim of Right for Scotland, which is this period's intellectual pinnacle, and whose incorporation of such universalized principles as equal parliamentary representation for men and women are (as far as I know) unprecedented in world constitutional history: who could deny this as the happiest mix of nationalism and modernity?

But it is also undeniable that part of the popular Arab legitimation – the hundreds of thousands in the streets of the region, not
their national political leaders – for Saddam Hussein's actions is his
claim to establish the Arab nation as a means of recasting Western
development in the region, on Arabs' own terms. Within the fascist
terms of Ba'athist ideology, this 'Arab nationalism' justifies gassing
separatist Kurds in your own boundaries, excluded from citizen-
ship as 'all persons who take a political, economical or intellectual
attitude hostile to the Revolution and its programme'.

But an Arab nationalism could also mean, in the words of PLO
executive member Bassam Abu Sharif, (who first mooted
Palestinian recognition of the Israeli state), a reckoning for the
Arab world similar to the upheaval in Eastern Europe: 'This is a
time for democracy', he exults in August 1990, 'for freedom and
the redistribution of wealth!' One can only wonder at the moral
confusion which could abstract these universalised values from
Iraq's aggression; perhaps fifteen years of fruitless diplomacy is
some kind of explanation.

The most compelling recent perspectives on nationalism and
modernity in the Middle East have come from those Arab writers
who, in an increasing tone of bitterness and despair, arraign the
Arab world for its intellectual mediocrity. In a piece in the
*Guardian* last week, Edward Said talks of 'the supreme irony' that
'Arabs are of this world, hooked into dependency and
consumerism, cultural vassalage, and technological secondariness,
without much active volition on our part. There has to come a
point when we cannot accuse the West of Orientalism and racism,
and go on doing little about providing an alternative.'

Said rejects the aggrieved, unfulfilled Arab nationalism that he
has experienced since his post-war youth, which places too much
emphasis on simple identity and is not critical enough about the
national programme itself – being Syrian and Saudi and Egypt
before being democratic and universalistically progressive. But his
disheartenment at the way that the Arab masses support Iraq's
invasion of Kuwait seems a little blind to the capitalist history of
the area: the extent of how Western support for undemocratic
regimes in the region – ensuring steady oil supply, untroubled by
any potential egalitarian demands over wealth-distribution (but
certainly troubled by fascist ones) – has pathologised civil society in
the Arab world.

I would argue that the possibility of a just settlement in the
Middle East – economic, cultural, political, territorial – is more
likely to come through the taming of Western capitalism in the region,
and the application of democracy as a means of ascertaining real

national interests, than any overarching pan-Arab structure: either the garrison of US troops cracking its whip at its surly, mutually-loathing oil-producing nations, or an Iraqi reich which would obliterate all national boundaries in the name of a fascist purism. An Arab modernity could be effected through mutually-cooperating nations freed from the lethal grip of Western capitalist energy demands to determine their own attitudes to the inexorable processes of development. But I would point the present finger at capitalism for the present atrocity: not nationalism.

More precisely, I should say American capitalism, and Arab nationalism. For I find myself returning to the ultimate banality of nationalism and modernity – its Janus-face, taking a nation forwards into progress or backwards into protected tradition: that there are nationalisms and nationalisms, socialisms and socialisms, capitalisms and capitalisms, specific to their historical conjuncture and evaluable only in these specifities. Nationalism, I would finally argue, is simply part of the terrain of global society: a component of how we move into the future, not a discardable element.

# ☆ Scotland By Starlight

## 1.

For as long as I breathe, a small but irreducible area of my life will be devoted to bringing about an independent Scotland. It's something I want to see in two years' time rather than twenty: the prospect of my daughter becoming an adult during a period of probably uninterrupted Tory rule from Westminster is an immediate spur to any nationalist activist. But no matter the political climate, I'll always be convinced of the necessity of a Scottish nation-state – or, to put it no vaguer, a fully empowered and properly democratic Scottish Parliament. Short of death or violence, there's nothing I wouldn't do to make it happen.

Finally thumping down onto a sincerely-held belief, in the midst of these fragmentary and relativistic times, gives you a satisfying ache in the rear; the pain of knowing that you're right does not go away – however masochistically it's endured in the less encouraging moments. But I've fallen a long way, through thick mists of ideology, experience, debate, hope and emotion, to land on the rock of Scottish sovereignty. I need to recall the journey, to be clear of where I am now.

☆ ☆ ☆

When do you first become aware of a national identity? When do you feel able to describe yourself as a Scot? It builds from details at first: a growing pile of similarities and differences. Later, you can start to sift through this mound, discern structures and attack excrescences – until the 'Scottish identity' you have becomes rational and justifiable, rather than a psychological, half-thought out reaction to circumstances. But at first, there are the tough wee memories of childhood and adolescence – indissoluble, formative.

A wedding reception in the Home Counties: I was a three or four year old, watching the blank incomprehension of strange adult faces as I asked once, twice, third time very clearly, fourth time with painstaking elocution and a rising anger, for another glass of 'ginger'. Their laughter, not unkind, but turning away from the strange Scottish child: my mother saving me, whispering in a way I'd only heard her do in church: 'They don't understand 'ginger' down here, Patrick. Ask for leh-mon-ayde next time.' Who didn't know what ginger meant? Didn't everyone have the same words for the same things? And where was 'down here'?

As a TV kid, Scotland was defined for me through the small screen, which throughout the Seventies was a montage of embarrassments. Shows like *Thingummyjig* brought down a storm of protest and derision in our house – whether from my father's obscurely passionate hatred of 'heedrum-hodrum', or even via my own media sensibilities: look at how cheap those sets are, how canned that laughter is, how fusty those jokes are about 'glens' and 'lassies' and 'bachles'! The very squeeze and exhalation of an accordion was enough to launch several fingers for the other channel – *Kojak*, Morecambe and Wise, *Fawlty Towers;* anything other than this tartan-rimmed black hole of Scottishness. We were Sinatra and Wonder and Italian Opera fans; we were second-generation Donegal Irish, the first Catholics in our aspirational street, sensitively aware of class and ethnic achievements. We were *not* these bumpy-faced men in dresses, with their forced conviviality and barely adequate talents.

Yet television also bound us into a community of Scottishness in one obvious way – through football. I dimly remember pitch invasions of Wembley in the early Seventies at the end of Scotland-England games; the circle of men and boys that huddled round these television spectacles in our living-room clucking occasionally, but chuckling more often as another crossbar broke under the weight of several bare-torsoed Scottish fans. I remember Archie Macpherson, the commentator, his muted shame and my own nine-year-old puzzlement – why are they doing this? Isn't it only a game? I can't understand this excess.

☆ ☆ ☆

Four or five years on, a pustular teenager, and I am watching the Scotland-Peru match, our first fixture in the 1978 World Cup. We put our bodies as well as our souls into the fortunes of the Scottish World Cup team: an over-investment in the abilities of eleven men to 'put Scotland on the map' in world terms. (My own unforgettable tabloid fact of that time: the Brazilian president of FIFA saying that he thought the final would be between Brazil and Scotland. Imagine!). Only retrospectively, through reading the accounts of older Scottish commentators, have I made the connection between the run-up to the devolution referendum in 1979, and the degree of unrealistic fervour for Scottish World Cup hopes. At the time, as a teenager, my nationalism was utterly focused on the soccer prospects of men in shorts: a young male's intensity about sporting ideals and perfect masculinity, wrapped up in a Lion Rampant flag for the sake of cheering and communual identification.

And as for the referendum itself? A small, unusual scatter of leaflets and booklets across our dining table; a cloudy exchange with my father about 'the Kirk ruling Scotland', 'putting us back to the bad old days', and that's why he was voting NO; some night-time dreams about Scotland being an oil-fuelled Utopia – modernist streets filled with prosperous, sensitive citizens, new inventions and humanitarian initiatives in the Scottish national papers every day, a wee jewel of a country admired by all. But so far as the result and its aftermath was concerned – the one per cent majority, the forty per cent rule, the Nationalists bringing down the Government and the election of the Conservatives, that whole '79 narrative of the devolution debacle – I have only the dimmest memory: literally, a shoulder-shrug on the way to school one morning, registering the latest tragedy that had befallen the world of adults.

(I sometimes wonder whether my own adult passion for Scottish self-determination stems from my lack of mental and emotional injuries from this period – wounds and injuries which seem to put painful limits on the imaginations of so many older Scottish politicians, activists and writers I've met over the last few years. Independence in Europe is a coherent, informed political position, and I have no reticence in proposing it as an option to any Scot (or anyone) I meet. But the number of forty-somethings who recoil from that position – who don't deny its viability or even its eventual desirability, but warn about going 'too fast too soon', the 'lack of maturity' of Scottish political culture, the need for careful progress – is too many to be coincidental. This reaction is the common trauma of a generation of late-seventies devolutionary activists, who become uncomfortable when the stakes in the eighties and nineties are raised higher – aiming towards independence – than the devolution they tried to wrest from the British state.)

University was excessive consumption of all kinds – books, sex, drink, more books – but in an omnivorous, cosmopolitan way: American classics and French literary theory was more urgent than cobwebbed seventeenth-century Scots makars like Dunbar and

Henryson, part of the same Eng. Lit. curriculum. However, I did
hook up with a magnificent woman, who confronted my soul-boy
sneering at her 'over-done Scottishness' with a relationship ultima-
tum of such severity that I was faced with two choices: out in the
cold with my cosmopolitan snobbery, or in the warmth with an
acceptance of the centrality of Scotland – past, present, future – to
my partner's concerns.

There was no choice, and we both headed for London after
graduation in 1985, following our journalistic ambitions and
nursing a Scottish identity that was more than merely parochial or
hand-knitted. A few months living in the metropolis, and that
identity revealed itself to be mostly composed of political differences; I couldn't believe how uninterested in the contest of public
affairs were the music journalists and media hacks I mingled with.
When one fey Northerner suggested we start up a style-glossy
called *SLAM!*, with Auberon Waugh ('he's *sooo* extreme')
contributing a column, I knew that I was at best in the wrong
political community, if such thoughts could even be campily
entertained. The unspoken left-of-centre assumptions of student
days and home life in Scotland began to emerge from the
background of my consciousness, clearer on every domestic visit.
Yet this was still no more articulable than the cosiness of the
'Heimat', the known and formative community; a warm glow held
in a shortie tin, to take back down to Tufnell Park.

And the metropolis still had all the best ideas, as far as I knew.
When the music business break came, in '86–'87, the record that
hit the Top Ten – 'Labour of Love' – carried an explicitly anti-
Thatcherite lyric. But the allegory behind the romantic narrative
on the surface wasn't some kind of subaltern Scottish radicalism.
'Withdraw my labour of love', the hookline, was a straight Leftist
metaphor, the summit of an argument derived from Gramsci (and
shamelessly cribbed from *Marxism Today*) about how Thatcherism was exercising 'hegemony' over the working classes: 'loved
you putting me down in a totally new way', said the song's
speaker, a reference to the way Thatcher's rhetoric of individualism was a new and immensely subtle exercise of authority over the
popular consensus. Academic Stuart Hall's gloomy judgement that
there must be a deep streak of masochism running through the
portion of the UK's working class who regularly endorse
Thatcherism, also informed the lyric; and the hope contained in
those three and a half minutes, was that the Tories' attacks on
public services and housing, on employment and industry, on
enemies without and within, would finally come across as 'too
much pain, for too little gain'.

The record's arc of success spanned the June '87 election – some adroit nodding and winking kept it on the airwaves – and, of course, made not a damn bit of difference, as the Tories thundered into power again. Many things began to smell rotten in the London that I worked in and passed through at that time: how do you cope with the prole record plugger, the sensitive journalist, the worldly video maker, all as modish and cutting-edge as the metropolis can manage, and all admitting they've voted Conservative? Not very well, in my case. But more importantly, in terms of my Scottish identity, the attraction of metropolitan thinking began to wane too. Scores of issues of designer socialist magazines, the efforts of the star-studded Labour pressure group Red Wedge, conference after imprint after Sunday article – how much had all this brilliantly-informed agitation, education and organisation changed any of the minds of the crucial South-Eastern and Midlands English voters? Hardly at all. Take your Gramsci, your Foucault, your Barthes, your Peter York's and your Stuart Hall's, take every paste jewel studding the critical discourse of the thinking London Left and stick them up your arse, I said to myself. I'm going home – physically, socially, emotionally and intellectually.

The first three were easily done. But the last was a whistling gap in my solidifying commitment to Scotland. It was clear, at least in electoral endorsement, that Scots had more socially-oriented, ethically militant values than the elephantine Tory majority of Southern England. Why? A crude proclamation of 'because we're different/better' wasn't anywhere near satisfying the standards of justification that London cut-and-thrust demands of you (one of the metropolis's few technical advantages). So, between record releases at the tail-end of the eighties, I began to haunt empty universities and deserted libraries, rain-sodden demonstrations and woolly conferences – digging for the deep structures that might explain, but also sustain, the daily kindnesses, passions and solidarities of my fellow Scots. I found much treasure; actually, an inexhaustible resource.


2.


'The democratic intellect', 'generalism', "common sense' philo-sophy', 'inferiorism', 'independence in Europe', 'secular Calvinism', 'civil society', 'Tartanry' .... This is some of the conceptual short change of Scottish intellectual debate around culture, politics and society over the last three decades. In one sense, my delving into such Scottish theory is motivated by the crudest political statistic:

why do Scots vote overwhelmingly for non-Tory parties – 75% at the last General Election? Given that 60% of that particular vote was for professedly social-democratic/democratic-socialist parties of the Left (the Labour Party and the SNP), there is even majority support for what would probably be the most socially-oriented polity in Western Europe, if it ever got the chance to govern itself. What are the roots of this consistent Scottish refutation of the famous Thatcherite dictum, election after election, asserting that there *is* such a thing as society?

For me, the most important contemporary locus of Scottish political difference is the idea of the Scottish nation itself. For Scots to see themselves as members of a nation, rather than a region or principality, is to directly tie their identity as Scots to issues of democracy and rights. A nation implies a people, a national community, who could be expected to have a consensus on a range of issues affecting modern life – economic, political, cultural, social, military, etc. But if you are members of a *stateless* nation, a people without the political means to realise their consensus on how they should collectively live, then you face two options.

Either demote your sense of being a nation, or there being something like the will of the people, so that there won't be such a painful disjunction between the rhetoric of the Scottish nation and the reality of its powerlessness. (This is the strategy of those opinion-formers in Scotland who, feeling the strains of nationalist invocation, like to divide the national left-of-centre consensus along geographical, linguistic, or even subcultural lines – Central Belt lefties, Highland Liberals and Tories, mutual East and West Coast suspicions: a patchwork of localisms and parochial emnities.)

Or – the other option – you let the painful denial of the socio-economic consensus of the Scottish people feed into a strengthening commitment to Scottish self-government: the desire for a nation worth the invocation, able to act on its collective wishes. (This is the process which all those in Scottish politics and culture who assert the Scottish mandate – the idea that Scots should get the government they vote for – implicitly support. The sovereignty of the Scottish people is thus asserted over the sovereignty of Westminster; and a virtuous circle ascends towards the attainment of the maximum amount of power a people can have over themselves in the modern world – that is, as a nation-state.)

These are the consequences of a nationalist politics in Scotland – either a growing rejection of the claims of nationhood, or a growing intensification of them. The specific post-election developments in June '92 – specifically the Labour Party in Scotland's

support of the idea of a multi-option referendum (with independence on the ticket), conceding to SNP policy under pressure from
their own ranks – shows that asserting the rights of the Scottish
nation is a vortex, into which all Scottish-oriented parties are
drawn towards a position of strong self-determination, or national
liberation.

It would be narrow to understand the Scottish nationalist perspective as purely an ideological trap for those who get caught up
in its inexorable logic. The right of peoples to national self-determination is indeed an article of international law – and calling down
this kind of authority for Scottish self-government would seem the
ultimate end-point of democracy movements within Scotland,
party or non-party. But Scottish nationhood is justified not only as
a matter of democracy, of good and fair self-governance as a global
right, but also as a matter of the development of its own traditions
of thought and practice.

I agree with the words of SNP leader Alex Salmond in the
campaign run-up to April 1992, that we should not just be 'for
Scotland, for its own sake: we should be for Scotland *for* social and
economic justice.' Yet Scotland's cause is not just a matter of socio-
economic nationalism or constitutional patriotism, being loyal to
our national modernity and political sophistication. One of the
great joys of having a confident Scottish identity, is the willingness
to treasure and proclaim those aspects of the cultural and
intellectual past which make Scotland historically continuous, right
up to the present. That is to say, we can link our rejection of the
anti-society, anti-communal, atomising Tory regime of the 1990s
with the writings of our greatest writers and thinkers from the last
three hundred years and beyond.

Some would see this link as not necessary to the conduct of an
oppositional Scottish politics. David McCrone, in *Understanding
Scotland*, describes current expressions of Scottish political
difference as having developed 'without the encumbrance of a
heavy cultural baggage ... No icons need to be genuflected at, no
correct representation needs to be observed in this journey into the
future' (McCrone, 1992, p. 196). It is true that nationalist politics,
across the parties and movements, is primarily concerned with the
practicalities of decision-making and control, and not with
preserving or restoring the 'essential Scottish identity', cultural,
historical or otherwise.

But if there are intellectual resources in Scotland's past which
can be deployed in the public challenge against the current UK
Tory Establishment, they should be used – and promoted widely.
The Scots may well be 'travelling light', in McCrone's phrase, into

the twenty-first century: even still, our bags should be full of the best stuff to hand. Some of that stuff is already in our possession.

☆ ☆ ☆

Quite the most fruitful legacy of Scottish thought for present anti-Tory argument lies in the common sense tradition of philosophy, represented by Thomas Reid (1710-96), Adam Smith (1723-90) and James Ferrier (1808-64). What is so useful about this tradition is the way that it can radicalize and make critically specific one of the most hackneyed popular clichés: shut your eyes, recall every besuited politician from whatever mainstream party validate their policies by belching up the authority of 'common sense', and your heart will sink at the prospect of the phrase.

The notion of common sense, in the hands of Reid, Smith and Ferrier, has two precise philosophical meanings, both of which are above and beyond the colloquial meanings of gut reaction or self-evident convictions. The first is as a *unifying* sense behind all the other five senses whereby we experience the world. This sixth, or *common* sense, is the area which our identity and individuality inhabits; all our sensory experiences of the outside world are made coherent by this common bond between the senses. It is our 'common sense', understood this way as our total experience of the world, which makes us feel autonomous, in control of ourselves, comprehending of our surroundings and society.

But the other meaning outlined is of common sense as *sensus communis*, public or shared sense. As Richard Gunn renders it: 'It is through interaction with others that I achieve a sense of my identity... [this] identity includes an ability to relate and distinguish the various aspects of my experience in a coherent way' (Gunn, 1987, p. 48). We exist as individuals only if we are recognised as such by others; they, in their turn, rely on our recognition of them to confirm their individuality. This is a sense of everyday acknowledgement, of 'mutual recognition' as Hegel would put it (Hegel, 1977, p. 112), without which it would be difficult to exist as a coherent self.

The important thrust of Scottish commonsense philosophy is that these two meanings of the term – 'the common bond or centre of the five senses', and 'the general sense of a community' (Oxford English Dictionary) – *are utterly interdependent*. 'Only if our sensory experience is coherent [common sense as identity] are we competent to interact with our fellows; but it is only through such interaction [common sense as mutual recognition] that we can make our sensory experience, and ourselves, "add up"' (Gunn, 1991, p. 80).

What is interesting, from a political perspective, is the way that common sense philosophy strikes an exact balance between an excess of individual experience and an excess of communal experience. If common sense is too private, too personal, it risks being unintelligible to the outside world; if it is too public and general, common sense becomes orthodoxy, the assumed status quo. The individual who sincerely believes, for example, that television news is an actual physical oppression, may well need to interact with his or her fellows, so that this disorder of experience can be worked out; a stimulus (television) that affects the senses of sight and hearing is being understood through the sense of touch. This might imply that there is something out of kilter in his or her 'republic' of senses – far too closed and insular in relation to the general *sensus communis* of the world.

But these others may well need to interact with such an apparently malfunctioning individual, just as much as he or she does with them. There is always the possibility of this initially incoherent view being integrated into the social conversation, rather than being rejected as incomprehensible. For example, a certain conceptualisation of how mass media operates – the way it induces passivity, atomisation, demoralisation, making the citizen inactive and therefore affecting his or her *physical* presence in movements and demonstrations of protest in the public realm – *could* plausibly equate television news with real, physical oppression, and in this way be accepted a legitimate subject for general discourse.

The human interaction at the heart of the philosophies of Reid, Smith and Ferrier helps them steer a path between totally individualist dimensions of common sense – which could lead to *pathologies* of perception like the above – and a totally communitarian idea of common sense – which could lead to *conformism*, the acceptance of collective, unchallenged wisdom, without the vitalizing input of the marginal voice. So the full functioning of common sense is like a circular process of meaning, a perpetual and open enquiry – an interaction between persons, or 'dialectic of experience' without end.

'To see ourselves as others see us': Robert Burns and Adam Smith, whether in poetry or in works like *The Theory of Moral Sentiments*, both claimed that the 'general sense of a community' formed individuality, and vice versa; common sense should be always understood in its *double* sense. 'Sympathy' amongst humans is the great theme of Smith's moral argument in the *Sentiments*. His promotion of mass education was reacting to the way that eighteenth-century industrialisation was destroying the well-springs of such natural sympathy. The specialisation of jobs in the new economy meant that people gained prosperity at the cost of solidarity and mutual recognition: benefiting from their specific skills and work-regimes as wage-labourers, but cut off from that 'general conversation' of the pre-capitalist community. Extensive education programmes would be needed to keep all workers informed of others' special tasks and conditions, to comprehend the ever more expanding division of labours and knowledges (Smith, 1979, pp. 788ff).

So the supposed patriarch of 1980s Thatcherite innovations – pouring aplenty from the opportunistically named Adam Smith Institute – was, in fact, intensely concerned with the existence of 'society': the threatened dimensions of mutual recognition and communication in rapidly developing and modernizing nations. This is a fact which cannot be too often stated in the current battle to define Scotland's present and future in relation to its past.

This focus on education was one of the most specific practical prescriptions of Scottish commonsense philosophy, and was seen as the means whereby that mutuality of perspectives which made for a rich individual and social existence could be sustained, in the face of the specialising and atomising effects of industrial expansion. Do Scots want, then or now, a society split between 'over-specialized boffins on the one hand, and unthinking proles on the other', as George Davie puts it in *The Scottish Enlightenment*? The specialisation of tasks and knowledges may be necessary to material growth, but the 'common sense' of the country – as Adam Smith claimed – will only be maintained by a kind of 'general studies mentality', which would 'counteract atomisation by building an intellectual bridge between all classes', creating an 'educational democracy' (Davie, 1991, p. 58).

In these hi-tech times, such an educational democracy could only exist in a condition of real, general democracy. A shrinking class of privileged information innovators and electronic experts stand atop a vast majority of servile/service workers in most developed Western countries, including Scotland. The high-technological liberation from labour should mean that the reduced workload is shared equitably amongst an educated citizenry, releasing more leisure time to be 'mutually recognitive' and nurture common sense. Instead it is being used to increase the profits of capital, via an ever-worsening social division.

The debate that Scottish commonsense philosophers of the eighteenth century had with radical English utilitarians like Joseph Priestley and William Cobbett is strikingly contemporary, resting on what are basically metaphysical or philosophical judgements on what makes the 'good society'. Scots thinkers saw humans living in two worlds. The first world was composed of persons-in-relation and mutual recognition, our identities formed in an inescapable movement towards others – in 'social acts of mind' as Thomas Reid said (modern Critical Theorists would call this the 'lifeworld', the 'realm of solidarity' – Davie even terms it 'almost a socialism, in its spiritual productivity'). The second world was that of facts and science, composed and identified systematically by experts and specialists (these days, this realm would be designated as 'steering systems', 'media of power and money', by contemporary social theorists). English radicals, like Joseph Priestley and William Cobbett, saw only one world – a world in which 'man' was infinitely 'perfectible' in all his realms, material and spiritual, through the rigorous application of science and technology in production and social organisation.

Cobbett had fun with the Scots' 'feelosophy' – asking the working man to put Bacon with a capital B before bacon with a small b. And those hard-headed populist pragmatists are still having fun with our feelosophies – witness the right-wing Scottish Tory press jibes at the 'middle-class proletarians', who despite statistically occupying a lofty strata within the division of labour still feel a profound 'sympathy' with their fellow disadvantaged Scots. Writers like William McIlvanney express this old Scottish obsession with the 'godly commonwealth', the 'spiritual utopia', in the most casual tags to their popular journalism of the moment. As I write, McIlvanney is raising up a 'spiritual socialism' to his Sunday *Observer* readers, asking them to answer to the 'desire to be the best that we can be' in the face of post-election Tory dominance and the disorganisation of the opposition. His closing comments reverberate through the centuries:

> What we have to remember is what that best is. It is not in possessions or career. It is in how we are as people and how we live towards others. (12 July, 1992)

This sounds like classic commonsense philosophising to me; and it does no harm, and perhaps some good, to relate such apparently off-the-shelf moralisms to a continuous Scottish tradition of mutualist thinking. We need all the ballast we can find in the present storm; the 'talent of the nation' (Alexander Brodie) for intersubjective, inherently social thought can be a small but worthy weight.

### 3. A New Generalism, a New Scotland
*(An edited version of my inaugural address as Rector of Glasgow University, April 1990)*

My rectorship comes at a time when Scotland's future is at stake – politically, economically, and culturally. What part will the universities of Scotland play in this unfolding national drama? Surely not that of the stage extra, nor the armchair critic. I call on Glasgow University, along with the other great Universities of this country, to join the vanguard fighting for the future of Scotland as a culture, economy and polity. The universities are crucial to this fight, for the simple reason that the distinctiveness of Scottish education expresses the distinctiveness of Scotland itself – all our best values, all our most worthwhile traditions.

George Davie's writings on the 'Democratic Intellect' and its crises, remind us of the intellectual traditions we should be striving to defend and extend. Scottish education has always had a strong conception and practice of serving the community as a whole – both in a historical comparison with England and Europe from the late sixteenth to the early twentieth century, right up to the greater proportion of Scottish over English school leavers able to enter Higher Education at present.

But much more germane to the current crisis is the cultural content of the democratic intellectual – the 'generalist' tradition of education. At its most radical, this is more than an argument about lengths of degrees and discrimination against Scottish Highers, however practically relevant these matters may be. Scottish generalism encodes a whole relationship between education and society which is not only distinctively Scottish, but absolutely necessary for the progress of Scottish society as we head towards the next millennium.

The educational debates of the inter-war years in Scotland which George Davie focuses on in his latest book might seems distant and arcane today, dealing with long-forgotten Ordinances and dead controversies. But from them can be extracted a powerful clash of competing philosophies of education.

On one side the Anglo-American-influenced utilitarians, wanting to make education a training for specific vocations – teachers, professionals, the scientific specialists needed for a productive and efficient society. On the other side the indigenous generalists, defensive of a more broadly-based higher education, philosophical, interdisciplinary and eclectic; an education able to provide the student with a critical distance on the society in which he or she would be an active citizen.

The result of the struggle, a compromise – but one which Davie believes meant the devaluing of the Scottish generalist tradition to this day. The three year general degree continued as a vestige of generalism, downgraded in regard to the four years Honours course. The limited scope for general studies in the first two years of Honours narrowed down into tight specialization for the last two. Here Davie relates a narrative of decline, where only the ghosts of former glories haunt the cloisters and lecture rooms of Scottish universities.

Having completed an Honours degree in English Literature and Language at this University, I'd have to disagree slightly with Professor Davie's doom and gloom about the eclipse of generalism. Central to his criticisms is the displacing of philosophy as a compulsory subject in the Scottish degree courses. This had provided the ability to reduce all matters studied to 'first principles', a commitment to theoretical reasoning as the 'common sense' behind all subjects. To discuss general, fundamental issues like the nature of aesthetic experience, the aims of education or the worth of a particular technology, would mean a discussion that the student and the teacher, the educated and the layperson, might all make a contribution to.

I found that kind of general, comparative reasoning a scarce practice in my years at Glasgow. But the corners in which it did flourish perhaps point to a new rationale for the defence of generalism, one which connects it up to the most burning intellectual and political issues of our times.

I entered University as a child of the television age; my formative experiences are as much Doctor Who and the Flintstones as they are Robert Louis Stevenson and *Lord of the Flies*. If people of my generation have any common or shared sense, it is their sensitivity to the conventions and themes of broadcast television. The course I chose in my first year that seemed to address this experience was Film and Television Studies.

The course was a revelation: interdisciplinary, eclectic, it revealed what had seemed the most lowly of media to be an incredibly complex phenomenon. Theoretical reasoning was often the only way to open out the workings of this previously most banal of cultures; I learned to apply an understanding of economics, technology, psychology, cultural analysis, politics, history to any particular art work or situation, trying always to advance on several disciplinary fronts at once.

As far as my future career went, this would seem like a classic case of utilitarian, vocationalist training – learning the media theory to go into the world to make money in media practice. But as far as my intellectual development went, Film and Television Studies was as generalist a start in education as any Humanities student could hope for. Its inherently comparative method, and the broad range of its approaches, has given me an analytical training which I have found enriching and invaluable.

How does this course relate to my demands for a modern generalism? And how might a modern generalism relate to this critical moment in Scotland's future?

One of the signal virtues of the Film and Television Studies course was the way that no strict division was made between the study of science and the study of culture. To look at film history is also to consider the possibilities for expression enabled by film technology – and also the political and economic pressures that promoted or repressed that technology. George Davie's lament for the loss of the compulsory syllabus of mathematics, philosophy and language in the Scottish degree system is partly answered by interdisciplinary courses like these; here, the realms of science and society are no longer sundered by the evils of specialization, are linked together in a way accessible to the layest of laypersons.

But think of the range of pressing issues of the day, which might benefit from this kind of eclectic, generalist intelligence. Green politics has engendered a whole new awareness of how science has become fatally sundered from ethics and social morality. In these times, how can one conceive of a new way of making energy, of communicating, of manufacturing goods, of transporting people, of destroying waste, of reproducing humans, without considering matters of control and social effect?

Such new technologies force the humanities and the sciences to draw much closer together. The ethical and political issues over, say, genetic engineering or information technology must enter into the purportedly 'objective' world of the scientist; and scientific advances like these present an awesome challenge to humanist understanding, demanding new moralities and new frameworks of judgement.

The task for Scottish education is to build upon its traditions to meet these demands of the twenty-first century. These are not demands that require universities to be narrowing and specialising, filleting their generalism to fit an outgoing politician's vision of an 'enterprise culture', meaning social progress as a headless chicken. These demands are for an education which conceives of society as needing ever more sophisticated models of planning and rational understanding, to cope with the explosion of social possibilities in the nineties and beyond.

Much of this end of millennium enlightenment might not seem

to have much specific relevance to the drama Scotland is playing out at present. This would be wrong. For example, the relationship between new productive technologies and old productive industries is one which bedevils Scotland at the moment. If steel production were to leave this country, what would be the future for indigenous manufacture in Scotland? Do we abandon any vision of producing high-technology goods for social use, and satisfy ourselves with assembly of Japanese, American or Continental parts for indiscriminate global consumption?

Where is the utopian perspective on new productive technology coming from in Scotland – that we might use scientific advance to liberate people from alienating work, into the pleasures of – perhaps – education? Jimmy Reid, in his 1972 Rectorial Address, expressed his 'earnest desire that this great University of Glasgow should be in the vanguard' of airing such perspectives. The inaction of this University to practically join such a vanguard, eighteen years on, is something I hope my Rectorship will begin to reverse. An inter disciplinary School of Studies in Technology and Society would be one practical step; an extension of the Technology and Society course across all the faculties, as a continually available and prioritised study option in the humanities and sciences, would be another.

And if we are to constructively go 'back to the future' in Scottish education, then surely a restructuring of the degree system is a viable option? Continental higher education can bear its students staying on for five or six years in a science or humanities course. In the context of a sympathetic education policy of a Scottish parliament, the return of the general degree for all students of whatever faculty cannot be seen as too far-fetched, within the interdisciplinary generalism I've been sketching. Perhaps a three year general course, followed by two or more years of specialism, would be the ideal form? A truly modern generalism demands no less, if the students of this University and other Scottish Universities are to shape, not shirk these new, volatile times.

Looking beyond the university for a moment, it's clear that some preparation for the generalist intellect would have to begin in secondary schools. A philosophy qualification should at least be an option for these students, dealing with the history and practice of theoretical reasoning from the classics to contemporary media theory-like the classe de philosophe in France, if a lot more flexible in its ambit of topics.

Why deny philosophy and theoretical understanding to working-class children? As James Kelman has recently written, the analytical skills required to operate several bingo cards simultaneously, or

studying form in a sprint handicap at Ayr, or doing a weekly
shopping on a limited budget with a large family – all these skills
are in no way essentially different from the competence needed to
be 'expert' in an academic discipline. One must also state that such
democratic intellectualism could only flourish in a more just and
equitable society; basic economic security, implying the freedom to
pursue knowledge without it having to keep you surviving, is the
precondition of popular enlightenment.

So, if we are in a fight for Scotland's future, then at least
educationally and intellectually, we now know what we are
fighting for. But if Universities are to take a lead in Scottish society,
they should themselves be exemplars of that new Scottish society
they wish to help bring about. If the impending Scottish parliament
implies a 'radical democratization' of Scottish society, it should be
foreshadowed by a radical democratization of the University of
Glasgow.

This Rector is foolish enough to think that an institution whose
function is to spread enlightenment, should be itself enlightened in
its organization. In opposition to managerial models for University
administration, typified by the recent Coopers and Lybrand report,
we should be arguing for an effective 'community of scholars' –
consisting of students, teachers and administrators – with collective
control and decision over University resources and course
formation.

As a student-elected rector, I am violently opposed to any kind
of new decision-making processes that will treat students like mute
objects, incapable of making informed decisions about the
direction and nature of the institution they are such a crucial part
of. One of my tasks as Rector over the next few years is not only to
resist any moves to turn Glasgow University into G.U. plc, but to
mobilise and inform students of their rights to participation in the
University's new direction, both institutionally and educationally.
If a new generalism cannot come from the top, then it must come
from below.

## 4. *Scotia Moralia*

*Back, biology!* – 'The Scots are a proud race', droned John Major in the midst of the '92 General Election clench. One expects such a doltish conjunction of biology and nationality from a mind exercised by nothing other than institutional pragmatism: no shafts of theory have ever illuminated the dark office gloom of the Prime Ministerial intellect, nor are likely to. But the appeal to the species, as a justification for the existence of nations in particular or in general, surfaces from even the most fragrant theoretical waters.

Tom Nairn – 'Scotland's only intellectual', by repute – has recently invoked the authority of *Scientific American*'s L. Cavalli-Sforza, tentatively suggesting that there may be some biological or hereditary element to explanations of nationalism, 'in a way that has nothing to do with blood or race'. Africa is determined by Cavalli-Sforza as being 'the original homeland of [all] hominids'. The 'demographic success' of waves of subsequent migrations is now much more likely to be based on 'cultural developments' than biological ones, given this 'common genetic inheritance' of humankind. Thus humans have become a diverse species 'through cultural means', through 'differential cultural development (including language)'. This, says Nairn, is an affront to those historians and theorists who saw cultural diversity as a kind of Babel, an 'accident that got in the way of more rational evolution'; nationalism was seen by them as a brutish and obstructive 'throwback' to this random, meaningless particularism. But if our common biological 'human nature' has featured such cultural diversity throughout its existence, then it may be the case that the 'isms' of nation or region *do not* 'derive so totally from the circumstances of modernity', from the moment of 1789 and global industrialisation (Nairn, 1992, pp. 31-2).

We can draw out the conclusions. The variety of ethnicities and languages could be a fundamental condition of the human species; the persistence of nationality or regionalism, as a form of human organisation, could be sourced in biology. Nationalism's economic causes – the strains of uneven capitalist development forcing ethnic variety into political and defensible nation-states – might finally evaporate, in the midst of global prosperity and equality; but the basic human need for nations may still remain, even beyond such an end of history. Nairn concludes his scientific excursion: 'As yet, this area of theorising is too little developed to affect current politics'.

Too dangerous to cite it, then, in a journal of 'current politics'. Why, as a 'Scottish Nationalist and a British Marxist' (Beveridge

and Turnbull, 1989), does Nairn need to reach down to the spe-
cies-being? There are many social, historical, philosophical justifications for nations and nationalism to hand; contestable in the
public sphere of debate, surely, but still coherent enough in themselves – as theories of human action and intention, rather than of
biological human nature – to be adequate for any political or
cultural nationalist.

Science can be used as ideology, Habermas once said. The accuracy of its processes are mythically assumed, and its uncheck-able
results mediated into the public realm by Gramsci's 'organic intellectuals', here rotting a little under the burning sun of 'current
politics'. Nairn's article, appearing in the context of a study of
Europe's borderlands, has trawled a shoreline too far, and brought
up a coelecanth. As an ideologist for Scottish self-determination,
but also as 'detached' and 'intellectual', Nairn has to find some way
to *normalize* the 'ethno-linguistic variety' presently active, both
benignly and malignly, in post-Communist Europe. For him, this is
all 'liberation-chaos', another phase of 'creative but disruptive life'
in the order of the world. As a political metaphor, it is usefully
corrective to counterpose the necessary cacophony of a new 'Age of
Nations' to the monotone of the Cold War of the superpowers:
that fearful, oscillating hum of nuclear deterrence. Is it worse to
have more borders in the world of the future, than to have no
world at all?

This may well be a new global normality of proliferating
'contrasts and conflicts, previously repressed and distorted'. But
there is *simply no need* to describe the areas repressed and
distorted, or understand their energies, through any kind of biological
or species-hereditary determinations. The only universally-binding
terms which might help us through this international liberation-
chaos are not our hominid instincts, but those 'circumstances of
modernity' which Nairn foolishly attempts to go behind: the
expectation that new nation-states, or effective national groupings,
measure up to those modern standards of human rights and democracy instituted by the French in 1789. Pursuing a progressive-
nationalist game with the cards of biological science means that
your opponent may defeat you, still playing poker – but with
higher, more terrifying stakes, holding infinitely dirtier and
dishonest hands. The packet of nationality and biology should be
left unopened, in the drawer of the first half of this century.
Political dullards will always find jokers slipping out of their cuffs.
But an intellectual should know better.

☆ ☆ ☆

*Pinnochio Unbound.* – Like a marionette, Scotland's economic future is understood as dancing to a fistful of inescapable strings. Before we regain some of the powers of our wooden limbs, through the merest exercise of national sovereignty – but expecting no Good Fairy to grant us our self-empowerment – we have to test the flexibility and strength of our joints, gauge the steps we can take without crashing to the floor of the world stage. What form of self-government would best develop Scotland economically? What powers can a small nation really exercise over its affairs, in a thoroughly multinational and globalized economy?

As with all Scottish self-interrogations, we can be too hard on ourselves; even God's own children have serious doubts in this area. American business guru Bob Reich (presently economic adviser to Bill Clinton) has written in *The Work of Nations: preparing for 21st century capitalism*, that the future economic strength of nations – even America – will not reside in the amount of giant companies they have at 'home base'. A growing cadre of supranational corporate players – Japanese, American, European, sometimes all three at once – will start to claim allegiance to their worldwide performance, rather than any one nation's economic success.

All that developed nations – even Americans – can do is to maximise the skills and insights of their citizens. Western living standards will rest on clever innovators and qualified operatives ('symbolic analysts', Reich calls them) satisfying mega-corp demands for new product and ideas – built anywhere on the globe where the labour is cheapest, and the profit is greatest. But these symbolic analysts, possibly earning half a nation's income by the early years of the twenty-first century, will only make up twenty per cent of any population. Aloof and cosmopolitan, they'll have no civic connection with the majority of their countrymen and women, sunk in routine production and service jobs. The biggest recent expansion in the US service industry is in private security; the gilded problem-solvers are beginning to keep their distance from the manual hordes at the gates of their laagers.

American intellectuals are as good at dystopias as they are at utopias – and Reich does pour on the post-industrial nightmare scenario a little thickly. But there are local accounts of Scotland's economic future which express some of the same anxieties. How does a 'peripheral' economy like ours – on the edge of Europe, without substantial planning powers as yet – negotiate a hi-tech industrial future, where most of the main employment comes from outside investment?

A gloomy prognosis comes from Jeffrey Henderson, who looks at 'the globalisation of high technology production', taking

Scotland as a case study. Semiconductors are the most vital sector
of any electronics industry – and at first glance, Scotland's array of
American and Japanese multinationals is impressive, giving us the
status of 'probably the most important semiconductor production
complex in Europe.' But Henderson reminds us of how weak a
position this is. Scottish semiconductor plants have no research and
development facilities of their own, working to the foreign
corporations' designs, and therefore can't build up the expertise
that might survive companies withdrawing due to a global contraction in their activities. Even the components they make – for example, circuit wafers – are a stage in a global process, which involves
exportation to low-wage East Asian companies for final assembly
and finishing.

The separation of world corporations from their national bases
– that growing interrelationship and autonomy which Reich talks
about – poses a very direct limit to the prospects for semiconductor
production in Scotland. These giant companies are forging 'strategic alliances' on commonly-developed hi-tech – Motorola and
Toshiba, Texas Instruments and Philips, Toshiba and Siemens, to
name only a few alliances. Even the most advanced semiconductor
industries, including the US and Japan, will be locked into
structures of mutual development, innovation and finance. With
this level of transnational unity, Henderson concludes, 'it may soon
become unlikely that any country' – meaning Scotland – 'will again be
capable of developing a fully autonomous semiconductor industry'.

There are enough innovations coming out of Scottish university
departments and indigenous companies to cast at least some doubt
on the depressing academic certainties of Mr Henderson. Our
expertise in optoelectronics – which could increase computing
speed a thousand-fold – might open out the same world-shattering
market opportunities as the semiconductor did for Silicon Valley in
California. Yet without the conditions by which Scottish
innovations can be turned into Scottish finished products – not just
hi-tech ideas and patents, but hi-tech manufacturing, marketing
and selling from this country – how can we defy the good
academic's foreclosure of our future? The next millennium may
demand that we be a nation of symbolic analysts, spreading our
licensed inventions and touting our skilled workforce amongst the
global corps. It can demand all it wants of us – but how can we
negotiate such demands?

An effective Scottish Parliament – that is, an independent one –
is the only negotiating tool that would be any use. The STUC's
1990 document *Scotland's Economy: claiming the future*, argues
for a devolved Parliament; it presumes a Labour Westminster

government, able and willing to act on Scotland's behalf to pressurise UK companies, never mind European, American or Japanese ones, to honour their commitment to Scottish workers. 'It would require a government that had the economic muscle and market power to resist and, if need be, reject EC regulations', say the writers robustly.

You'll get pie in the sky when you die if you're resting Scottish economic control on the prospect of that kind of interventionist Labour UK government, let alone any kind of British Labour administration. It's not that the SNP's policies on industrial strategy are qualitatively different from the Labour Party's, however quantitatively greater the resource commitment of the Nationalists towards Scotland. Both propose investment funds for industrial expansion and modernisation, research and development programmes for home-produced high value goods, expenditure on infrastructure and education – precisely the kinds of conditions which would support the indigenous hi-tech industry Scotland needs.

But the political argument must be – which state will deliver? A permanent Tory Westminster government, perhaps offering us 'administrative assemblies within the Union', with no power to initiate policy? Or an independent Scotland in the EC, with both real power and guaranteed resources to enact the policies we want?

There is one aspect to the glorified hi-tech horizons we travel towards which must not be forgotten. The electronics industry only rose in employment by five thousand – from 42 to 47,000 – from 1980 to 1990; in the same period, over 150,000 manufacturing jobs were lost. Scottish Enterprise is right to claim that the rise in service industries is more than just a fast-food and laundry service soak-up of these kinds of job losses. As their document *Strategies for the 1990s* says, half the service industries are 'inputs' to the final production and sales of goods. But job security and wage levels in the private service sector are still much less than in the mass manufacturing industries they have occluded.

If Scotland is heading towards an innovation-based, high-knowledge economy, we have to recognise that a purely market-led direction will dump millions of Scots in low-skill, low-initiative jobs. As Christopher Harvie says, 'our economic strategies have to go out from our evaluation of society: what holds it together, what it can do without' (Harvie, 1992). Bob Reich's hard-headed, even frightening analysis of American late capitalism concludes with a rather hopeful call to 'positive economic nationalism'. If the educated, innovative twenty per cent of symbol analysers don't act as duteous national citizens as well as global functionaries, their societies will rip apart. Half altruistically, half in self-interest, Reich urges them to give larger parts of their income at present over to public schemes of education, health and housing, so that others may enter their symbolic élite.

Didn't something like that clearly not happen amongst a large part of the population of these islands on April 9th, 1992? If Scots have the social cohesion to cope with the disintegrative twenty-first century, then let's entrench it in a state – and devise ways to shape our own century, our own way. Let the transnational puppet-masters feel some resistance in the strings: and if not Prometheus, then at least Pinnochio.

☆ ☆ ☆

*Come awa' wi' me.* – Scottish statehood has much to morally commend it – not least the power independence would give us to resist the imposition of Trident, and to use our contributions to its funding for 'bairns not bombs', as the Scottish National Party slogan has it. But this anti-militarist morality could go much further. Why shouldn't we also argue for 'bairns not frigates', 'bairns not field artillery', 'bairns not tanks'? Need a Scottish state be burdened with any of the armoury that Labour's UK nationalists would take for granted in the British state?

It's a measure of the popular grip of national military identity, that a left-wing party like the SNP has to work out credible, or in any case coherent defence policies, to hold their own on the hustings of the media. This means manifesto-talk about 'strong conventional forces', 'fulfilling international peace-keeping obligations', 'not destabilising European defence interests' – all this bullishness while still wishing to opt out of NATO's strategy on nuclear deterrence. One grand act of demilitarisation must surely lead to others, including our precious, blood-soaked Regiments.

But raise the possibility of a 'defenceless Scotland', and you step off the plateau of party politics – even your own – and into the realm of clouds, angels and ideals. Must the conscientious objection to war – potential or actual, defensive or offensive – always only be the decision of principled individuals? It's not inconceivable that a collective, national conscience could object to the armed state. In the irreversible thaw of the Cold War, a pacifist Scotland is at least a possibility to be worked for.

No doubt tough wee defence spokesmen of all parties would knock heads like mine together: Get real, son! By their own metaphors may they be damned. We want the demilitarization of Scottish society so that we can remove one major source of the general violence of our times – and that is our assent to the use of armed force in the national, or even international interest.

One Scottish *Daily Record* front cover during the Gulf War will be immemorial: 'In for the killing!' snarled the headline, over the picture of a 'marauding Scots Guard' starting the land war in Iraq. The populace was supposed to be proud of Scottish adult males being first in to slaughter, or be slaughtered by the Arabs. What a pathetic self-image the battling Scot is! Kilt-wrapped by the English to butcher for the British Empire in his heyday, and maintaining his thick-necked pre-eminence in the contemporary frontline: the pit-bull terrier of a decorative UK Gulf presence, gasping its Imperial last as a world power. The United States, cloaked in UN resolutions, now has as one of its regular signals a willingness to discipline the less pliant Middle-Eastern powers with military intervention. If independent, would we chip our Jocks in with such a thinly-legitimized 'peace enforcement' again? There is no worse appeal to modern Scottish national identity than the call to arms.

There are surely other ways a free Scotland could increase global peacefulness apart from letting regimental Highlanders join the latest blood-for-oil crusade. A close public monitoring of our industries' touting for military trade, whether it be hi-tech field communications systems or heavy industrial components, should be backed up by disciplinary action from government. The amorality of free-market defence capitalists – Despots! You got the authoritarian ends, we can sell you the technical means – screams out for some effective regulation by a moralized state.

With Northern Ireland exploding off our shores, we should be more sensitive than most of our European partners to the dangers of sending apparently 'neutral' peace-keeping forces to deal with civil wars like the Balkans'. It's the silent agreement of all that a negotiated settlement in N. Ireland, implying a withdrawal of troops, is the only lasting solution. Our independent efforts in the EC would be informed by the Troubles; encouraging an approach to Central European or Eurasian disputes which put a priority on easing the economic and political conditions at their root, not crude military attempts to sort out disorder and violence.

So where does our basest desire for the trappings of small-nationhood stop, and our minimum duties to European 'common security' begin? Adrian Hyde-White, sketching out 'four scenarios for the year 2010', makes the point that 'there can be no military-technical solution to the security problems of the continent'. The concept of 'security' must be expanded, placing the military alongside economic, political, social and cultural factors. What would create another violent continent more speedily than an economically impoverished Eastern and Central Europe, politically external to the EC, socially disintegrating and culturally extreme? It's these sources of insecurity that Scotland would be better trying to help solve, by our political and economic efforts – as a 'higher exporter per capita than both Germany and Japan', after all. A military commitment has to be the very least of our contributions to the European and world community.

Scotland bristles with war-readiness: Nato killer squads train in our glens, intelligence stations calculate the probabilities of invasion via the Faroes, and – most ludicrously – Faslane readies itself for a poisonous, pointless nuclear hulk in its waters. Is this absolutely necessary? A Scottish 'peace politics', to paraphrase one of CND's chairmen James Hinton, should be about 'building bridges between utopian thinking and effective action in the world as it is'. One such bridge is the prospect of an independent, and therefore nuclear-free Scotland.

☆ ☆ ☆

*Scotland by starlight.* – Michael Marra sings a song about Sandy Kidd, a Dundee garden-shed inventor, who developed – through a combination of strings, springs and gyroscopes – a working anti-gravity machine. Kidd's contraption produced upward thrust without downward reaction, thereby making infinite movement possible... '*And* interstellar flight', as Marra will growl in his stage introductions. 'So Scotland has invented the first starship, the first flying saucer.' Kidd attempted to get funding from Scottish universities and enterprise agencies, but to no avail. Then an Australian corporation stepped in with resources and a program: and Sandy departed, to realise his world-shattering innovation in another country. (At time of writing, mid-92, he is in California, 'edging towards a breakthrough'.) 'We'll get by selling cars', rails Marra gently at his careless compatriots, 'we know what we are'. His song is entitled *Australia instead of the stars.*

What is truly enraging about Kidd's story is not just the standard argument about our impoverished and over-specialized research culture, however pertinent. It is that Kidd's deepest scientific motivations are ones that a Scotland aware of its own intellectual traditions should have recognised immediately, and supported fully – presuming we had the means, and the powers, to do so.

Passages in *Beyond 2001,* Kidd's autobiography, express his rapt awe at the infinity of the cosmos, his calculations scattering its worlds and stars unimaginably far from each other, statistically almost unknowable in terms of our access to them. But Kidd's response to this alienating prospect of our cosmic loneliness – the mental downfall of many an introspective astrophysicist – is to try and conceive of as direct a means of contact, and therefore *communication* with this vast universe, as possible. It is this spirit of communication that leads Kidd to challenge the basic rules of motion and force in the material universe. If the friction, decay, and finitude of conventional spacetravel, in its propulsive struggle with gravity, makes the knowing of the universe unattainable, then reduce the problem to first principles – the elimination or reversal of gravity and friction – and proceed from there. Ever, ever upwards.

The scientific jury may still be out on Kidd's astral escalator – his project is now only one of several similar gyroscopic explorations across the world – but at least in terms of a Scottish tradition of the intellect, he's not the only aspirant spacetraveller, who dreams of standing on other worlds, the better to improve self-knowledge. In his centenary year, let us attend to Hugh MacDiarmid, in *The Innumerable Christ* (1925):

> *Wha kens on whatna Bethlehems*
> *Earth twinkles like a star the nicht*
> *An' whatna shepherds lift their heids*
> *In its unearthly licht?*

George Davie in *The Crisis of the Democratic Intellect* talks about MacDiarmid's almost science-fictional tone at the end of his great poem, *A drunk man looks at the thistle* (1926), desirous that our 'thocht' might transcend our terrestrial standpoint – 'To grow wings that'll cairry it/Ayont its native speck o' grit'. All our theorizing made yet 'is to the Earth confined,/Poo'erless to reach the general mind/Poo'erless to reach the neist star even'. Davie relates these extraterrestrial perspectives in *A drunk man* – where we can assess the possibilities and limitations of our existence by occupying a completely alien position – to an independent Scottish tradition of 'comparative' thinking.

Beginning with the pre-Reformation logician John Mair, developing in the Enlightenment with David Hume and Adam Smith, and coming up to the present in the work of thinkers like John Anderson and Alastair MacIntyre, its most pithy formulation sounds like a challenge whispered in Sandy Kidd's childhood ear:

> *O wad some Pow'r the giftie gie us*
> *To see oursels as others see us!*

Burns's comparative axiom is echoed in Adam Smith's *Theory of Moral Sentiments*: 'If we saw our selves in the light in which others see us, or in which they would see us if they knew all, a reformation would generally be unavoidable.' And David Hume also, when he writes that 'the minds of men are mirrors to one another'. It may seem forced to situate Sandy Kidd within this whirling constellation of Scottish connections. How far can one man's life-long dream of reaching the stars, and his scientific efforts to make it possible, be related to an enduring Scottish tradition of comparative – or as MacIntyre would say, 'intersubjective' – understanding?

Other famous Scottish inventions and inventors partake richly of this kind of thinking. What is John Logie Baird's television – an electronic journey through space itself – other than a realization of Hume's notion of the minds of humans being 'mirrors to one another'? The media spectacle which television underpins all too clearly possesses the 'Pow'r' of seeing ourselves as others see us – and it is exactly *who* has the power to determine our self-representations that media politics is all about. This Scottish fascination with the limits of the self, the way that we can only truly understand ourselves by our connections with, and immersions in, the lives and worlds of others, inevitably bears on language as its medium. It was a phonetician and physiologist working for the deaf in Elgin, Alexander Graham Bell, who later developed his insights about human communication into the century's other most communicative technology.

But the comparative method of Scottish thought is more relevant to our current situation than just the tracing of a broad philosophical-artistic-scientific tradition, or a citation of Scottish firsts in various fields. There are, as Davie might say, educational, cultural and political fundamentals at issue here. What kind of value are Scots placing on knowledge – not only how much we know, but the way in which we know it? What kind of intellect do we wish to foster amongst our citizens; a narrow specialization of skills-per-person, everyone an appropriate cog in the social machine? Or do we wish to encourage eclectic, speculative, comparative minds? An interdisciplinary, generalist education – fostering a democratic intellect – should give Scots the equipment to make new connections between realms of knowledge: a capacity ever more necessary as science and politics continuously shape and reshape our world.

And perhaps a future Scottish state – sensitive to the quality and productivity of its own intellectual traditions and institutions, and more able to relate resources to innovators more effectively –

wouldn't let another Sandy Kidd go. Will we get by just selling cars? Do we know what we are?

☆ ☆ ☆

Theodor Adorno, most wracked of those Jewish Marxist intellectuals living in the shadow of Auschwitz, described his philosophical and theoretical method as proceeding by 'constellation' – an arrangement of explanatory concepts surrounding, illuminating and framing the object of analysis. The explanation would therefore not be singular, or conclusive, piercing to the heart of the object and ripping out its essence – which would kill the object, and therefore distort our knowledge of it. Instead, the constellation would render up a complex meaning, aware of its contradictions, its brightness and darkness, its adequacies and inadequacies of description and causality. The constellation aims at a coherence – it is not a surrender of logic – but will always regard itself as fallible, open to the next critique, wishing most of all to maintain a dialogue amongst others about its area of concern.

Adorno's most important constellation of concepts was that which described what he called, 'peace'. Martin Jay, has called it 'a three-starred constellation, composed of collective subjectivity, individual subjectivity and the objective world' (Jay, 1984, p. 65). Adorno puts it more pithily: 'Peace is the state of distinctness without domination, with the distinct participating in each other' (Adorno, 1978, p.500).

I want Scotland to live by the starlight of this constellation. That is, to become a state of peace, a peaceful state – where we can be both individualist and socialist, distinct from each other but mutually enjoying each other's distinctiveness. A republic of love, in other words.

What does it feel like, reader of the future?...

# ☆ Acknowledgments

We are grateful to the following for permission to reprint copyright material:

CUT
The Guardian
The Herald
The Independent on Sunday
Radical Scotland
The Scotsman
Scottish Child

# ☆ Bibliography

Theodor Adorno, 'Subject-Object', in *The Essential Frankfurt School Reader*, ed. A. Arato and P. Piccione (Oxford, 1978)

—, *Minima Moralia* (Verso, 1986)

—, *The Culture Industry* (Routledge, 1991)

Neal Ascherson, *Games Without Frontiers* (Radius, 1988)

Nicholson Baker, *Room Temperature* (Granta, 1989)

Roland Barthes, *The Grain of the Voice* (Jonathan Cape, 1985)

Jean Baudrillard, *Revenge of the Crystal* (Pluto, 1991)

Zygmunt Bauman, *Modernity and the Holocaust* (Polity, 1989)

Craig Beveridge and Ronald Turnbull, *The Eclipse of Scottish Culture* (Polygon, 1989)

Robin Blackburn, ed, *After the Fall: The Failure of Communism* (Verso, 1991)

Robert Burns, *Complete Works* (Oxford, 1987)

Chris Carlsson, ed. *Bad Attitude: the Processed World Anthology* (Verso, 1990)

George Davie, *The Crisis of the Democratic Intellect* (Polygon, 1986)

—, *The Scottish Enlightenment* (Polygon, 1991)

Guy Debord, *Comments on the Society of the Spectacle* (Verso, 1990)

Don DeLillo, *Mao II* (Vintage, 1992)

Jacques Derrida, *A Derrida Reader*, ed. Peggy Kamuf (Columbia U.P., 1991)

Terry Eagleton, *The Ideology of the Aesthetic* (Blackwell, 1990)

Michel Foucault, *A Foucault Reader*, ed. P. Rabinow (Penguin, 1988)

*Five by Five: the Films of Spike Lee* (Stewart, Tabori and Chang, 1991)

Simon Frith, 'Art Ideology and Pop Practice', in *Marxism and the Interpretation of Culture*, ed. C. Nelson and L. Grossberg (Macmillan, 1987)

Janice Galloway, *The Trick is to Keep Breathing* (Polygon, 1989)

Anthony Giddens, *Modernity and Self-Identity* (Polity, 1991)

Ralph Glasser, *Growing up in the Gorbals* (Chatto and Windus, 1986)

Andre Gorz, *Critique of Economic Reason* (Verso, 1989)

Jonathan Green, ed., *Cynic's Lexicon* (Sphere, 1986)

Richard Gunn, 'George Davie' Common Sense, Hegelianism and Critique', in *Cencrastus,* Autumn 1987

—, 'Marxism and Common Sense', in *Common Sense 11,* Winter 1991.

Jurgen Habermas, *The Philosophical Discourse of Modernity* (Polity, 1987)

—, *The New Conservatism* (Polity, 1990)

—, *Autonomy and Solidarity* (Verso, 1992)

Vaclav Havel, *Disturbing the Peace* (Faber, 1991)

G.W.F. Hegel, *Phenomenology of Spirit* (Oxford, 1977)

Adrian Hyde-White, *European Security Beyond the Cold War* (Sage, 1991)

Martin Jay, *Adorno* (Fontana, 1984)

Paul Johnson, *Intellectuals* (Weidenfeld and Nicholson, 1988)

James Kelman, 'A Reading from Noam Chomsky and the Scottish Tradition in the Philosophy of Common Sense', in *Edinburgh Review* 84, 1990

Peter Labanyi, 'Images of fascism: Visualisation and Aestheticization in the Third Reich', in *The Burden of German History,* ed., Michael Laffan (Methuen, 1988)

Dave Laing, *One Chord Wonders* (Open University, 1986)

Hugh MacDiarmid, *Selected Poetry,* ed. by A. Riach and M. Grieve (Carcanet, 1992)

Alasdair MacIntyre, *After Virtue* (Duckworth, 1987)

—, *Whose Justice? Which Rationality?* (Duckworth, 1991)

Thomas McCarthy, *The Critical Theory of Jurgen Habermas* (MIT, 1978)

David McCrone, *Understanding Scotland: the sociology of a stateless nation* (Routledge, 1992)

William McIlvanney, *Surviving the Shipwreck* (Mainstream, 1991)

Douglas Mair, ed., *The Scottish Tradition in Economic History* (Aberdeen U. P., 1990)

Dave Marsh, *The Heart of Rock and Soul* (Penguin, 1989)

David Martin, *'Borderlands',* in *New Statesman and Society,* 19 June 1992

Richard Middleton, *Studying Popular Music* (Open University Press, 1991)

Tom Nairn, *The Break-up of Britain* (Verso, 1983)

—, 'Borderlands', in *New Statesman and Society,* 19 June 1992.

Sylvia Plath, *Collected Poems* (Faber, 1981)

David Rasmussen, ed., *Universalism vs. Communitarianism* (MIT, 1990)

Simon Reynolds, *Blissed Out* (Serpent's Tail, 1990)

Barry Richards, ed., *Crises of the Self* (Free Associations, 1989)

Richard Rorty, 'Towards a More Banal Politics', in *Harper's Magazine*, May 1992

Jacqueline Rose, *The Haunting of Sylvia Plath* (Virago, 1991)

Jon Savage, *England's Dreaming* (Faber, 1991)

*Semiotext (e) USA* (Johns Hopkins, 1988)

Jim Sillars, *Scotland: A Case for Optimism* (Polygon, 1987)

Peter Sloterdjik, *Critique of Cynical Reason* (Verso, 1988)

Adam Smith, *The Theory of Moral Sentiments* (Clarendon, 1976)

—, *The Nature and Causes of the Wealth of Nations* (Oxford, 1979)

*Socialist Sunday School Song Book*, Glasgow Clarion Federation, 1957

Rev. Ivan Stang, *High Weirdness by Mail* (Firestone, 1988)

Elizabeth Wilson, *The Sphinx in the City* (Virago, 1990)

Slavoj Zizek, *For They Know Not What They Do* (Verso, 1991)

# ☆ Index

Adamski's *Killer*, 27
Adorno, Theodor, 63, 80, 119, 207
AIDS crisis, 73, 80
America/Americans, 166-7
 and the Clyde, 147, 148-9
 Fringe, 85-6
 the left, 87
Arab nationalism, 176-80
Art, tastes in, 135-8
Ascherson, Neal, 69, 84, 170
Asians, 162
Autocues, 141
Autographs, 139-40

Ba'athism, 178, 179
Baker, Nicholson, 103-6
Banal, elevating the, 117-19
Barcelona concert 1991:, 50
Barthes, Roland, 33-4, 57
Baudrillard, Jean, 83, 84
Bauman, Zygmunt, 73
Behan, Brendan, 59
Belfast, 19-22, 90
Bell, Alexander Graham, 206
Bell, Ian, 163
Bernal, Martin, 168
Beveridge, C., and R. Turnbull, 145,
 168
Big Day, The, 27, 49-50
Biondolillo, Jimmy, 4-5, 6
Black nationalism, 166-8
Bowie, David, 77
Brecht, Bertolt, 112, 116
Brighton concert 1987:, 48
Brixton, 144
Brotherhood, dynamics, 40-3
Bruce, Lenny, 100
Burns, Robert, 44, 45-6, 189, 205-6
Business supplements, 93

Callinicos, Alex, 67-8
Camden, 144
Capitalism, 63, 92-4, 164
Carson, Ciaran, 21
Cavilli-Sforza, L., 197
*Charley's War*, 75
Chimes, The, 26, 27
Clyde, river, 147-8
Cobbett, William, 190, 191
Coltrane, Robbie, 161
Commerce and art, 51-2
Communication, art and, 58
Computer hacking and sabotage, 96,
 98
Computer-related injury, 97
Connery, Sean, 129
Connolly Jimmy, 160
Costello, Elvis, 48
*Crises of the Self*, 80
*Critique of Economic Reason*, 69
Currie, Ken, 160
CUT magazine, 71 n., 76-8
Cynicism, 100-2

Davie, George, 119, 190, 191, 192-3,
 194, 205, 206
Deacon Blue, 160 n., 161
Debord, Guy, 57, 128, 129
DeLillo, Don, 107-9
Demilitarisation, 202-4
Diogenes, 101

Eagleton, Terry, 67, 69-70, 119
Eastern Europe, 10-12, 17, 68-9, 83,
 122-3, 164-5, 177
Edinburgh, 154
Elton, Ben, 111
Engelmann, Bernt, 73
*England's Dreaming*, 30-1

Fanon, Frantz, 145
Fascism, 71-4, 76-8, 80, 178, 179
    films about, 74
    reasons for success of, 73
Feminism, and the left, 69-70
Ferrier, James, 188, 189
Football
    Glasgow Celtic, 156-9
    Glasgow Rangers, 157-8, 159, 162
    international, 181-3
Forshaw, Mark, 27
Foucault, Michel, 57
French Foreign Legion, 17-18
Freud, Sigmund, 81
Frith, Simon, 60, 63
Funny Farm, 161

Gallagher, Tom, 163
Galloway, Janice, 105
Gates, Jr, Henry Louis, 166
Germany, 13-14, 16-17, 124, 177
Giddens, Anthony, 119
Glasgow
    architecture, 153-5
    articulacy of people, 161-2
    City of Culture, 125-6
    concerts 1990:, 48-50
    Empire, 152
    Mayfest:, 50-2, 150
    and the new technology, 95
    Partick, 150-2
    see also under Football
Glasser, Ralph, 151-2
Goldberg, Harvey, 4
Gorz, Andre, 69, 70
Gourock, 147-9
Gramsci, Antonio, 35, 184, 198
Graphic fiction, 75-6
Gray, Muriel, 102, 161
Greenock, 147-9, 172
Gulf War, 203
Gunn, Neil, 141
Gunn, Richard, 188

Habermas, Jurgen, 69-70, 119-25, 175,
    176-7, 198
Harvie, Christopher, 201
Havel, Vaclav, 68-9, 118, 120
Head/heart split, 58
Hegel, G. W. F., 188
Henderson, Jeffrey, 199-200
High theory, 61-2
High Weirdness by Mail, 85-6
Hitler, Adolf, 71-4

Hitler, The New Adventures of, 76-8
Holden, Anthony, 170
Honeymooners, The, 7
Hong Kong immigration issue, 80-1
Howson, Peter, 160
Hue and Cry, 5, 25, 27, 31, 44-5, 46-8,
    160 n.
Hughes, Simon, 169, 170
Hughes, Ted, 38
Hume, David, 206
Hussein, Saddam, 178, 179
Hyde-White, Adrian, 203

Ideology of the Aesthetic, The, 67, 69
Ignatieff, Michael, 110-11, 112
Information technology, 95-8
International corporations, 200
Israel, 177-8

Jackson, Joe, 50
Jay, Martin, 207
Jews, 78
Jobson, Richard, 31
John Rae Collective, 28
Johnson, Paul, 111-12
Jungle Fever, 166, 167

Kane, Gary, 43, 156, 157-8
Kane, Gregory, 5-6, 40-3, 45, 46, 49
Kane, John, 99-100
Kane, Patrick
    early years, 23, 103, 181-3
    at university, 183-4, 193-4
    and America, 23-5
    as broadcaster, 125-7
    as canvasser, 139
    goes into Europe, 13-18
    in London, 184-5
    recordings, 44-6
    Rectorial Address, 192-6
Kelley, Kitty, 112
Kelman, James, 105, 106, 125-6, 160,
    195-6
Kilroy, 80-1, 111
Kuwait, 176

Labyani, Peter, 77-8
Laing, Dave, 76
Lally, Pat, 154
Laughter as weapon, 72, 93
Lee, Spike, 166
Left theory and 'humanist' values, 67
Life-as-art, 64
Live concerts, 46-8

Lochhead, Liz, 161

McCrone, David, 187-8
MacDiarmid, Hugh (Christopher Grieve), 205
McGrain, Danny, 157
Machoism, 52-6
McIlvanney, William, 160, 191
McLaren, Malcolm, 32
McStay, Paul, 157
Madonna Ciccone, 37-8, 39
Mair, Douglas, 94
Major, John, 197
Manhattan Bar, Partick, 150-2
Mao II, 107-8
Marra, Michael, 204
Marx, Karl, 112, 113
Marxism Today, 88-9, 144-5
Materialism, 103-6
    in fiction, 103-6
Maus, 77
Mezzanine, The, 103, 104, 105
Middleton, Richard, 34
Mills, Pat, 75-6
Miming, 27-8
Monroe, Marilyn, 39
Morrison, Grant 71 n.
Motherwell Train Depot, 113
Mulgan, Geoff, 88

Nairn, Tom, 141, 170, 174, 177, 178, 197-8
Neil, Alex, 139 n., 141
New Left Review, 144-5
New Statesman and Society, 89-90, 144-5
New technology, and strikes, 96
New York, 3-9, 24
    art market, 5
    beggars, 3
New York, working-class, 8-9
Nuclear waste disposal, 167-8

Odd Couple, The, 7

Paris, architecture, 153-4
Partick, 150-2
Peace defined, 207
Pencil sharpeners, paradox of, 103
Picard, Captain Jean-Luc, 7
Plath, Sylvia, 37, 38-9
Pleasure, universalizing of, 64
PLO (Palestine Liberation Organization), 176, 177-9

Poland, 10-12, 17
Poll tax, 139, 161
Pop
    differing tastes in, 59-60
    journalism, 60-1
    philosophy of, 32-6, 45-6, 58
    post-modern, 61
Post-modernism, political, 68
Post-punk, 31
Priestley, Joseph, 190
Prince, 28, 63
Psychoanalysis, 79-80
    pop and, 35
Punch, 71, 72
Punk, Nazi symbolism in, 76-7
Punk rock, 30-2
Pynchon, Thomas, 108

Racism, 80-1, 172-3
Radical Scotland, 89, 141
Referendum 1979:, 183
Reich, Bob, 199, 200, 201-2
Reich, Wilhelm, 79, 80
Reid, Charlie, 141
Reid, Jimmy, 160, 195
Reid, Thomas, 188, 189, 191
Religious institutions, 145, 183
Revolution, 68
Reynolds, Simon, 33, 34, 35
Rock Against Racism, 76
Romania, 82-3
Room Temperature, 103, 104
Rorty, Richard, 117-19
Rose, Jaqueline, 38-9
Ross, Ricky, 49-50
Rugby Union, 174-5
Runrig 160 n.

Said, Edward, 179
Salmond, Alex, 187
'Samplers', 28
Sartre, Jean-Paul, 112
Savage, Jon, 30-1
Scotland, 1980s culture, 160
Scotland
    intellectual magazines, 145
    see also Edinburgh; Glasgow; Greenock
Scotland, self-determination, 119-21, 124-5, 127-31, 163-5, 166-8,
    see also Salmond; Sillars
Scott-Heron, Gil, 82
Sectarianism, 162
'Semiconductor' production, 199-200

Sex Pistols, 30-2
Sexual politics, 52-6
Sillars, Jim, 139 n., 141, 158, 163
Simple Minds, 161
Sinatra, Frank, 23, 25, 112-13
Sloterdijk, Peter, 72, 100, 101
Smith, Adam, 125, 188, 189-90, 206
Smith, Elaine C., 161
Socialist Sunday School Movement,
   114-16
Song-writing, 6
Soul music, 26, 27
South Africa, 172-5
'Space to fill', 63
*Sphinx in the City, The*, 154
Spiegelman, Art, 77
*Spitting Image*, 101
Stage fright, 50-1
STUC (Scottish Trades Union
   Congress), 200-1
*Studyinq Popular Music*, 34

Tebbit, Norman, 80
Television, 80-1, 189, 193, 206

Scottish, 83-4, 182
*Tender is the Night*, 57
Thatcher, Margaret, 48, 58, 81, 93,
   118, 126, 161, 184, 186
*The Trick is to Keep Breathing*, 105
Tin Pan Alley, 63
Tom Robinson Band, 30
Tschumi, Bernard, 153·
Turnbull, R., 145

Vidal, Gore, 85

Wangford, Hank, 20
War comics, 75
Wark, Kirsty, 161
Weimar Republic, 72
Welfare state, 122
Wembley concert 1987:, 46-8
Wet Wet Wet, 161
Wilson, Elizabeth, 154-5
Women, attitudes to, 52-6
Wyllie, George, 148

Zizek, Slavoj, 164-5